Understanding Global Terror

WITHDRAWN

Understanding Global Terror

Edited by

Christopher Ankersen

with

Michael O'Leary

polity

First published in 2007 by Polity Press

Polity Press
65 Bridge Street
Cambridge CB2 1UR, UK.

Polity Press
350 Main Street
Malden, MA 02148, USA

ISBN-13: 978-07456-3459-3
ISBN-13: 978-07456-3460-9 (pb)

A catalogue record for this book is available from the British Library.

Typeset in 11 on 13 pt Berling
by SNP Best-set Typesetter Ltd, Hong Kong
Printed and bound in Great Britain by MPG Books Ltd, Bodmin, Cornwall

The publisher has used its best endeavours to ensure that the URLs for external websites referred to in this book are correct and active at the time of going to press. However, the publisher has no responsibility for the websites and can make no guarantee that a site will remain live or that the content is or will remain appropriate.

For further information on Polity, visit our website: www.polity.co.uk

Contents

Notes on Contributors

Christopher Ankersen has written on a wide array of defence and security topics, earning awards from such organizations as the British Ministry of Defence, the United States Naval Institute, the United States Department of Defence, and the Royal United Services Institute of Defence Studies. He was Lord Dahrendorf Scholar at the London School of Economics and Political Science (LSE) from 2001 to 2004 and a Security and Defence Forum Scholar from 2002 to 2004. He has taught at LSE, the London Centre for International Relations, King's College London Department of War Studies, and Carleton University, and has acted as an academic advisor at the Canadian Forces Command and Staff College and Royal Roads University. For twelve years, he was an officer in Princess Patricia's Canadian Light Infantry, serving in the Balkans with the United Nations and NATO.

Alexander Bialsky is an M.A. student at the University of Haifa. His research deals primarily with Palestinian suicide terrorism.

Philip Bobbitt is A. W. Walker Centennial Professor of Law at the University of Texas (Austin). He has published several books, not only on constitutional law but also on international security and the history of strategy. These include *The Shield of Achilles: War, Peace and the Course of History* (2002) and *The War against Terror* (2005). Professor Bobbitt is a Fellow of the American Academy of Arts and Sciences, and a Fellow of the Club of Madrid. He has served as Associate Counsel to the President, the

Counselor on International Law at the State Department, Legal
Counsel to the Senate Iran-Contra Committee, and Director for
Intelligence, Senior Director for Critical Infrastructure and Senior
Director for Strategic Planning at the National Security Council.

James Boutilier is the Special Advisor (Policy) at Canada's Mari-
time Forces Pacific Headquarters in Esquimalt, British Columbia.
He has held posts at various universities throughout his career,
including the University of the South Pacific in Suva, Fiji, Royal
Roads Military College in Victoria, British Columbia, and the
University of Victoria. He lectures nationally and internationally
on political, economic, and security developments in the Asia-
Pacific region.

Chris Brown is the author of *International Relations Theory:
New Normative Approaches* (1992), *Understanding International
Relations* (1st edn 1997, 3rd edn 2005), *Sovereignty, Rights and
Justice* (2002), and editor of *Political Restructuring in Europe:
Ethical Perspectives* (1994) and (with Terry Nardin and N. J.
Rengger) *International Relations in Political Thought: Texts
from the Greeks to the First World War* (2002). He was Chair of
the British International Studies Association in 1997 and 1998,
and has served on the Governing Council and Executive
Committee of the (US) International Studies Association. He
is currently Convenor of the International Relations Department
at LSE.

Michael Cox is Professor of International Relations at the London
School of Economics and Political Science. He is also Director of
the Cold War Studies Centre at the LSE, the Chair of the Euro-
pean Consortium for Political Research and the United States
Discussion Group at Chatham House (the Royal Institute for
International Affairs). His main areas of research interest are
American foreign policy, transatlantic relations and E. H. Carr.
Professor Cox was formerly editor of the *Review of International
Studies* and is the current editor of *International Politics* and of
two book series, Rethinking World Politics and Great Thinkers
in International Relations.

Lawrence Freedman has been Professor of War Studies at King's College London since 1982. He has recently been appointed to the position of Vice Principal (Research) at King's, having previously been Head of the School of Social Science and Public Policy. Elected a Fellow of the British Academy in 1995 and awarded the CBE in 1996, he was appointed Official Historian of the Falklands Campaign in 1997. He was awarded the KCMG in 2003. Professor Freedman has written extensively on nuclear strategy and the Cold War, as well as commentating regularly on contemporary security issues. His most recent work includes an Adelphi Paper entitled *The Revolution in Strategic Affairs*, edited books on strategic coercion and terrorism, and an illustrated book on the Cold War, a collection of essays on British defense policy, and *Kennedy's Wars*, which covers the major crises of the early 1960s over Berlin, Cuba, Laos, and Vietnam. In addition, he published a book on deterrence in 2004 and *The Official History of the Falklands Campaign* in the summer of 2005.

Margot Light is Emeritus Professor of International Relations at the London School of Economics and Political Science. She has been teaching and writing about the former Soviet Union for the past 30 years. Her current research investigates the relations between the European Union and NATO and their new European neighbours, Russia, Belarus, and Ukraine. Among her recent publications are "Russia and the West: Is There a Values Gap?" (with Stephen White and Ian MacAllister) in *International Politics*, and "Belarus between East and West" (with Roy Allison and Stephen White) in *Journal of Communist Studies and Transition Politics*.

Christopher Mackmurdo is a doctoral candidate in the Department of International Relations at the London School of Economics.

Kerry Lynn Nanikvell provides analysis of the Asia-Pacific region to senior naval staff at Canada's Maritime Forces Pacific Headquarters, in the office of the Special Advisor (Policy). She has published a wide array of articles discussing issues ranging from the crisis on the Korean peninsula to the small arms trade in Asia's ports. Her current areas of interest include security in the developing world, international security cooperation, and port security.

Martin S. Navias is Senior Research Associate at the Centre for Defence Studies, King's College London. He is the author of a number of books, including *Ballistic Missile Proliferation in the Third World, Going Ballistic,* and *Tanker Wars.*

Ami Pedahzur is Associate Professor in the departments of Government and Middle Eastern Studies, University of Texas at Austin. He is also a Senior Fellow at the National Security Studies Center at the University of Haifa, Israel. His main fields of interest are terrorism and political extremism. Dr Pedahzur serves as an associate editor of the journals *Studies in Conflict and Terrorism* and *Democracy and Security.* He is also the book review editor of the *Civil Wars* journal. His latest book, *Suicide Terrorism,* was published in 2005.

Arie Perliger is adjunct faculty at the School of Political Sciences at the University of Haifa, where he is the coordinator of terrorism studies at the National Security Studies Center. He is the author or coauthor of articles and papers in areas as diverse as extreme right political parties, terrorism and political violence, political socialization, and civic education.

Dinah PoKempner is General Counsel at Human Rights Watch, one of the largest non-governmental monitors of human rights around the globe. She lectures and publishes regularly on international humanitarian law and war crimes, transitional justice, the UN system, and many other topics in the field of human rights. Dinah PoKempner is a graduate of Yale University and Columbia University School of Law.

Timothy M. Shaw taught Political Science and Development Studies at Dalhousie University for three decades and has been

Professor of Commonwealth Governance and Development at the University of London for five years. He holds visiting professorships in South Africa (Stellenbosch) and Uganda (MUST), and previously did so at universities in a number of countries round the world. His most recent coedited titles are *Twisting Arms and Flexing Muscles* (2005), *Political Economy of Regions and Regionalisms* (2005), and *A Decade of Human Security* (2006).

William Wallace is Emeritus Professor of International Relations at the London School of Economics and Political Science. He has written extensively on European international politics and transatlantic relations.

Preface

Philip Bobbitt

The Terrorist War

We are not winning the war against terrorism. We are not winning because the forces that empower terror are gaining – as markets increase, as weapons technologies diffuse, as clandestine communications become more effective – at a faster pace than our defenses and our preemptive strategies are strengthening. There is a widespread sense in the West of the inevitability of further major terrorist attacks on the scale of the 9/11 atrocity, and many analysts believe that terrorists will acquire and use weapons of mass destruction such as biological pathogens or even nuclear arms, and that it is inevitable that they will do so.

Since September 11th, the US has declared war; it has received the unprecedented invocation of Article 5 of the North Atlantic Treaty by its allies on its behalf. The US Congress and the British Parliament have passed various statutes aimed at making the prosecution and detection of terrorists easier. In the United States the bureaucracy has been reorganized and vast new funds have been authorized. US/UK-led coalitions have invaded and conquered Afghanistan and Iraq in lightning campaigns, and the UN has sanctioned, for the first time, the invasion of a member state in order to suppress terrorism. The first acknowledged targeted assassination by coalition forces against terrorists has taken place. Much of the senior leadership of al-Qaeda has been killed or detained, with all the fruitful possibilities for interrogation. What remains – the senior figures of bin Laden and al-Zawahiri – is in desperate flight.

And yet at the same time, al-Qaeda has continued to strike; indeed there has been a drumbeat of violence, and since the invasion of Iraq, far from abating, it has picked up momentum. The year 2003 was the deadliest year of terrorist violence in 20 years, and if we exclude terrorism waged by states, it was the deadliest year on record. In Bali, Kenya, Pakistan, Tunisia, Afghanistan, Iraq, Israel, and in Morocco as many people have been killed and wounded in terrorist attacks since September 11th as died on that date, which was itself the most deadly terrorist attack in history. Virtually every week, US soldiers are killed. Almost as frequently, Arab television networks and al-Qaeda websites show the beheading of innocent civilians, a grotesque *coup de théâtre* never depicted before on television. The statutory rights of US and British citizens, and of those persons who, while not citizens, are in their custody are less than before. We have seen countless alerts, color-coded to indicate their threat levels, and one can reasonably conclude that Americans are less safe than before, and some believe perhaps less safe than ever.

We must step back and ask the most basic questions about winning the war on terrorism. Do we know what we are doing, in the way that we knew what we had to do to defeat Germany and Japan in the Second World War? Are we developing new strategic doctrines of the kind we had to develop to confront the Soviet Union in the context of mutual assumed deterrence in the Cold War? Are we writing new international law and creating new institutions to cope with global problems in the twenty-first century in the way we did when we faced similar global challenges in the twentieth century? I think the answers to all these questions are evident. Our legal and strategic habits – which are enshrined in international institutions like the UN and NATO, in military plans that contemplate invasion and conquest, and in intelligence operations that are geared toward renditions and prosecutions – are not appropriate to the decentralized operations of a mutated market state like al-Qaeda, which finds lucrative targets in the emerging market states of the West.

Secretary of Defense Donald Rumsfeld put it well in a memorandum of October 2003 that asked, "Does the US need to fashion a broad, integrated plan to stop the next generation of terrorists? The US is putting relatively little effort into a long-range plan, but we are putting a great deal of effort into trying to stop terrorists. The cost–benefit ratio is against us. Our cost is billions against the terrorist's cost of millions."

This is the right question, and it applies to both the United States and the United Kingdom. One may ask, however, whether the US administration of which the Secretary was a member has fully appreciated the degree to which the September 11th attacks were a violent reaction to America's preeminence; for there is much in recent American behavior that suggests an aggressive neglect of perceptions of US hegemony abroad, indeed of the critical importance of public perceptions in the emerging world of mediacentric market states. Writing in 2004, the International Institute for Strategic Studies in London concluded that

> the manner of US preponderance had to change . . . the appearance of American unilateralism needed to be tempered. Strategic ends had to be more adeptly coordinated with tactical means. The necessary tools included more nuanced public diplomacy, which could portray a less parochial and chauvinistic society while emphasizing religious pluralism; less doctrinaire political and economic conditionalities attached to foreign assistance . . . and an approach to international law that – after more than two years delay – openly admitted that the older standards of intervention and the laws of war that applied to state-based security problems and standing armies did not easily fit new security problems and that these required systematic, collegial reconsideration on a multilateral basis.[1]

With equal validity, the Institute might also have concluded that "the manner of much European behavior in collective institutions like NATO and the UN has to change. The appearance of strategic neglect must be tempered. Legal and diplomatic means have to be better coordinated with the strategic goals of the Alliance, which include the defeat of terrorists and the anti-Western states that support them. At times it appears that French, German, Belgian and now Spanish policies have little other strategic goals than thwarting wherever possible the efforts of the US and the UK, and place a total tactical reliance on institutional maneuvering to the neglect of the instruments of force, whilst insisting on an international law that plainly does not fit our current circumstances."

These wholesome rebukes cannot really result in positive reform, however, until we first undertake an examination of the most basic questions surrounding the issue of waging war against terrorism. For it isn't simply a matter of the transatlantic styles. It is clear that the US, owing to its great economic and military presence, is the chief cause of twenty-first century, networked terrorism. That is not a matter for blame, any more than one can blame urbanization for the black plague in the fourteenth century. It is equally clear that a lack of sincere collaboration with the US is the chief reason the terrorists think they can win such a war. This too calls more for reflection on basic issues than tirades against the leadership of any state, because all the advanced states will ultimately be threatened by twenty-first century terrorism and it is understandable that some would want to protect their publics by disassociating themselves from the most prominent political target in the West, alliance with the US.

The Unwritten Script

Let me very briefly outline what I take those basic questions to be, and indicate how I believe they should be addressed.

First, we have defined the problem of winning the war against terrorism in a way that makes winning impossible. The ways we conventionally understand "winning" (a victory with an armistice agreement followed by occupation and a peace treaty), "war" (a conflict between nations over issues of statehood and sovereignty), and "terrorism" (a criminal act by the disenfranchised or the psychopathic) mean that we simply cannot defeat terrorism. "The War on Terrorism" becomes little more than a metaphor for propaganda purposes; we can no more win such a war than we can win a war against disease or disillusionment. We must reconceptualize each of the key ideas to bring them into accord with the changing nature of war, terrorism, and victory.

We are going to have to understand terrorism from the supply side, not simply the demand side. By that I mean we must change our exclusive focus on who is the terrorist and what troubles him, to what vulnerabilities we have created and how to reduce them. This will become ever more urgent, regardless of what happens to al-Qaeda, as we enter a period in which it will be increasingly difficult to determine precisely who is striking at us and from what remove.

We shall have to abandon the nation-state's dichotomy of crime and war – the inner and outer dimensions of state violence – and replace this with a worldview that admits a free flow between these two dimensions. The IRA were criminals, who hungered to be treated as soldiers; the Waffen SS were soldiers who behaved like criminals, and deserved to be treated as such. But the atrocities of September 11th, though crimes of historic proportion, were not committed by mere criminals. These actions were plotted with military precision, against military and political targets, by perpetrators willing to sacrifice themselves for purely political goals.

Second, we must be clear about what we are fighting for, and what that fight requires of us, lest terrorists effectively defeat us through our own misguided attempts to protect ourselves. This determination is not nearly as easy as it is made to look by those civil libertarians who alarm us by claiming that any diminution in our liberties means "the terrorists win," or by those bureaucrats and politicians who soothingly reassure us that all the necessary measures can be taken without compromising our civil freedom of action.

In every era of the state, throughout the evolution of its constitutional orders, societies have confronted the problem of determining the proper relationship between strategy and law. Outside its territorial domain the state seeks to be free of external coercion; this is strategy. Inside its boundaries, the state seeks to monopolize legitimate violence; this is law. But what measures are appropriate, within its territory, to prosecute the war outside when inside and outside have lost their clear boundaries?

Governments must explore the changing relationships between the intelligence agencies (as they become more dependent on open sources) and the media (as they become more powerful purveyors of secrets); between the political parties, who seem to have shunned the traditional bipartisanship of governance during war; between federal unions and their constituent parts (both in the US and the European Union), where intelligence in the case of the US is not shared *by* the central union, and in the case of the EU, not shared *with* the central union owing to national distrust. Governments will have to learn how to find and work with private sector collaborators, partly because they own most of the critical infrastructure that we must make less vulnerable, and partly because they are market-oriented and global, thus arcing some of the gaps between the nation-state and our al-Qaeda adversaries. Governments must rethink ideas like "Homeland Security" when the threats to security cannot be neatly cabined as in or out of the homeland, just as the American and British governments must revisit the issues of cooperation between the CIA and the FBI and between MI5 and MI6 – issues that arise owing to jurisdictional divisions between domestic and international operations – because these agencies are so completely defined by the Long War[2] and its basis in the territorially defined nation-state.[3]

States must measure their tactical and strategic policies against the impact such policies are likely to have on their legitimacy. If the United States were to abandon its Executive Order prohibiting assassinations, what is the cost to its legitimacy as a state that follows the rule of law, one principle of which is that no criminal penalty can be levied without a fair and open trial? On the other hand, if the US is at war, is the Executive Order even relevant? By such means, the domestic environment of states is steadily militarized. Similarly, does it matter what we are fighting for, or is "one man's terrorist another man's freedom fighter"? We do not apply murder statutes to soldiers in battle, even enemy soldiers. Soldiers are permitted to maim and kill civilians if that is not their aim, while we condemn the terrorist whose objective is to kill civilians. By such means, the foreign environment can be degraded into a sea of "collateral damage." Put the two together and the war on terror can make our soldiers into organized vigilantes, using the methods of warfare against civilians, domestic and foreign.

If our governments engage in torture, perhaps by turning over prisoners to less squeamish national intelligence services, are they substantiating the charges made against them by those who say ours are the true rogue states,[4] and that the state terror of the US and its allies, including Israel, is every much a threat to mankind as the terrorism of al-Qaeda? These are essentially constitutional issues: not matters of civil liberties but rather of the self-definition societies achieve through their constitutional development. They are matters of constitutional legitimacy because they are matters of self-respect. States must have clear answers to these questions in order to decide what legitimacy as law-abiding institutions they are willing to risk to meet the threat posed by terrorism, because if the legitimacy of the state is compromised it will seed its own terrorists who will take up arms against it in revulsion.

If the US and the UK ally themselves with undemocratic autocracies who share our fear of al-Qaeda but with whom we have little else in common, are we simply borrowing against a future in which those peoples we have helped to suppress rise up and blame us – much as we are blamed for collaborating with dictators in the Third World to fight communism (though we are seldom blamed for the equally awful collaboration with communism to defeat fascism)? Is there a realistic choice? If it is true that full and fair elections in a dozen Islamic states would bring bin Laden to power, does the international community dare to risk such an election? And if it does not, does this make us hypocrites to claim that the sovereignty of other states, like Iraq, is forfeited owing to its undemocratic practices, and then to turn a blind eye to questions over the legitimacy of regimes that are allied to ours but which deny their citizens basic human rights? Or does it mean that our commitment to globalize the systems of democracy itself – or what we mistake for the pluralistic system we have evolved and called "democracy" – must be rethought? Answering urgent strategic questions about terrorism will also require us to give some thought to larger constitutional questions about sovereignty, democracy and the laws of war, because if we ignore these issues we will find we have decided them, inadvertently, in the unthinking acts of crisis that ultimately determined their outcome.

Third, while the United States must play a leading role in winning the war against terrorism, that war can only be won with the collaboration of many states, including some states that fear and even loathe American hegemony. The risks of leadership are twofold: if the US is out in front, it becomes the target for every terrorist group that simply wants a free hand for its local predations, while, at the same time, America becomes the focal point of charges by other states that it is seeking an empire. Some of those who make the latter charge believe simply that overwhelming power necessarily leads to empire, indeed that that is the very definition of empire.

The United States is very powerful, economically and militarily. It has the world's largest economy, greater than those of all the other members of G8 combined, and it is growing at a faster rate than they are. The US is the only state that can settle its debts in its own currency. It is, militarily, the only remaining superpower, owing to the collapse of the Soviet Union and US defense budgets that approach half a trillion dollars. Yet we should not be misled by these figures; like the much-cited increase in the gap between high and low income earners, these statistics conceal an equally important truth – that the development gap between high and low is closing. This means that while the US has a large army equipped with infinitely superior weaponry and communications, the harm that can be done to the nation is growing more quickly (as technology disperses and becomes cheaper) than its lead is growing. In other words poor states – or rich terrorist groups – who could not begin to mount a challenge by invading across a contested plain, can hope to do enough damage to dissuade the US or any other powerful state from attempting to coerce them. This paradox – the increasingly greater power and greater vulnerability of the US – means that America is the indispensable leader of the war on terrorism (because it alone has the resources) and that it has a vital interest in being such a leader (because it is also very vulnerable).

Yet American leadership actually tempts disarray and nonco-operation. The former French foreign minister Hubert Vedrine spoke for many when he said, "We cannot accept a politically unipolar world."[5] This conclusion is shared by many outside the US. It was widely reported that when, in the midst of ongoing hostilities in Iraq, the French foreign minister Dominique de Villepin was asked which side he wanted to see win that war, he simply declined to answer, after a long and irritated pause. Indeed there are many who see the war on terrorism as a kind of stalking horse for the creation of an American empire. One research center has provided a list of what it considers to be America's true intentions in the war against Saddam Hussein's regime. The war, the center maintains, was undertaken in order to:

- instigate a "clash of civilizations" that will provide the US with an excuse to reorganize the world under the tutelage of an American empire;
- secure control of the oil and gas rich lands of Central Asia and the Middle East;
- undermine the political and economic development and inte-gration of the Eurasian landmass;
- maintain economic power during the course of the current financial crisis by using US taxpayers' money (and lives) to force on the world an unchallenged American economic and political supremacy.[6]

One must shudder at the consequences for the world, to say nothing of the war on terrorism, of such attitudes, for they invite an anti-American multipolarity with which the worst and most retrograde forces can tacitly combine. Multipolarity is not simply a condition of mutually affecting forces but of mutually opposed forces. How many persons who have called for a European army in order to achieve multipolarity to "balance" the Americans have actually thought through what such an army would do to achieve the objective of thwarting US unilateralism? If that army were to join American expeditions then it might well have influence on allied policy. But this is not what the opponents of US hegemony have in mind. Indeed they have frantically (and successfully) tried to keep NATO forces out of Iraq. If, however, the objective is to prevent US forces from intervening in Serbia or Afghanistan or Iraq or the Sudan, then such an army must be used to threaten the use of force. What other role could it possibly play in achieving such an objective? That was how multi-polarity checked US policies before 1989, when the Soviet army stood ready to oppose any allied attempts to liberate Eastern Europe. Is it possible that any sane person would want to recreate the conditions for such an armed confrontation in the twenty-first century?

If neither unipolarity nor multipolarity is acceptable, what about multilateralism? Should the war against terrorism be prosecuted under the auspices of a multinational organization such as the United Nations, or perhaps NATO or the EU? Or should what have come to be called "coalitions of the willing" become an acceptable means of fighting this war? There is, at present, no more important question before the world because failure to resolve the question of legitimate cooperation will frustrate not only our efforts against global terrorism but also regional climate change, regional and global epidemics, and great power confrontation.

What constitutional and strategic models can we look to for the reconstitution of societies that have been ravaged by conflict and have sheltered terrorists? It may be that we can revive the otherwise outmoded provisions of the UN Charter that create trusteeships for failed states like Afghanistan or postwar Iraq. Or it may be that we will need new models that are less territorial and exclusive, such as free trade zones for both the US and the EU that embrace areas such as Palestine, Kashmir, the Koreas, Iran and Iraq, incentivizing rather than coercing these societies toward humane constitutional development. The EU's market in sovereignty is one such model, admission to which has been used as a successful incentive to achieve human rights reforms in states wishing to join.

Fourth, we must urgently develop legal and strategic parameters for state action in the war on terrorism. This will be a matter, ultimately, of drawing the links between successfully warring on terror and the evolving legal concepts of sovereignty and its relationship to lawful, legitimate governance. We might start with a pragmatic definition of what constitutes terrorism. Perhaps this: "terrorism is the use of violence to prevent persons from doing what they would otherwise lawfully do when that violence is undertaken for political goals without regard to the protection of non-combatants." Beginning with such a definition, we can then work out what a state is permitted to do in its search for terrorists, and its efforts to suppress them. With such a definition we could seek an international convention universally outlawing terrorism as we outlaw piracy. With such a definition we could determine when a group are terrorists or "freedom fighters," and when other states may intervene to stop them.

We might then be able to address the new US National Security Strategy and its call for preemption in light of its obvious conflict with Article 2(4) of the UN Charter which prohibits the use of force by any state outside the Charter's carefully circumscribed limits. These provide that it is unlawful for a state to use force in the absence of an actual or imminent attack[7] or authorization by the Security Council. Does this mean it is also unlawful – in the absence of a Security Council resolution – for one state to preempt another's warmaking capabilities before these are ever put to use? Yet in the era we are entering of disguised attack using terrorist networks, preemption is an absolute necessity where the proliferation of weapons of mass destruction (WMD) to violent groups is concerned. For once any state, no matter how repugnant, acquires nuclear weapons, a moment that no UN or US monitoring seems capable of predicting with precision, it is too late to compel de-proliferation. The genie cannot be put back in the bottle and must do the bidding of its new master. The chief reason why Saddam Hussein is not in power and Kim Jong Il is – at least of this writing – is because the latter got to the nuclear finish line before he was preempted (despite, it should be noted, UN inspections).

Nor should a search for such parameters exclude the consideration of the so-called "root" causes of terrorism. I do not believe that the developed world should seek to aid the peoples of the less developed states – to improve their health and longevity, their per capita incomes and education, their human rights and political liberties – on the grounds that this will reduce the threat of terrorism. The tie between such causes and effects is too tenuous. A "supply-side" approach to terrorism better fits the global, anonymous networks we shall have to face in the twenty-first century than the "demand-side" approaches that were relevant to the national liberation movements of the twentieth. The search for root causes, however, has led me to an unexpected conclusion: it is the United States's position as world leader, economically, politically and militarily, that is the principal root cause of twentieth-century terrorism. This uncomfortable fact may have misled some into concluding that this is so owing to American state terrorism. If the assassinations and torture by allied states are countenanced, indeed financed, by the United States, either because we support their war aims or because they are our proxies, then, it is argued, the US is rightly subject to the same accusations of terrorism it would hurl at any other state that employed such methods. Can the United States persuade its citizens and its allies that these tactics are the only effective means of protecting a society at war with those who can easily infiltrate it, and whose operations prefigure the tactics we will ourselves be forced to adopt? If the US does adopt these methods, are they more like the strategic bombing of the Second World War, which relied on an *in terrorem* effect to achieve its military goals (as at Hiroshima and Nagasaki), or more like the bombing of civilian populations that we now condemn as war crimes (like the blitz against London, or the Allied bombing of Dresden)?

We must develop new rules of international law that incorporate these parameters. The rules would be used to determine when it is permissible for one state to intervene in another's affairs in order to protect itself or its allies from terrorism (*jus ad bellum*). Similarly they would govern the ways states may lawfully treat prisoners during the war on terrorism (*jus in bello*). Obviously we need to amend the Geneva Conventions to deal with the question posed at Guantanamo: what treatment is to be accorded prisoners of the war on terrorism? They are not combatants in uniform, with a publicly acknowledged chain of command. But they are not spies or partisans either. As soldiers, even if unlawful ones, who are captured on the field of battle they can be held in prisons until the end of the conflict without trial or arraignment. This scarcely makes sense, however, when there is no nation-state with which to agree to end the conflict, or to make arrangements for prisoner exchanges – when, that is, these prisoners may be held perpetually because the field of battle is everywhere and the conflict is perpetual.

Fifth, we must confront the possibility that we will not extinguish global terrorism because we and the rest of the international community will be unable to transform our ideas successfully. We must, that is, consider the question: if winning the war against terrorism is not losing, what constitutes losing? Much important work remains to be done on the question of *losing* the war on terrorism. The use of global scenarios – a technique pioneered by Royal Dutch Shell, and eloquently recommended by Joseph Nye when he was head of the US National Intelligence Council and imaginatively implemented by his successor Robert Hutchings – is an appropriate but at present under-utilized means of anticipating such failures and coping with or even preventing them.

Plague in the Time of Feast

The emergence of market states will bring greater wealth to mankind than has ever been known. This new constitutional order will make life more abundant by increasing productivity; more spacious by increasing accessibility to more varied environments; and more connected by means of a global network of telecommunications. Although it will bring important cultural challenges to societies, as an engine of wealth creation the market state surpasses all of its predecessors. Its raison d'être is to maximize opportunity. On this basis it lays claim to power. It has the potential to bring a kind of perpetual feast to much of the world.

It is also responsible for creating the conditions for twenty-first century terrorism. That is because the dramatic growth in wealth and productivity that is harnessed by the market state has as its concomitant a parallel growth in vulnerability; and because market states provide the model for global, networked and outsourcing terrorism; and because they enable the commodification of weapons of mass destruction. It is the global presence of the United States, the first and most dynamic of the emerging market states, that has been the main target as well as the main precipitating factor of twenty-first century terrorism. American military power, American empathy and ideals, and American ubiquity have brought forth both American hegemony and al-Qaeda, and will bring forth other global, networked terrorists in the future. The appearance of mutated market states like al-Qaeda represents the emergence of a form of plague, propagated by the very conditions that brought us feasts.

We are not winning the war against terrorism because we don't understand its deep connections to historic changes in the nature of the state that are currently underway as the state makes a transition from the constitutional order of the nation-state to that of the market state. Terrorism will become the continuation of diplomacy by other means, waged by state proxies and entities that are not controlled by conventional states, and which seek to influence the politics of states by theatrical killings and atrocities. Strategy and law, which were carefully separated in the twentieth century of nation-states, will have to be reintegrated in the twenty-first century of market states.

We are neglecting the symbiosis between strategy and law which is reflected in the revolution in military affairs that is underway and the transformation of the state that is both a cause and consequence of that revolution. Owing to this two-way relationship, terrorism is one of the principal drivers destroying the legitimacy of the nation-state and leading to the market state, and the market state is a principal driver in transforming twentieth-century nationalistic terrorism into twenty-first century global, networked terrorism. Because we have neglected this relationship we in the West have delegitimated our own efforts in international and domestic affairs – by our behavior in the UN, at Abu Graib, at Guantanamo – and abandoned strategic initiative to our enemies – on September 11, 2001, in Baghdad in the winter of 2003, and in Madrid in the spring of 2004.

Neglecting these tasks is yet another reason we are not winning this war. We have not lost the war either, however. It is time for a serious rethinking of first premises.

Notes

1 International Institute for Strategic Studies, *Strategic Survey 2004/5*, at p. 18.
2 The Long War (1914–90) is a term applied to the group of wars fought that ultimately determined whether the nineteenth-century imperial constitutional order would be replaced by nation-states governed by communism, fascism or parliamentarianism. See Philip Bobbitt, *The Shield of Achilles* (New York: Knopf, 2002), book 1, part 1.
3 See for example the provisions forbidding the CIA to investigate persons within the US.
4 A survey by Eurobarometer conducted for the European Commission of the European Union asked respondents which of 14 countries presented a threat to peace in the world. Among EU respondents, North Korea and Iran were tied with the United States. See http://europa.eu.int/comm/public_opinion/flash/fl151)iraq_full_report.pdf.
5 R. W. Apple, "Power: As the American Century Extends its Run," *New York Times*, Jan. 1, 2000.
6 Center for Cooperative Research, New York, see www.cooperativeresearch.org.
7 Article 51.

Acknowledgments

The production of this edited collection has been marked by periods of joy and tragedy, of birth and death, in my life and in the world around me. All of this has taught – and humbled – me greatly.

I have been honoured to work with an extraordinary group of scholars throughout this project. For their brilliance and, above all, patience I have nothing but the highest respect and gratitude.

Speaking of patience, and adding professionalism, I must thank all the people at Polity who helped me at every stage of this project, especially Louise Knight, Ann Bone and Emma Hutchinson.

Goodenough College provided the original idea and venue for the discussions which led to this volume. The College is an extraordinary community of scholars and artists, tucked away in the heart of London. Its name belies its excellence. Its former Director, Major-General Timothy Toyne-Sewell, its Development Manager, Roger Llewellyn, and its Senior Academic Fellow, Professor Christopher Coker, deserve thanks for their part in making this project possible.

I have been extraordinarily fortunate to have the support and assistance of Michael O'Leary and another colleague, who wishes to remain anonymous. They have offered much and I have taken it all, giving them very little in return. To them both, my apologies and thanks.

Without my wife, Denise, this book would have been neither started nor finished. For this, and everything else good in my life, I thank her with all my heart.

Christopher Ankersen

Abbreviations

Abbreviations occurring in more than one place in the book:

AFP — Armed Forces of the Philippines
AGOA — African Growth and Opportunity Act (US)
ASG — Abu Sayyaf Group
CIS — Commonwealth of Independent States
DRC — Democratic Republic of the Congo
EU — European Union
FATF — Financial Action Task Force
G7 — Group of Seven: Canada, France, Germany, Italy, Japan, UK, USA
G8 — Group of Eight: G7 plus Russia
HIPC — heavily indebted poor countries
ICG — International Crisis Group
IMU — Islamic Movement of Uzbekistan
IPE — International Political Economy
IRA — Irish Republican Army
KMM — Kumpulan Mujahideen Malaysia
LURD — Liberians United for Reconciliation and Democracy
MILF — Moro Islamic Liberation Front
MNNA — Major Non-NATO Ally
MNC — multinational corporation
NEPAD — New Partnership for Africa's Development
NGO — nongovernmental organization
OECD — Organization for Economic Cooperation and Development
OIC — Organization of the Islamic Conference

OSCE	Organization for Security and Cooperation in Europe
PLO	Palestine Liberation Organization
POW	Prisoner of War
PSR	Palestinian Center for Policy and Survey Research
SAP	Structural Adjustment Program
UMNO	United Malays National Organization
WMD	weapons of mass destruction
WTO	World Trade Organization

1

Introduction

Christopher Ankersen

International Terrorism and International Relations: Understandings and Responses

International terrorism is a defining feature of contemporary international relations. The attacks on the United States of America in the fall of 2001 and the invasions of Afghanistan and Iraq are but three of the most obvious hallmarks. Beyond these iconic events, others have been added, changing our interpretations of time and space. Shorthand notations like "9/11" and "7/7" are all that is required to begin a flood of emotional remembrances. Similarly, places like Bali and Madrid are now tinged with connotations of violence at the hands of Muslim extremists. The threat from terrorism and the impact that it and states' responses to it have on our lives have come to define "the new normal."[1] There is certainly no shortage of information available on terrorism: to use the prevailing currency, a Google search on "terrorism" indicates more than 134 million hits, nearly 100 million of them relating to "new terrorism." It is vital to note that this phenomenon is not merely a Western one. Writing in India seven months before September 2001, Poonam Mann declared, "Terrorism today has emerged as the most potent threat to the international community. It has engulfed the entire world in one way or the other."[2] International terrorism and the "war" against it are the leitmotif of our times.

The role of the academic community, though, must be to explore and interrogate such a zeitgeist, not merely to record it. James Der Derian believes the challenge for scholars is "to understand the celerity and alacrity by which our age has now been defined by terrorism."[3] To do anything less would relegate academic inquiry to nothing better than slow journalism. The first aim of this study, then, is to *understand* terrorism, or at least understand how terrorism is understood throughout the world. It is both a founding assumption and a strongly held conclusion of this book that there is no one understanding of terrorism, but rather a plethora of differentiated meanings. These meanings vary across the spectrum of terrorist perpetrators, victims of terrorist violence, decision-makers aiming to respond to terrorism, and the "rest of us." So, while Mann writing in India may claim that international terrorism is the most potent threat, can we be sure that his notion of terrorism is the same as ours, or anyone else's for that matter? The second aim is to examine how, in light of those understandings, countries are responding to terrorism. Given our view on several interpretations of terrorism, it should come as no surprise that we also conclude there is no one war on terrorism, either. Variegated understandings necessitate variegated responses.

It does not take much investigation, of course, to determine that terrorism is an ambiguous term. Terrorism has developed such a polysemic quality that it runs the danger of becoming an "analytical hatstand," where anyone can use it to mean anything, therefore rendering it meaningless.[4] Michael Ignatieff has tried to provide a useful conceptual definition of a terrorist from which many (including several in this book) would dissent: "A terrorist targets non-combatant civilians to achieve a political goal. Those who undertake political actions that target civilians are terrorists."[5] Parsimonious it may be, but it is indicative of the difficulties associated with bringing rigorous definition to the subject. One might ask Ignatieff whether the political actions in question must be violent in order to be considered terrorism, and that would only be the beginning of a long and frustrating interrogation. The authors in this book are left to use (or not) their own definitions of terrorism in reflection of their point of view and line of argument.

Perhaps more than anything else, terrorism as a topic of study has become a question of questions. The titles of scholarly articles across a number of fields are revelatory. Some look for definition: "What is Terrorism? Redefining a Phenomenon in a Time of War."[6] Others search for definitions and answers to moral questions: "What is Terrorism, Why Is it Wrong, and Could it Ever be Morally Permissible?"[7] Perhaps this trend is best captured in a book chapter title: "Questions, Uncertainties and Ambiguity: Discussing the Phenomenon of Terrorism."[8] Such a high degree of questioning creates a great deal of space for exploration. There is little orthodoxy here and this means that different authors may pursue the subject as they see fit, without fear of bumping into barriers or boundaries. The result is a richer discussion.

The potential for a more wide-ranging intellectual exploration must be weighed against the fact that there is little consensus on terrorism, and what little there is can be seen to be inaccurate and informed more by bias than information. This has profound ramifications for the practice of international relations. If, as Weber says, there can be no effective social action without shared social meaning, then the fact that what little we think we know about terrorism is contentious poses serious obstacles to policy-makers.[9] For instance, while most people in the West and elsewhere are opposed to the idea of killing innocent civilians, Ignatieff points out, "We're all in favour of moral clarity and clear lines on terrorism, and when we get down to the business of choosing, we actually disagree profoundly."[10]

Part of any disagreement arises from a profound misunderstanding. When confronting a global phenomenon such as terrorism, there are myriad reasons for confusion and misapprehension. For those in the West, Robert Jervis believes, "there are many barriers to understanding, starting with the fact that the terrorists come from different cultural and religious backgrounds than we do. Even if we can trust the translations of their statements, they metaphorically as well as literally speak a different language." Misunderstanding, though, goes beyond mere linguistic incompatibility. Jervis claims "there are political and psychological inhibitions to understanding why one is hated, since this may lead to asking whether there is some validity to the grievances" which spur people to terrorism.[11] Categorical statements such as Bush's now famous "Either you are with us, or you are with the terrorists"[12] have served to delimit the legitimacy of searching for the meaning underpinning terrorism. This has been a shame and reflects a fallacy. Simon Glynn helpfully reminds us that "to attempt to explain individuals' behaviour by understanding how they interpret or make sense of situations which motivate them, in no way implies either that one necessarily shares their view, or, even if one does, that one condones their chosen response."[13]

In a sense, by failing to understand terrorism, we aid the terrorists in their quest. If, as Philip Heymann contends, "the object of terrorism is . . . to use *magically exaggerated* fear, anger, and anxiety that even a few terrorists can create as a megaphone to speak to audiences that would not otherwise hear or listen,"[14] then our ignorance provides the terrorist with a good portion of the magic required. The brand of terrorism on offer from groups like al-Qaeda thrives on a skewed appreciation of Islam which relies on Muslims and non-Muslims alike having a "less than complete" perspective on the religion. In that way, symbolic terms such as jihad and fatwa help leaders like Osama bin Laden to create and maintain what Der Derian labels "mythoterrorism," which is "conducted for an imagined collectivity, looking backwards to a supposed Golden Age, or predicting a future paradise."[15] By labeling all Muslims, for example, as "potential terrorists," we swell al-Qaeda's ranks with billions of "bogeymen," quite apart from the fact that we may be encouraging a small number to actually take up arms. Lest we think such comfort to the terrorist comes only from bombastic politicians, we might ask what is the real impact of statements from scholars, appearing in peer-reviewed journals, such as this: "Terrorism is a diverse and complex phenomenon for which there is no one overarching psychological explanation . . . [however] this paper emphasizes that for the radical Islamic fundamentalist terrorists and the nationalist-separatist terrorists, 'hatred has been bred in the bone.' "[16] Such demonization is at once shocking and unhelpful. One thing is clear: sticking our heads in the sand and proceeding on the basis of our own limited experience, rumour, and supposition is unlikely to produce positive results. The warning of Zimmermann and Wenger is particularly instructive here: "Labelling . . . terrorism 'irrational' is in fact more than a result of inappropriate intellectual transposition: It is an act of self-deception."[17]

Taken more broadly, this warning instructs us that ideas matter. This is the essence of Weber's conceptualization of social action and forms a key thread in the thesis of this collection. Perhaps because of the "homegrown" nature of the two attacks in London in the summer of 2005, there has been a palpable shift away from trying to determine the identity of potential terrorists toward a focus on their motivations. Turi Munthe asserts that "we have no stock answers anymore to the 'who' question: who are those attacking us? Who joins the global jihad against the West?" We know now that they are as likely to be West Yorkshire cricketers as they are Afghan or Saudi mujahedin. "If we can no longer ask 'who,'" Munthe continues, "then we must ask 'why?'"[18] In this vein, British prime minister Tony Blair, speaking after the London bombings of July 7, 2005, concluded: "This is the battle that must be won, a battle not just about the terrorist methods but their views. Not just their barbaric acts, but their barbaric ideas. Not only what they do but what they think and the thinking they would impose on others."[19] If we are to target terrorist ideas, then it is of prime importance that we first find out what they are and then discover what they mean. As Glynn notes, "it must surely be evident that an understanding of the causes of terrorism is, from a purely pragmatic standpoint, indispensable to any attempt to protect ourselves from it."[20]

Pragmatism notwithstanding, we must be careful not to think that "understanding" is a process by which we try to retrieve some objective truth. Our own subjectivities will mean that when we do begin to follow Munthe's advice and ask "why," "the way we answer that question will determine our policy approach."[21] Put another way, there is a great deal of our current understanding that will be implicated in our further attempts to understand. What we find important, frightening, or unintelligible will shape the way in which we prepare and organize for, and react, in the current struggle with terrorism: "Security . . . is not only about 'who is against us,' but also . . . about 'who we are' and whom we do not wish to be."[22] At the international level it is possible to observe that "the security environments in which states are embedded are in important part cultural and institutional, rather than just material."[23] We must, therefore, be doubly conscious of ideas: conscious of how they motivate terrorists *and* how they motivate the wide variety of societies affected by terrorism around the world – and therefore be wary of constructing a "monolithic conception of national security."[24]

While this book delves into understandings of terrorism, the focus of this study is on the impact terrorism has on international relations. In terms of the level of its analysis, for the most part it deals with effects that terrorism, and states' reaction to it, produce within the international system. Therefore it is concerned, in the main, with grand concepts such as whether or not America's supposed trend toward empire is a cause or result – or both – of international terrorism. It interrogates propositions such as that offered by Deepal Lal, that "empires . . . through their pax . . . provide the most basic of public goods – order – in an anarchical international society of states. This is akin to maintaining order in social life."[25] At the same time, though, the book questions whether or not the United States really is on the road to "universal empire."[26]

Following on from the notion that "ideas matter," this study is sympathetic to the notion that ideas help to shape the identity of states, which, in turn, has an effect on "national security interests and policies."[27] This is manifest in three main ways: first, changes in identity "may affect states' prospects for survival"; second, such changes may alter "the modal character of statehood in the system over time"; and third, new meanings may "cause variation in the character of statehood within a given international system."[28] An early attempt to deal with these issues led Jervis to conclude that "terrorism reinforces state power more than it undermines it or exemplifies the decreasing importance of states," that "the claims for reducing terrorism at its root causes are largely tendentious," and that "the world is not likely to unite against terrorism."[29] The authors in this book grapple with issues – ranging from the foreign policies of countries to the changing nature of international law – through a series of larger and smaller lenses questioning terrorism's impact on what Lipschutz calls "the *logic* of the state system [and] *interpretations of position* and *responses to interpretations* that arise from the logic of the relationship."[30]

The intended audience of this work is a mixed one, comprising both scholars and decision-makers. Jervis claims, "the need for understanding is almost self-evident. Intellectuals seek understanding for its own sake; policy makers need understanding to establish an appropriate policy."[31] Some policy-makers would welcome a stronger link between academic inquiry and political action. Paul Nitze believes "it is by action – in my terms, by the practice of politics – that theory . . . can be kept in touch with reality . . . The two are inseparable; theory and practice being complementary, they constitute harmonic aspects of one whole."[32] There are those who would not agree, however. Christopher Hill, for instance, observes that "the more [scholars] strain for policy relevance, even if only to justify our existence in the eyes of society at large, the more difficult it becomes to maintain intellectual integrity."[33] If there is truth in Hill's statement then it can be found in the idea that it is the *strain* that is potentially damaging, not the mere fact that academics work in areas of policy interest and concern. As Lepgold and Nincic put it, "The issue . . . is whether the production of knowledge with concrete bearing on practical problems may undermine the intellectual foundations on which that knowledge rests."[34] While several of the authors introduce International Relations theory in their chapters, the work as a whole addresses the happenings in what might be called the "real world," as opposed to the academy. It captures the underlying ideas which manifest themselves in the execution of international affairs, and in this way straddles the gaps across the gulfs of theory, policy, and practice. Readers may decide for themselves to what extent the authors are straining for policy relevance and the degree to which any intellectual foundations have been undermined.

The reader will note that the chapters in this study are written in the style of essays. They are not, by and large, studies of exhaustive empirical detail or positivist methodology. Rather, they may be considered to lie within Hedley Bull's "classical" tradition, following an

> approach to theorizing that derives from philosophy, history, and law, and that is characterized above all by explicit reliance on the exercise of judgement and by the assumptions that if we confine ourselves to strict verification and proof there is very little of significance that can be said about international relations, that general propositions about this subject must therefore derive from a scientifically imperfect process of perception or intuition, and that these general propositions cannot be accorded anything more than the tentative and inconclusive status appropriate to their doubtful origin.[35]

It is hoped that the reader finds this approach satisfactory and that this book serves Bull's several purposes: "communication between specialists seeking understanding of the subject . . . education, persuasion [and] public entertainment."[36]

This volume begins by looking at how global terrorism has affected the international system. In that sense, it begins with a "top down" analysis, focusing on how the international community has reacted both to terrorist acts and to state responses to them. Chris Brown's examination looks at changes – and continuities – at the systemic level of analysis. Has terrorism, al-Qaeda, or the War on Terror fundamentally altered the makeup of the international system? Early commentary was split: 9/11 could be seen as the genesis of a new age, one where traditional rivalries and differences would be swept aside in the name of solidarity and common action. Another possibility could have seen the end of the state, challenged now by a nonstate, global, transnational threat with a demonstrated ability to inflict damage and death on the most powerful nation on the planet.

Of course, there is no right or wrong answer. In the time that has passed since the autumn of 2001, the world has seen cooperation, marked by coalitions of the willing and by regional arrangements for information sharing. At the same time, in many aspects and in many parts of the world, as Brown points out, "there is less of an international consensus on the way to combat terrorism now than there was on 10 September, 2001." Brown's focus is on the "war on terror," perhaps the most divisive concept facing the international community at present. War has long been an institution of the international system, and most theoretical understandings of International Relations revolve around differing understandings of when it is justified, how it should be conducted, and what to do once it is over. Purists will say that the War on Terror is no war; it is simply too abstract and multifarious to deserve the term. Here, Brown takes the contrary position and objects: if the international community's greatest contemporary challenge does not fit the definition, redefine the concept of war. In this sense, 9/11 may well change things at the systemic level, but no more so, perhaps, than other "war defining" events, such as the signing of the United Nations Charter.

In contrast to Brown's systemic perspective, Pedahzur, Perliger, and Bialsky illustrate the logic at work at the level of the individual; in this case, the individual suicide bomber. In keeping with one of the key themes of this book, Pedahzur, Perliger, and Bialsky highlight the interrelation between understanding and response. How a potential suicide bomber interprets the world around him or her does not *determine* the course of future events at the global level, but it certainly contributes in a significant way. Just as the field of military studies has its "strategic corporals" – low-ranking personnel who, by dint of being in the right place at the right time, take actions that have profound implications – the field of international relations has felt the effect of "strategic bombers" in New York and London, but also in Colombo, Tel Aviv, and Bali. It seems that the suicidal nature of many of the terror attacks serves to heighten their impact, to intensify the terror. These bombers walk among us, fear no deterrent, and unleash gruesome destruction at close hand.

Pedahzur, Perlinger, and Bialsky's work also points out the deeply subjective nature of a great deal of our understanding of terrorism. Indeed, how can we, as observers, ever really know what goes through the minds of young men and women who decide – who actively choose – to sacrifice themselves in the name of something "greater"? The kind of understanding that is required to fully appreciate this phenomenon is beyond most of us. Instead, we insert stereotypical images as substitutes for understanding. Pedahzur, Perlinger, and Bialsky illustrate that far from being a mere tactic, chosen for instrumental means, suicide bombing is deeply emotive, capable of achieving – at least for its perpetrators – some existential ends as well.

Moving inward from the pole of the international community at one extreme, and the individual suicide bomber at the other, Michael Cox addresses the issue of empire through the lens of the American response to global terror. In this sense, Cox moves our analysis to the level of the state, but keeps a sharp eye on the context within which states must act. Dealing with the United States as an actor on the world stage means coming to grips with the issue of hegemony, whether as an up and comer in the nineteenth century, as a sleeping giant in the early part of the twentieth century, or as a superpower for the last half of that century. America since 2001, Cox believes, is an extension of that trajectory, traced as it has been through the ether of global terrorism. In many ways, it has acted as a quintessential state, defending its own interests as it understands them. But it has been more: it has tried to shape the entire discussion about terrorism, and by extension, the "legitimate" reactions to it. As a state it is debatable whether or not its interests are being addressed: it is possible, especially since the invasion of Iraq in the spring of 2003, to make the claim that more Americans are dying now than for many decades. However, as a shaper of the world order, the track record of the United States appears less ambiguous. It has not "won over" many within the international community, and far from commanding an empire, it can now be seen to be defending itself, not only from terrorists, but from challengers (albeit Lilliputian ones) in places like South America and Europe. As Cox points out, though, "any assessment as to whether the United States is, or is not an empire, has to address the problem of perception." How the United States understands itself and the world must come into contact with the corresponding (and often conflicting) understandings of how the world sees the United States.

William Wallace's chapter on the European understanding of terrorism and war on it is largely predicated on this interplay. Much of what he reports as European thinking is defined largely in opposition to American reactions. Terrorism is nothing new to Europeans, Wallace tells us, and Americans would do well to temper their reaction with a healthy dose of Continental pragmatism. Does this dichotomy mean that Europeans are "backwards looking," mired in history, while the Americans are taking care of today, with an eye on tomorrow? Wallace believes that, to a large extent, opposition is a defining feature of Euro-American affairs now, ranging from secularism to interventionism. But there are signs that this is changing. Some Europeans, feeling overwhelmed, are beginning to lose their liberal bent, opting for policies meant to shore up their European identity.

On the issue of international terrorism, Russia can appear to be, as is often the case, reading from a different page. As Margot Light illustrates, the way in which Russia understands terrorism and the fight against it is shaped by a number of agendas. From one perspective there is a desire to connect with the United States (and indeed the rest of their partners in the G8 club of industrial countries) and "join in" the War on Terror. But as Light is quick to point out, "Russia's war is very different from America's." This stems from a dissimilar understanding of the problem posed by terrorism. Thanks to the Chechen conflict, Islamic fundamentalism represents a threat to the territorial integrity of Russia in a way not found in the American imaginary. Russia may be standing shoulder to shoulder with the US for the common goal of eradicating the threat of terrorism, but it is doing so with its own interests foremost in mind.

Similarly, as Kerry Lynn Nankivell and James Boutilier point out, the "common front" subscribed to by most countries around the world is not as unified as it may appear. Once it is probed, national interests – which are formed by, and in turn form, particular, if not unique, understandings – can be seen to be in play. Nankivell and Boutilier employ the metaphor of refraction when looking at two Asian countries embroiled in the War on Terror. For both the Philippines and Malaysia, their particular historical and cultural identities are determinants in their national strategies against terrorism. For both countries, the "international" dimension of terrorism provides a convenient prism through which they can channel their domestic security concerns. The result for the United States, as the "leader" of the war, is an "alliance of convenience" as much as it is one of the "willing."

Not only is the understanding of how to fight terrorism different in different environments, the impact of international terrorism is also variable. Perhaps nowhere is as affected by this as Africa. As Timothy Shaw points out, Africa can be seen as a "victim" of terrorism, as well as a "source" of it. The diversity of the continent, ranging from the Maghreb to the Horn, from the Niger Delta to the Cape, tends to be ignored in light of the homogenizing narrative of terrorism. Development and human security, ascendant perhaps for the first time in a meaningful way in Africa in the 1990s, are jeopardized by competing "strategic calculations," akin to those made during the Cold War. Those countries who are "on side" get help; those countries who pose the biggest threat (often correlated to their degree of lawlessness) receive attention of a different sort.

If Africa represents a geographic casualty in the War on Terror, then law (international and domestic) represents a conceptual one. The post-9/11 world is one of extraterritorial detention camps, covert renditions, and an erosion of civil liberties. Putting it mildly, Dinah PoKempner states that "the law governing the conduct of hostilities is an important normative area under pressure." At times, that pressure has been intense, inflicted by occurrences of "necessary torture" and other expediencies. PoKempner is careful to point out that when these incidents are reported, and remedied, liberal norms – which form the heart of what most states claim they are defending in the fight against terrorists – are strengthened. The converse, of course, is equally true and the damage done to that liberal foundation has not yet been fully appreciated.

Despite the fact that terrorism is fought with guns, bombs, and even airliners, it relies on money. The illicit flow of financial resources, often through legal but nontransparent means, was quickly identified as a target in the global war on terrorism. In so doing, the shady depths of drug trafficking, money laundering, and corruption had to be plumbed, as did mundane matters, such as money transfers, and charitable fundraising. Martin Navias traces the initial steps taken following September 2001, some conceived of in the earlier "war on drugs," others developed explicitly to combat terrorism. Despite the centrality of terrorist financing and the breadth of international cooperation in the War on Terror, Navias concludes that the financial front may not be the front where the most progress is made.

Much attention has been focused on the role of intelligence in the War on Terror. Languishing in the lull following the end of the Cold War, the global intelligence community was thrust into the spotlight on September 11, 2001. This attention has largely raised questions: What did we know? When did we know it? How did we know? Could we have known more? Christopher Mackmurdo reminds us that reform has been the order of day, and the theme of that reform has been on "breaking down boundaries," within domestic bureaucracies as well as between countries. That process has shown remarkable progress internationally; progress, however, must be understood in the context of individual understandings and agendas. Of course, cooperation has its limits and not all barriers to information sharing have been eliminated. Secrets *not* shared can have as much of an impact as those that are.

We live in a globalized world, one supposedly marked by a convergence of cultures, tastes, and perspectives. Globalization, while not completely understood, has been connected to the rise of international terrorism in a host of ways. Some see the various terrorist attacks of the twenty-first century as a reaction to the onslaught of an American-cum-global culture. Others credit the ease with which information and money can be created and shared – advancements due to globalization – as the accelerant to terrorism. Still others talk about how the reaction to terrorism, spanning countries and civilizations, boosts the fate of globalization. Lawrence Freedman addresses each of these arguments, supporting some and dismissing others. International terrorism has more to do with a debate within Islam than with a clash on a "civilizational" scale. To subsume terrorism and the fight against it under the slogan of globalization (or any other convenient label) is to overlook both the continuities and the irregularities that are in play, shaping our understandings of, and reactions to, the issue of global terrorism.

Notes

1   The term is taken from a speech by American Vice President Dick Cheney and has been taken up by human rights groups as evidence of a change in the role that civil liberties play in social life. Lawyers Committee for Human Rights, *Assessing the New Normal: Liberty and Security for the Post-September 11 United States* (New York: LCHR, 2003).

2   Poonam Mann, "Fighting Terrorism: India and Central Asia," *Strategic Analysis*, 24.11 (2001): 2035.

3   James Der Derian, "Imaging Terror: Logos, Pathos, and Ethos," *Third World Quarterly*, 26.1 (2005): 26.

4   This turn of phrase was first used with reference to "civil society," but the sentiment holds equally true in this case. See Allison Van Rooy, "Civil Society as an Idea: An Analytical Hatstand?" in Allison Van Rooy (ed.), *Civil Society and the Aid Industry* (London: Earthscan, 1998), pp. 6–30.

5   Carnegie Council on Ethics and International Affairs, "Edited Transcript of Remarks: Interview between Joanne Myers and Michael Ignatieff," Jan. 23, 2004, at www.cceia.org (accessed Apr. 20, 2004).

6   Benjamin Grob-Fitzgibbon, "What is Terrorism? Redefining a Phenomenon in a Time of War," *Peace and Change*, 30.2 (2005): 231–46.

7   Alison M. Jaggar, "What is Terrorism, Why Is it Wrong, and Could it Ever be Morally Permissible?" *Journal of Social Philosophy*, 36.2 (2005): 202–17.

8   Doron Zimmermann and Andreas Wenger, *The Transformation of Terrorism* (Zurich: International Relations and Security Network, 2003).

9   Max Weber, *The Theory of Social and Economic Organization*, trans. Talcott Parsons and A. R. Henderson, vol. 1, part 1 of *Economy and Society* (New York: Free Press, 1964).

10 Carnegie Council on Ethics and International Affairs, "Edited Transcript."

11 Robert Jervis, "An Interim Assessment of September 11: What Has Changed and What Has Not?" in Demtrios James Caraley (ed.), *September 11, Terrorist Attacks and US Foreign Policy* (Washington: Academy of Political Science, 2002), pp. 184–5.

12 George W. Bush, "Address to a Joint Session of Congress and the American People," Washington DC, Sept. 20, 2001, at www. whitehouse.gov/news/releases/2001/09/20010920–8.html (accessed Feb. 2, 2002).

13 Simon Glynn, "Deconstructing Terrorism," *Philosophical Forum*, 36.1 (2005): 113. Jervis makes the same point when he says, "Understanding and even empathy is not inconsistent with the strongest possible condemnation" (Jervis, "An Interim Assessment," p. 185).

14 Philip B. Heymann, *Terrorism, Freedom, and Security: Winning without War* (Cambridge, MA: MIT Press, 2004), p. 5, emphasis added.

15 Der Derian, "Imaging Terror," p. 31.

16 Jerrold M. Post, "When Hatred is Bred in the Bone: Psycho-Cultural Foundations of Contemporary Terrorism," *Political Psychology*," 26.4 (2005): 615–16.

17 Zimmermann and Wenger, "The Transformation of Terrorism," p. 23.

18 Turi Munthe, "Terrorism: Not Who But Why?" *RUSI Journal* (Aug. 2005): 8.

19 Tony Blair, "Remarks to the Labour Party Conference," July 16, 2005, at http://news.bbc.co.uk/1/hi/uk/4689363.stm (accessed July 17, 2005).

20 Glynn, "Deconstructing Terrorism," p. 113.

21 Munthe, "Terrorism," p. 8.

22 Ronnie D. Lipschutz, "Negotiating the Boundaries of Difference and Security at Millennium's End," in Ronnie D. Lipschutz (ed.), *On Security* (New York: Columbia University Press, 1998), pp. 214.

23 Ronald L. Jesperson, Alexander Wendt, and Peter J. Katzenstein, "Norms, Identity, and Culture in National Security," in Peter J. Katzenstein (ed.), *The Culture of National Security: Norms and Identity in World Politics* (New York: Columbia University Press, 1996), p. 33.

24 Keith Spence, "World Risk Society and War against Terror," *Political Studies*, 53 (2005): 284.

25 Deepal Lal, *In Defense of Empires* (Washington DC: American Enterprise Insitute, 2004), p. 2.

26 David C. Hendrickson, "Toward Universal Empire: The Dangerous
     Quest for Absolute Security," *World Policy Journal*, 29.3 (2002):
     1–10.
27 Jesperson, Wendt, and Katzenstein, "Norms, Identity and Culture,"
     p. 33.
28 Ibid., p. 34.
29 Jervis, "An Interim Assessment," p. 179.
30 Lipschutz, "Negotiating the Boundaries," p. 212, emphasis in the
     original.
31 Jervis, "An Interim Assessment," p. 185.
32 Paul H. Nitze, cited in Jospeh Lepgold and Miroslav Nincic, *Beyond
     the Ivory Tower: International Relations Theory and the Issue of Policy
     Relevance* (New York: Columbia University Press, 2001), p. 1.
33 Christopher Hill, cited in Lepgold and Nincic, *Beyond the Ivory
     Tower*, p. 1.
34 Lepgold and Nincic, *Beyond the Ivory Tower*, p. 81.
35 Hedley Bull, "International Theory: The Case for the Classical
     Approach," *World Politics*, 18.3 (1966): 361.
36 Ibid., at 365.

2

Global Terror and the International Community

Chris Brown

In response to the atrocities of 9/11, President George W. Bush announced a "War on Terror" and invited the international community to join the US in this venture.[1] The initial response was positive, but now the mood is rather different; at least in Europe, and amongst progressively minded people more generally, there is a widespread feeling that the project of a war on terror was and is misconceived, while, even in the US and among those more supportive of the project, there seems to be a sense that the war is going badly.[2] A few years ago the excellent satirical magazine *The Onion* ran the lapidary headline "Drugs Win Drugs War,"[3] and there is a similar tendency in some quarters to argue that the terrorists are winning the war on terror. In this essay, I will argue against the current mood. First, I will argue that the War on Terror is worthwhile, necessary and unavoidable. Second, that while, for reasons I will shortly suggest, the notion that such a war can be won needs to be heavily qualified, the campaigns so far have been relatively successful – although the involvement of the "international community" in the war has been highly problematic, and, in certain respects, there is less of an international consensus on the way to combat terrorism now than there was on September 10, 2001.

As a preliminary to this discussion, however, some exegesis on the key terms "war" and "terror" is required. This may seem a semantic exercise, but semantics are important; how words are understood defines expectations, and expectations are important in shaping action. If, as many have suggested, the notion of a war on terror is conceptually incoherent, this has important real-world implications.

The Metaphor of War, Applied to Terror

As *The Onion* headline referred to above illustrates, over the last decade or so we have had "wars" against all sorts of social evils – the war against drugs, but also the wars against, *inter alia*, poverty, crime, and AIDS. War in this context is an extended metaphor, referring to a sustained, ongoing project that can be seen as composed of campaigns fought on many fronts against a powerful enemy. Why is this metaphor widely thought to be inappropriate when applied to terror, given that, on the face of it, it would appear to be more appropriate in this case than in the others mentioned? The answer, I think, lies in the way in which war is usually conceptualized.

The case against the "war" metaphor as applied to terror rests on the common perception that wars have a beginning, a middle, and an end; that they are declared (explicitly or tacitly); that campaigns are fought by recognized combatants, and a winner is determined; and that in the history books they can be dated with reasonable precision. It is noted, quite rightly, that none of this can be applied easily to the War on Terror. Who can say when this war began – certainly well before 9/11 from the perspective of the terrorists – and who will ever be able to say it is over? We can say with certainty that there will be no ceremony of surrender on the deck of a convenient aircraft carrier.

So, better, perhaps, to change metaphors and see the war on terror as analogous to police action against crime? In that context, everyone knows that there is no beginning and no ending. The police may succeed in eliminating one particular gang of criminals, but another will soon take its place. However many muggers, burglars and fraudsters are caught, there will always be mugging, burglary and fraud. Accordingly, the purpose of police actions is not to eliminate crime but to lower its incidence by preventive measures and by increasing the likelihood that any particular criminal will be caught, even if crime as such will continue. In the same way, the campaign against terrorism will not end terrorism, but it may get rid of some specific terrorists and make the cost of terrorist acts higher for the rest, thereby reducing their incidence.

This is a sensible position, but it is not, I think, incompatible with the idea of a war on terror, so long as the notion of war is redefined, which, in any event, it should be. The model of a war presented above has been very much in evidence for the history of the European states system, but it is by no means the most prevalent in history.[4] The kinds of small wars that are pushed to the margin of Western thought (low intensity conflicts, guerrilla campaigns, savage wars of peace, and so on) are actually much more typical, as are the long struggles with exterior barbarians that characterized imperial China's wars, or the wars of the later Roman Empire. Moreover, and this is the crucial point, these latter wars are also more typical of the post-Westphalian international order that we now inhabit. Very few modern wars have actually ended with a surrender and/or a peace treaty. The current situation in Iraq demonstrates the point; *pace* President Bush's declaration of the end of the war on an aircraft carrier, Baathist militants have continued the struggle;[5] even though they have little popular support and were comprehensively defeated in conventional war, they see no reason not to continue the struggle by other means.

In this light, once we acknowledge that "war" in the modern world is no longer Clausewitzian, Western war, we ought not to worry too much about the announcement of a "war on terror." Such a war will look very like the kind of defensive imperial wars waged by China behind the Great Wall combined with the sort of low-intensity military campaigns that have been characteristic of both colonialism and decolonization. There is, however, one other objection to the notion of a "war on terror," and that is that it assigns too much importance to the phenomenon of terrorism; on a global scale, terrorism is not that important a problem compared to many others (world poverty, for example), and to dignify terrorists with the status of combatants (even so-called "illegal combatants") in a war is a mistake. There is a serious point here, but I think, ultimately, the criticism is misplaced; a war on terror would not be appropriate for all varieties of terrorism, but it is for the variety against which the present war is being, or ought to be, fought.

The Meaning of Terror

The term "terror" is too wide and insufficiently specified. In making this point I very definitely do not wish to endorse the oft-heard proposition that terrorism is simply a matter of definition and that, as the saying goes, one man's terrorist is another's freedom fighter. That is pernicious nonsense. The deliberate murder of innocents in pursuit of a political end is terrorism whether carried out by an individual, group or state, and, crucially, whether or not we approve of the cause. Of course, there will always be hard cases and grey areas, but the fact that day shades into night via twilight does not mean that we cannot distinguish between day and night, to paraphrase Dr Johnson.[6]

Still, there are different kinds of terrorism and different motives for terrorism, which should lead to different strategies for combating terrorism – and these differences have tended to be ignored in some of the rhetoric of the war on terror. The central point is that although some people may come to take psychopathic pleasure in terrorist activity and/or combine terrorism with straight criminality, as a rule they come to terrorism initially as the result of a political choice, and the basis on which this choice is made is crucial to identifying and specifying the threat that terrorism poses.

People of good will who think about this issue generally acknowledge that terrorists take up their calling for political reasons, but then proceed to make unwarranted assumptions about the politics in question. Terrorists, it is assumed, are driven to their appalling deeds because of oppression by the powers-that-be – terrorism, it is said, is a weapon of the weak, and no one would become, say, a suicide bomber unless they were already reduced to utter hopelessness.[7] From this perspective, terrorism is an *illegitimate* response to a *legitimate* grievance. Often this is so, but while true of some of those who turn to "propaganda of the deed" because, rightly or wrongly, they see no other way of opposing tyranny, it is by no means true of *all* terrorists, and in particular it is *not* true of the terrorists who ought to be on the receiving end of the war on terror.

While some terrorists engage in terrorism in pursuit of the kinds of freedoms and rights recognized by modern liberal-democratic and social democratic polities, others reject these freedoms, and pursue goals antithetical to these freedoms and rights. Sometimes the intolerable oppression and sense of hopelessness that drives the terrorist on can indeed be defined in terms with which any modern heir to the Enlightenment can identify, even without necessarily agreeing that the level of oppression taking place justifies the action. But sometimes this is not the case, and the "intolerable oppression" in question would not be recognized as such by progressively minded people of good will. The goals of the terrorist are crucial here, and sometimes these goals are themselves repressive, and, if achieved, would actually bring about more, as opposed to less, oppression.

This distinction is important for two reasons. First, when the rhetoric of human rights and Enlightenment values is employed, this very fact acts as a constraint on the kinds of actions carried out, if only because support from other people who share these values is sought. Second, the fact that terrorists use this rhetoric establishes a point of contact between them and nonviolent politics, and makes it easier to bring them into the democratic fold. Many of those who were on the fringes of the left-wing terrorism of the 1960s and 1970s have gone on to pursue legitimate political careers, most noticeably the former German foreign minister, Joschka Fischer. It has proved possible, just about, to involve the Provisional IRA in the political process in Northern Ireland, but, significantly, its more exclusively nationalist and antiprogressivist elements, now forming the so-called "Real" IRA, have proved impossible to co-opt. Similar differences exist between the Palestine Liberation Organization (PLO) and Hamas in the struggles in Israel/Palestine; a comparison between the Covenants of the

PLO, calling for a secular state in Palestine, and Hamas, which is overtly anti-Semitic, makes the point, although, as in Ireland, the reality may be a little less clearcut.[8]

The Real War against Terror

The relevance of this to the War on Terror ought, I hope, to be clear. The terrorists who ought to be the true targets of the War on Terror are *not* helpfully defined as all those who use terror as a political instrument. The kinds of terror campaigns that have emerged in, say, Ireland have emerged out of specific situations; essentially they are local campaigns and they require local solutions. Some mix of sticks and carrots appropriate in each case – the cost of terrorism must be increased for the terrorists via police action, but terrorists must also be given some reason for stopping their campaign. Insofar as the terrorists are ostensibly campaigning for political freedoms that are intrinsically desirable, there need be no qualms about making concessions to end these campaigns, so long as these concessions do not create new and greater injustices. In any event, this kind of terrorism needs to be dealt with on a case-by-case basis.

The campaign against the variety of Islamic fascism represented by Osama bin Laden, al-Qaeda and its allies is another matter; here a "war on terror" is indeed an appropriate response, because the campaign this enemy has launched is general in scope and most definitely not linked to progressive politics or any cause for which men and women of good will ought to have sympathy. Bin Laden and his followers have, somewhat belatedly, adopted the (potentially progressivist) cause of the Palestinian people, but this is pretty clearly opportunism. Al-Qaeda is not attacking America and the West because it supports Israel – France, for example, has been pretty consistently hostile to Israel and yet has been the victim of many attacks by radical Islam – but for much more fundamental reasons. Bin Laden's 1996 "Declaration of War against the Americans Occupying the Lands of the Two Holy Places" specifies the stationing of US troops in Saudi Arabia as the immediate cause of this declaration, but ranges widely over nearly 1,500 years of historical wrongs allegedly done to Islam by its enemies, of whom the American "crusaders" are simply the most recent manifestation.[9]

In short, America and the West are under attack not because of what they *do* but because of what they *are*. Of course, there are some Western policies that do increase support for the terrorists in the Islamic world, in particular the Western unwillingness to see Israel destroyed – which is widely misinterpreted as tantamount to presenting Israel with a blank cheque to oppress Palestinians – but while such factors may be important on the margin, the core reason for Islamic terrorism is that, albeit in an imperfect way, Western societies instantiate a set of principles that are anathema to bin Laden and other Islamo-fascists.

Fascism is not usually a term that should be used as a descriptor out of its original context, but here it is reasonably precise; al-Qaeda represents a particular authoritarian take on modernity in much the same way that the real Fascists did early last century.[10] The Fascist movements of the first half of the twentieth century wanted to create industrial societies devoid of irony, without representative institutions, and without extended human rights, and in this they are followed by contemporary "fundamentalist" movements. Such fundamentalists want a world with modern technology, but with scientific rationality confined to the technical, a world with information technology and mass media but with its content strictly regulated, a world where the community of Believers exercise political power and nonbelievers are disenfranchised and, a consistent theme of fundamentalisms of all varieties, a world where women remain subjected to men, and transgressive sexual identities are delegitimized. This is the basis for Islamo-fascism – and other fundamentalist fascisms, although in their cases the context is different, as will be noted later – and a global war directed against this kind of terrorism makes sense in a way that a war against "terror" plain and simple does not. Al-Qaeda's goals are not specific and they are not negotiable. Its aim is ultimately to bring the whole world under the sway of its particular brand of Islam, starting with the Gulf and moving out; mass conversion to Islam is hardly something that the West can offer to the terrorists as a carrot.

It might be – will be – argued that this overdramatizes the
threat from al-Qaeda: the kinds of terrorist actions it has carried
out have been broadly commensurable with those of other terrorists group and offer no genuine threat to the Western way of
life. It will be said that the attach of 9/11 was a terrible event,
but 2,750 deaths do not justify an apocalyptic response. There is
some truth to this criticism – although it is worth noting that
approximately the same number of people died in one hour on
9/11 in New York City as have been killed in the Northern
Ireland troubles since the mid-1960s – but what it leaves out of
the equation is the possibilities inherent in the potential avail-
ability of weapons of mass destruction to the terrorists. The
attack of 9/11 was carried out using box cutters to capture commercial airliners and turn them into flying bombs, but there can
be little doubt that if the terrorists can get hold of biological or
radiological weapons the next attack will be far more devastating;
equally, material captured in Afghanistan suggests the search for
WMD is an al-Qaeda priority.[11] The key point, returning to an
earlier observation, is that while, say, the Provisional IRA would
not have used WMD because they were looking for the support
of people who would have been alienated by such methods, and
because they, the PIRA, have been proud (sometimes unjustly
so) of the discrimination they used in their terror tactics, targeting only "representatives" of the British state or economic targets,
these restraints do not apply to al-Qaeda, who quite explicitly
regard *all* Westerners as legitimate targets not by virtue of what
they do, but because of who they are.

There are, of course, issues on the margin of al-Qaeda's campaign which look more like the Irish case, but here appearances
are deceptive. A peace deal between Israel and the PLO based
on a mutually satisfactory two-state solution or a single secular
state would be a good thing in its own terms, but it would have
very little effect on the wider picture. One can say with absolute
certainty that no deal in Palestine that would be acceptable to
even the most radical Israeli "Peace Now" member would be
regarded as satisfactory by al-Qaeda (or Hamas) – their goal is
not peace and justice in Palestine but the elimination of Jews and
"crusaders" throughout the Middle East, and that as a first stage

only of a wider program. In effect, what we have here is a war between two different conceptions of how life ought to be lived. The West, for all its faults, imperfectly instantiates a number of Enlightenment goals that are anathema to the Islamo-fascists, and it is precisely for this reason that the West is worth defending and must be defended. Hence the War on Terror is worth fighting and must be fought.

The Balance Sheet

But has the war been, so far, a successful project? The first point here that needs to be stressed is that success and failure in this context are relative terms – as will be clear from what has gone before, there is no question of an outright victory in this war. This needs to be stressed because the media in our age are dominated by a culture that chooses to deny the relativity of success and failure. The "tabloidization" even of most of what were previously the most serious-minded Western, especially English-speaking, media is a sad fact about our time. News has become "infotainment", and journalists and presenters have become showbiz figures, always on the lookout for the sensational story. This has produced a general bias in favour of bad news, which always makes a better story than good news, while, in order to demonstrate their "integrity" and preserve their professional reputations and self-images (all the while adding to the drama), the celebrity journalists who dominate the mainstream news and current affairs programs take every opportunity to magnify the incompetence and stupidity of their own national leaders.[12] Add to this the currently fashionable anti-Americanism which European reactions to the Bush administration have pushed to new heights, and it is unsurprising that reporting of the War on Terror has presented a seriously distorted vision of the world.[13]

This media culture obscures the picture vis-à-vis the war on terror because the main way in which the war is being fought is precisely via the kind of campaign that our media are least well equipped to report. The unprecedented financial measures taken by all the world's major economic actors against al-Qaeda go largely unnoticed by the press and the BBC.[14] The extensive active cooperation between the security services of the various supporters of the War on Terror cannot, by definition, be reported if it is to be successful, and the passive security measures designed to deny terrorists access to vulnerable targets only get reported when they fail.

How do we know whether these measures have been effective? The simple answer is, we do not – the security services may have some idea, but even they will not be aware of the plots that have never gone past the planning stage because of their efforts. All we can do is look at the record since September 2001, which has been, I think, in certain respects rather encouraging. The basic point is that immediately after 9/11 the universal assumption was that, as the expression has it, the other shoe would soon drop, and it has not. Since we can be pretty sure that al-Qaeda would have liked to have followed up 9/11 with other atrocities on a similar scale in the US and other Western countries, and almost certainly had plans to this effect, it seems as if, so far, it has been frustrated. Of course, all this could change by a single act – it is in the nature of terrorism that the terrorists only have to get lucky once – but for the time being it does look as if al-Qaeda is weaker than is usually supposed.[15]

Partly this is because of the relative success of the campaigns in Afghanistan and, more controversially, Iraq. Relative is, of course, a necessary qualifier here, but then no one should expect everything to work out perfectly – to reiterate, success and failure are always to be qualified. Prior to 2002, Afghanistan was a safe haven for Islamo-fascism; now it is not. It may well be the case that the new Afghan government only has effective control in relatively few areas, and that Taliban and al-Qaeda forces are still operating in the country, but the point is that these forces are now having to devote resources to their own survival that previously they could devote to killing Westerners. This is, as far as I am concerned, progress – and it is a bonus here that music can again be heard on the streets of Kabul, that the women of Afghanistan can use their education once more, and that the football stadium is nowadays used for football rather than public executions.

The Iraq case is obviously more complex; the doubtful legality of the action has clearly produced great stresses within the West and the outcome cannot be described as unambiguously positive. Still, there are at least some reasons to be cheerful. Saddam was a tyrant and removing him from power was a good thing – opponents of the war should always be asked whether they actually regret the fall of Saddam, and if the answer is no, how else this could have been brought about; the sanctions that were the main alternative way of containing his ambitions clearly hurt the innocent rather more than has the use of force.[16] Saddam was certainly no ideological bedfellow of al-Qaeda, but on the time-honored principle that my enemy's enemy is my friend they had occasionally cooperated in the past and might well have done so again in the future. His interest in WMD was apparent over a 25-year period; in the 1990s an effective inspection regime under Rolf Ekeus destroyed much of his arsenal, but the French and Russian refusal to reappoint Ekeus in 2002 and the establishment of a less enthusiastic regime of inspection under a weaker leader boded ill for the future had action not been taken.[17]

Critics of the war argue that subsequent events vindicate their stance and the guerrilla campaign currently underway suggests that the US is about to be trapped in a quagmire of potentially Vietnam-like proportions. In response to this it should first be noted that things are nowhere near as bad as prewar critics believed they would be; thus, for example, Amnesty International's account of what they believed could be the human costs of war – 50,000 civilian deaths, 500,000 civilian injuries, 2 million refugees and displaced persons and 10 million people in need of humanitarian assistance – has proved to be wildly out of line with reality.[18] Things could perhaps have been that bad, but they were not and are not.

The quagmire thesis seems unduly pessimistic for three reasons. First, fairly obviously, casualty levels are of orders of magnitude lower than during Vietnam – the US casualties that are taking place represent desperate tragedies for the individuals concerned, their families and friends, but they are not at levels that a super-power of 300 million people cannot sustain indefinitely, given the will, which is, of course, a very important proviso.[19] More to the point perhaps, it is actually rather better that the pool of potential al-Qaeda militants pour into Iraq and fight US and British soldiers than that they train up to kill US and British civil-ians in New York City and London. One of the real difficulties of the war on terror is precisely that of pinning down the enemy, getting them into one's field of fire – when George W. Bush said of the terrorist threat in Iraq, "bring it on," he was actually expressing a perfectly sensible point, albeit in a somewhat insen-sitive way.[20]

The third reason not to be too pessimistic about the situation in Iraq is the attitude of the Iraqi people, the majority of whom appear not to support the terrorists; within the so-called Sunni triangle to the north of Baghdad there may be more support for Saddam, this being the area from which nearly all of his clients were drawn, but in the country as a whole there seems little enthusiasm for a Baathist restoration.[21] This is a crucial point. Although things have not been going at all badly so far, strategic victory (see earlier qualifications) in the War on Terror probably does requires a substantial change in Middle Eastern politics, in particular the emergence of at least one Arab state that can provide a model of nonauthoritarian, nonfascist modernity.[22] The point is that, while the fundamentalist, fascist mind-set is not confined to Islamo-fascists, they are the most prominent of such groups – and the most ruthless and unpleasant – not because of any features specific to Islam as a religion, but because of the particular conditions to be found within the Arab world, espe-cially the failure of any state or society in the region to offer a convincing, nonfundamentalist, liberal model of modernity.

It may well be idealistic and unrealistic to think of the estab-lishment of a functioning liberal democracy in Iraq, but some such development is, I believe, possible, as long as one is not looking for Denmark-on-the-Euphrates but would settle for something rather less ambitious, perhaps on the model of Turkey.

Iraq is a country with a great deal of human capital and, I think, a desire not to revert to tyranny. More, the failure of the so-called Arab street to erupt during the war, or since, is significant. It does not signify support for the US or the West, but it does suggest that thinking Arabs are unhappy with their existing political order. For much of the last 50 years ordinary Arabs have been told by their authoritarian governments that all their ills can be put down to the Zionists and their American friends – perhaps now a realization that the fault lies elsewhere is spreading. One product of such a realization is support for al-Qaeda, which is also opposed to the authoritarian Arab regimes – this is why it is important that the US keeps its nerve in Iraq and tries to create a situation in which there is another model of what a noncorrupt Arab political order might look like. There is an awful lot riding on Iraq at the moment.

The International Community and the War on Terror

Examining the brief account of the War on Terror presented above it is clear that the degree to which the war has been fought by the "international community" varies from campaign to campaign. Economic and security cooperation has been widely supported, and NATO has accepted a major postwar role in Afghanistan, but the Iraq campaign has been highly divisive. The only effective military support for the American military campaign came from the UK and Australia, and the other major powers – France, Germany, Russia, and China – were in opposition, leading to a serious war of words at the United Nations.

How did this come about? Was this divide an inevitable result of the US's drive for primacy; does it tell us something about the failures of US diplomacy; or does it illustrate something more fundamental about the gap emerging between the US and Europe, as writers such as Robert Kagan and Thomas Friedman have plausibly implied? The "drive for primacy" thesis has points in its favor; it may well be that some people in Washington did regard 9/11 as an opportunity to pursue more forcibly an agenda they already supported on other grounds.[23] Still, and perhaps counter-intuitively, the problem with this thesis – and "Chomskyism" more generally – is that it insists on interpreting the world in American terms, promoting a kind of inverted account of "American exceptionalism" in which it is the exceptional evil of the US rather than its exceptional goodness that explains why things happen. You're so vain, you probably think this song is about you, one might respond; the determination to interpret everything as a response to US policy denies agency to other international actors – as suggested above, it implies that terrorists are solely driven by our wickedness, and in this context it implies that America's allies, rather than pursuing their own goals, are simply reacting to US policy.

More to the point is James Rubin's account of the failures of US diplomacy, which acknowledges that the goals of the US and its allies may well be different, but assumes that the role of diplomacy is precisely to bridge such differences, castigating the Bush administration for its failure so to do.[24] A strong case is made by Rubin, but there are, perhaps, more fundamental issues involved here. Thomas Friedman has argued that if a situation requires the use of military force, even NATO is no longer an effective international body; if peacekeeping, nation-building and training of personnel were what was required then there are many developed countries who can provide this, but only the US, the UK, and Australia, sometimes with France, are prepared to commit their soldiers to actual fighting.[25] Robert Kagan provides a more extended account of this thesis: in essence, Continental Europeans have been so successful in replacing military force by economic power in Europe itself that they have come to assume, wrongly, that the same strategy will be successful everywhere else in the world, rejecting the Anglo-American view that sometimes only force will suffice.[26] If this is so there are limits to what diplomacy can do.

In any event, the term "the international community" has always had a somewhat dubious ring to it – a term that diplomats employ when it suits them and ignore when it does not. The problem in the 2000s goes deeper than this however. The key point is that US military and economic superiority over everyone else is so great that we have to rethink the dynamics of international order.[27] The notion of an "international community" conveys the idea that the states that make up the international system have certain common values, and will, under some circumstances, coordinate their actions in order to pursue these values – but this process of coordination is no longer a matter of states "concerting" their actions, but rather of the leadership of one hegemonic power.[28] Other states have no effective capacity to prevent the US from acting, and, by the same token, can add very little to the effectiveness of whatever action the US is taking. Iraq 2003 was undertaken by the US and only two allies, while Kosovo 1999 was a NATO project, but in *both* cases the actual fighting (bombing in the case of Kosovo) was carried out overwhelmingly by US troops and warplanes, and the contribution of others was nominal at best.

This situation is hardly conducive to the effective operation of the international community. From the point of view of the US, multilateralism may bring substantial political benefits and a higher quality of decision-making, but, *pace* Joseph Nye, it is no longer a necessity.[29] The benefits are, in any event, accompanied by costs; understandably enough, many in the US military establishment – including former NATO commander, and former candidate for the Democratic presidential nomination, General Wesley Clark – have expressed a preference for unilateral operations, on the principle that allies impose restraints while adding nothing to capabilities.[30] But, of course, from the point of view of America's allies, more or less exactly the same calculus points in the direction of "free-riding," taking the benefits of US power while verbally condemning its excesses and attempting to disassociate oneself from the consequences of its operation. This has been the strategy adopted by most of the West Europeans – East Europeans, being less confident of American security guarantees, and having a greater need for them than their Western colleagues, have been more supportive of US action, whatever their private views. Those countries which have rejected the strategy of free-riding, such as Britain, have done so not because their contribution to actions is necessary or even particularly useful, but precisely because they have not wanted to see the US isolated, and because they believe, probably correctly, that they can gain more influence with the US by not free-riding.[31]

Does this all mean that the notion of an international community is now redundant, or at best translates into "the US and its immediate allies" – or perhaps the "Anglosphere," a term coined by the science fiction writer Neal Stephenson, but which is occasionally used to describe the English-speaking democracies, and sometimes extended to East Europeans and others who support similar values (and speak English as a second language)?[32] It may be that although 9/11 had the immediate effect of uniting the world in condemnation of al-Qaeda, the longer-term effect has been to expose the hollowness of the idea that there is a world community. As against this, it should be recalled that the military side is only one facet of the War on Terror; apart from the economic and intelligence cooperation noted above, the skills of the Western Europeans in "nation-building" contribute effectively to the "hearts and minds" side of the war. It should also be noted that relations between the West and both Russia and China have markedly improved, despite the quarrel over Iraq.

Conclusion

The War on Terror will last for a long time and four or five years is too short a period for anything other than the most provisional of summings up. It is, however, worth occasionally accentuating the positive, because there is a danger that the negativism of the popular media (which in Britain include almost everything apart from the *Financial Times*) will come to dominate popular perceptions and act as a self-fulfilling prophecy, sapping the will of the US and others to continue the struggle. Still, if things are not too bad, they are not too good either, and sooner or later there will be another major terrorist outrage in the West, and then another. There is, I think, no way of avoiding such atrocities, although we can hope that we get lucky as often as possible.

The key point is to realize that there is no magic way of making all this go away. It is not actually possible to stop fighting the war on terrorism – or, to be more accurate, we could stop fighting but the war will go on anyway and we will be simply victims not combatants. The War on Terror is not optional, because there is no accommodation possible with the terrorists; certainly projects for global social justice need to be pursued – and a solution to the Israel–Palestine problem – but because we ought to be in favour of social justice, not because they are going to have any effect on this war. The war is something we are going to have to learn to live with, whether we want to or not.

Notes

This chapter is based on a presentation given at Goodenough College in the fall of 2002. It was later published as "Reflections on the 'War on Terror', Two Years On," *International Politics*, 41.1 (Mar. 2004): 51–64, and has been further updated for this collection.

I am grateful for comments from fellow participants at the Goodenough Trust conference where this paper was first presented. The main text was written in October 2003; obviously much has changed since then, but rather than take advantage of the pleasures of hindsight I have allowed the judgments I made then to stand unrevised, with only the occasional later comment.

1   See, for example, President Bush's speech to the UN General Assembly on November 10, 2001: www.whitehouse.gov/news/releases/2001/11/20011110-3.html.

2   Thus, for example, the essays collected in a special section "Bush at Midterm" in the authoritative journal *Foreign Affairs*, 82.5 (Sept.–Oct. 2003) are uniformly pessimistic about the War on Terror.

3   Now available as a – very popular – T-shirt; Scott Dickers et al., *Our Dumb Century* (New York: Crown, 1999), p. 163.

4   A key reference here is Victor Davis Hanson, *The Western Way of War* (New York: Knopf, 1989).

5   Speech: "Bush: Iraq is One Victory in War on Terror," May 1, 2003, at www.cnn.com/2003/ALLPOLITICS/05/01/sprj.irq.bush.speech/index.html.

6   The best discussion of such hard cases is still Michael Walzer, *Just and Unjust Wars* (New York: Basic Books, 1977).

7   See, for example, the controversial comments of Cherie Booth, QC and wife of Tony Blair, on the subject of Palestinian suicide bombers: "As long as young people feel they have got no hope but to blow themselves up you are never going to make progress," June 18, 2002, at http://news.bbc.co.uk/1/hi/uk_politics/2051372.stm.

8   Both the Hamas and PLO Covenants can conveniently be found at the website of the Avalon Project of the Yale Law School, at www.yale.edu/lawweb/avalon/mideast/.

9   The Declaration of August 1996 is widely available on the web, as is the later 1998 Fatwah against the Infidels; see e.g. www.pbs.org/newshour/terrorism/international/fatwa_1996.html. Michael Scott Doran, "Somebody Else's Civil War," *Foreign Affairs*, 81.1 (Jan.–Feb. 2002), is a very good short account of the motivations of al-Qaeda.

10 This position is developed in Chris Brown, "Narratives of Religion, Civilisation and Modernity," in Ken Booth and Tim Dunne (eds), *Worlds in Collision* (Basingstoke: Palgrave, 2002). Paul Berman, *Terror and Liberalism* (New York: Norton, 2003), provides empirical evidence of the continuity between fascism and al-Qaeda.

11 See e.g. "Tapes Shed New Light on Bin Laden's Network," CNN.com, Aug. 19, 2002, at www.cnn.com/2002/US/08/18/terror.tape.main/.

12 Philip Bobbitt, *The Shield of Achilles* (New York: Knopf, 2002), writes to the same effect on the role of the media in the "market-state" (ch. 10).

13 Such anti-Americanism is often stoked by disaffected Americans: witness, for example, the extraordinary success of Michael Moore's comical fiction, the film *Bowling for Columbine* and his book *Stupid White Men* (Basingstoke: Penguin, 2001), which are both widely regarded as documentary works, in spite of their manifest inaccuracies; see e.g. www.spinsanity.org/columns/20021119.html for some of these inaccuracies.

14 See UN Security Council Resolution 1373 (2001), 28 September 2003 for the legal basis for these measures.

15 Since I wrote these words in January 2004, bombs have been detonated in Istanbul Madrid, and London, with major political consequences in the second case, but the general point holds – the second shoe has not yet fallen on a scale commensurate with the first on 9/11.

16 Christopher Hitchens, *A Long Short War: The Postponed Liberation of Iraq* (New York: Plume, 2003) is one of the best statements of this case.

17 See Rolf Ekeus, "Don't be Fooled, They Found More than You Think," *Sunday Times* News Review, Oct. 19, 2003, p. 7. (Subsequent inquiries by the US Senate and Lord Butler in the UK have thrown doubt on the intelligence that Saddam actually possessed WMD, but his intent to develop them given the opportunity has not been challenged; July 2004).

18 *Amnesty*, Mar.–Apr., 2003, front page.

19 As of October 30, 2003, the US has lost 354 soldiers, roughly half after May 1, the date at which President Bush declared "mission accomplished" (*Financial Times*, Oct. 30, 2003, sec. 1, p. 13). In Vietnam the US suffered 58,000 deaths over around nine years: in the worst year, 1968, there were 16,592 deaths, just over 45 per day. The current media policy of headlining every individual death draws attention to how few casualties there actually are in Iraq – such a policy would be impossible in a real war.

20 See "Bush Warns Militants who Attack US Troops in Iraq," CNN, July 3, 2003, at http://edition.cnn.com/2003/ALLPOLITICS/07/02/sprj.nitop.bush/.

21 It is obviously difficult to substantiate this position, but apart from the anecdotal evidence offered by, for example, the obvious delight in Iraq at the death of Saddam's sons and the capture of Saddam, there is some poll data from a Zogby International Poll conducted in August 2003 which supports a positive reading of Iraqi public opinion. See Karl Zinmeister, "What Iraqis Really Think," *Wall Street Journal*, Sept. 10, 2003. (The Provisional Government established on the return to Iraqi sovereignty on June 30, 2004 appears to enjoy quite wide public support.)

22 See Fouad Ajami, "Iraq and the Arab's Future," *Foreign Affairs*, 82.1 (Jan.–Feb. 2003).

23 See e.g. Noam Chomsky, *Hegemony or Survival: America's Quest for Global Dominance* (London: Penguin, 2003).

24 James Rubin, "Stumbling into War," *Foreign Affairs*, 82.5 (Sept.–Oct. 2003).

25 Thomas Friedman, "The New Club NATO," *New York Times*, Nov. 17, 2002.

26 Robert Kagan, *Paradise and Power: America vs Europe in the Twenty-First Century* (New York: Atlantic Books, 2003). Robert Cooper

argues a not dissimilar position in *The Breaking of Nations* (London: Atlantic Books, 2003).

27 William Wohlforth, "The Stability of a Unipolar World," *International Security*, 24.1 (1999); Charles Krauthammer, "The Unipolar Moment Revisited," *National Interest*, no. 70 (winter 2002–3).

28 Chris Brown, "Do Great Powers have Great Responsibilities?" *Global Society*, no. 1 (2004).

29 Joseph Nye, *The Paradox of American Power: Why the World's Only Superpower Cannot Go it Alone* (Oxford: Oxford University Press, 2002).

30 Wesley Clark, *Waging Modern War: Bosnia, Kosovo and the Future of Combat* (New York: Public Affairs Press, 2002).

31 See Peter Riddell, *Hug Them Close* (London: Politico's, 2003).

32 See www.wordspy.com/words/Anglosphere.asp for an interesting survey of the term, and, for a wide definition, Andrew Sullivan, "Come On In: The Anglosphere is Freedom's New Home," *Sunday Times* News Review, Feb. 2, 2003.

3

Explaining Suicide Terrorism

Ami Pedahzur, Arie Perliger, and Alexander Bialsky

The advent of suicide attacks in the early 1980s in Lebanon, and their rapid spread throughout the world in the past two decades, has attracted the attention of researchers from a large number of disciplines. They have sought to understand the processes and the factors that lead young people around the world to sacrifice their lives for political goals, through suicide attacks.

Early attempts to comprehend the suicide attacks phenomenon appeared in the late 1980s and focused on the individuals who perpetrated them. The first group of researchers tried to apply a wide variety of theoretical approaches based on personality psychology and suicide behavior, in order to examine whether the suicide attackers shared any similar character traits. Alternatively, they attempted to identify behavioral disorders or mental problems that were common to most of them. Despite the researchers' many attempts in this direction, their findings concluded that it was impossible to identify common personality traits which characterized the suicide attackers. Moreover, it seemed that the psychological profiles of most of them were no different than those of regular terrorists. Furthermore, unlike people who commit suicide in other life circumstances, and harm only themselves, suicide attackers do not tend to display early warning signs before their suicide attacks.

Alongside the considerable progress in various psychological approaches, other researchers attempted to account for suicide attacks via sociological explanations. Some researchers tried to explain the motivation of suicide attackers by categorizing them using Émile Durkheim's typology, which describes four different types of motivations that lead individuals to commit suicide. Others sought to explain the tendency among groups to groom suicide attackers by using the relative deprivation approach originally developed by Ted Gurr. As in the case of the psychological approaches, however, these theoretical approaches were also unable to provide a satisfactory explanation for the suicide attack phenomenon. Studies that attempted to confirm these theories found that even though suicide attackers sometimes come from deprived communities, they are not necessarily poorer or less educated when compared to "regular" terrorists.

In light of only partial success in finding an explanation for suicide attacks that focuses on the individual level, the researchers claimed that deciphering the phenomenon lay in the understanding that suicide attackers are simply weapons in the hands of others who direct their actions. This instrumental concept of the suicide attacker's role was the basis for the emergence of two additional approaches to the study of this phenomenon. The first is the cultural approach, whose advocates claim that the dominance of Islamic components in the groups perpetrating suicide attacks makes it impossible to avoid the recognition that the centrality of sacrificing one's life for religious values, which is deeply rooted in Islamic religion, heritage, and culture, contributes substantively to the increase in suicide attacks and their use throughout the world by Islamic fundamentalist groups. Even though this explanation seems reasonable at first glance, 31.5 percent of suicide attacks throughout the world were perpetrated by non-Muslims and another 25 percent were carried out by Muslims operating in the framework of secular groups, making it difficult to accept the cultural explanation. Furthermore, martyrdom in the name of religious principles exists in both Christianity and Judaism, and studies have shown that, in general, the suicide phenomenon itself is less common in Muslim countries than in the West.

The second approach that emerged is the rational organizational approach. This approach explains suicide attacks by focusing on their organizational framework, and mainly on the decision-making process of the organizational elite. It was first developed by international relations researchers, who suggested that suicide attacks are the response by a substate group in an extended, violent, and asymmetrical confrontation with a strong state. The organization can use suicide attacks to maintain a type of strategic balance with the state. Over time, this approach was expanded by political science researchers, some of whom claimed that the use of suicide attacks was intended to help the organization to garner support from the public it is interested in representing. On the other hand, there were those who argued that this was a rational decision-making process by the organization's leaders, who would use a suicide attack when they felt it was the most efficient means of achieving the organization's goals.

In recent years there seems to have been a decline in the ability of the rational organizational approach to explain suicide attacks. The above approach, used by researchers seeking to comprehend the suicide phenomenon, had ceased to be effective, as most of the relevant groups had either ceased operating, or stopped using the tactic of suicide attacks. At the same time, however, there has been a rise in the number of suicide attacks perpetrated by groups with a network structure, such as al-Qaeda, and by older groups that adopted a network structure, such as Hamas. The researcher who presented this change most succinctly was Marc Sageman, who used the network analysis approach in his study of the global jihad. This approach was expanded by sociology and computer science researchers, who tried to depict the structure of the networks, their characteristics, and their weaknesses.

In this chapter we will present a three-generational explanatory model for interpreting suicide attacks, which is based on three generations of studies of suicide attacks. The first part of the model is the individual-cultural generation, which consists of two dimensions, the individual and the community. In the personal dimension we will try to identify the main factors that motivate suicide attackers, and in the community dimension we will examine conditions that must exist in the community the terrorist group represents, in order to foster the development of suicide attacks. The second part of the model is the rational-organizational generation, which focuses on the strategic considerations that prompt terror groups to use suicide attacks. The third part is the network perspective generation, in which we will review studies which analyzed networks of suicide bombers, and will try to determine what motivates these networks to initiate suicide attacks.

The Individual-Cultural Generation

The individual dimension

One basic necessity for all suicide attacks is the recruitment of activists who will be willing to carry out such attacks. As noted at the beginning of this chapter, the suggestion that psychological or social factors motivate suicide attackers does not provide a satisfactory explanation for an individual's desire to end his life as a suicide attacker. However, in order to obtain some understanding of what motivates young people to act in this way, we conducted a systematic survey of the main motivations of the Palestinian suicide attackers, starting from the first suicide attack in April 1993 and ending in early 2005. In addition, we conducted a survey of the literature that focuses on the motivations of suicide attackers in other groups worldwide.

In general, the findings can be divided into two main groups of motivating factors: (1) motivations stemming from a personal crisis in the suicide attacker's life before his or her recruitment; and (2) motivations stemming from the feeling of deep commitment to the social network to which he or she belongs or the group of which he or she is a member.

In the first group of motivations, the individual's personal crisis could be connected with the loss of a close friend, relative, or familiar figure. In such cases, the desire for revenge is what leads the individual to participate in a suicide attack. The example of

Henadi Jaradat, who blew herself up in the Maxim restaurant in Haifa following the killing of her brother and fiancée by soldiers of the Israeli Defense Forces (IDF), is the most well-known instance of this type of motivation. Still, the personal crisis could also stem from the distress of the community of which the individual is a member.

The more an individual sees his community suffering, humiliated, and in a state of hopelessness, the greater his willingness to take radical action in order to gain release from or end the personal crisis he is experiencing through identification with his community's suffering. The individual essentially assimilates the community's distress and subsequently experiences severe personal distress, making him a preferred candidate for a suicide attack. Group recruiters will present the suicide attack to the candidate as the optimal solution for ending his personal distress, while at the same time aiding his community.

Sometimes the personal crisis has other causes. In many cases suicide attackers are people who suffer from social exclusion in the community in which they live. This could be due to abnormal external appearance or deviance from social or cultural norms. By participating in a suicide attack, such individuals can regain the social legitimacy they have lost and rehabilitate their name in the community. By their acts, their families are also relieved of the shame brought upon them by these persons in their deviance from the society and culture.

The second group of motivations explaining the consent of individuals to participate in suicide attacks is connected with the concept of commitment. The findings resulting from our survey indicate two main types of commitment among suicide attackers. The first is a commitment to some social network, while the second is a commitment to the group, its leaders, and the ideology the group represents. A great many of the suicide attackers operated within a social network whose members are closely affiliated with one another, and who develop deep loyalty to the group and its members through a wide variety of social projects. They live and study together, create symbols, share similar behavior and customs, so that eventually every member develops a high level of commitment to the network's values, goals, and other members. Research has found that the internal dynamics in such networks lead to a heightened ideology that guides them and to the radicalization of their members, each of whom aspires to show his friends loyalty and commitment to the network's values. This type of network spawned most of the al-Qaeda suicide attackers, who operated and were indoctrinated in various social networks in different locations throughout Europe. Examples of such networks can also be found in the Palestinian arena, such as a group of childhood friends from the village of Assira A-Shimaliya, three of whom participated in suicide attacks on the pedestrian mall in downtown Jerusalem during July 1997, after a fourth friend had participated in a suicide attack just over a month earlier.

Commitment to the group can also be an important motivating factor for a suicide attacker. When the individual feels a deep commitment toward the group and its goals, he becomes willing to sacrifice his life following incidents that may not directly affect him (or people close to him), but harm the group to which he belongs (such as attacks against the group's leaders or other members). It is also worth noting that most of the suicide attackers trained, lived, and operated alongside other members of the group, thus developing a sense of inner commitment to them. Therefore, when the time comes, they are ready to embark on suicide attacks, just like soldiers on the battlefield who sacrifice their lives for their comrades.

Figure 3.1 shows the division of the motivating factors among Palestinian suicide attackers. This figure indicates that 27.8

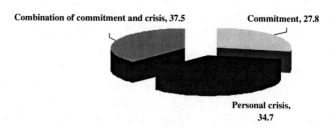

Figure 3.1   Motivations of Palestinian suicide bombers (percentages), 1993–2005

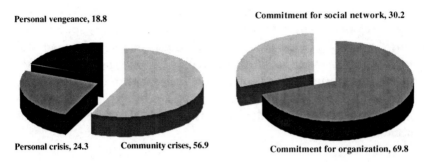

Personal vengeance, 18.8   **Commitment for social network, 30.2**

Personal crisis, 24.3   **Community crises, 56.9**   **Commitment for organization, 69.8**

Figure 3.2 Secondary motivations of Palestinian suicide bombers (percentages), 1993–2005

percent of the Palestinian suicide attackers were motivated by feelings of commitment to a group or social network of some kind, while 34.7 percent acted to end a personal crisis. Still, the largest group of attackers was motivated by a combination of factors: a personal crisis and a strong feeling of commitment toward the group or social network to which they belonged. Figure 3.2 shows the divisions within each of the groups in figure 3.1.

Regarding the type of commitment, it is evident that the overwhelming majority (69.8 percent) participated in suicide attacks out of commitment to their group, while just under a third (30.2 percent) acted through a commitment to their social network. The Palestinian suicide attackers who acted in response to a personal crisis are similarly asymmetrically divided. The crisis that motivated 56.95 percent of them stemmed from their identification with their community's suffering; 24.3 percent were motivated by a purely personal crisis, and 18.8 percent were motivated by revenge.

These figures lead to the conclusion that the combination of a sense of commitment and a personal crisis is the strongest motivating factor behind a decision by young Palestinians to become suicide attackers. In addition, almost half of them acted as a result of a personal crisis connected with their own history, indicating that the Palestinian groups seek out potential suicide attackers whose personal history makes them suitable for recruitment and increases the chances that they will consent to participating in a suicide attack. These were mainly young people who had suffered a loss or were socially ostracized. Finally, the findings indicate that external motivating factors (payment to the family after the death of the suicide attacker, promises of life after death) are less central to the individual's decision to participate in a suicide attack.

The community dimension

Alongside the understanding that the basic necessity for suicide attacks is the recruitment of people who are willing to sacrifice their lives, it is worth noting that there are a number of major conditions concerning the community from which those people come and which helps the group to recruit them and to execute the attacks.

First, all the communities that gave rise to the suicide attacks are communities that have been in a prolonged military conflict for many years and which suffer from harsh political, cultural, and economic deprivation. Thus, if we examine the extent of deprivation in the ethnic communities (by using the MAR dataset),[1] we will find that the combined measure of deprivation in the communities which resorted to suicide attack tactics stands at an average of 9.2, compared to 3.75 in communities which did not resort to suicide attacks. Furthermore, for many years these communities have been suffering from a sense of hopelessness and inability to change their political status.

The result of community deprivation is a feeling of frustration among members of those communities; a sense of hopelessness and lack of any expectation of being able to live a normal life. It is precisely these feelings that the terror groups exploit in order to prompt communities to support suicide attacks. The groups instill in these communities a culture of death and hatred, with an emphasis on the dehumanization of the enemy. The instilling of a death culture that praises and glorifies the self-sacrifice of suicide attackers gives community members a sense of political, cultural, and social empowerment that helps them to view suicide attacks as a genuine way out of their situation. Furthermore, the effective assimilation of a death culture helps the terror groups to recruit volunteers more easily for suicide attacks, and without the necessity for a long and complicated process of indoctrination. Also, the need for external rewards to suicide attackers becomes relatively small.

This means that in communities in which a terror group successfully instills a death culture that sanctifies the acts of self-sacrifice by the group's activists, and which sanctifies the suicide attackers' acts, there are longer and more successful campaigns of suicide attacks (as is quite evident in relation to Hezbollah, the LTTE in Sri Lanka, and the Palestinian groups). In cases in which a death culture is not effectively assimilated in the local population, the campaign will be relatively short, as happened in the case of the activities of the PKK (Kurdistan Workers' Party) in Turkey and among the Chechens in Russia.

In general, the marketing of a death culture is conducted via three main avenues: (1) the glorification of the suicide attackers themselves; (2) the glorification of the ideology and ideas in whose name they carried out the suicide attack; and (3) the dehumanization of the enemy and therefore the reinforcement of the moral legitimacy of the suicide attacks. All three components strengthen the social image of the community and lead to cultural and political practices that support the suicide idea as a tool for achieving political goals.

The various groups use a wide range of means for marketing the culture of death. The Palestinian groups, for example, market this culture through activities that advertise and market the suicide attackers in all possible mass media. Hence one can see photos of the martyrs in educational, cultural, and public health institutions (the walls of the waiting area outside the emergency room at the hospital in Jenin, for instance, are covered with posters of suicide attackers from the various groups). In addition, the terror groups exploit summer camps, hang posters in public places, write articles and biographies of the suicide attackers in the press (the children's newspaper of the Hamas movement, *Al-Fateh*, published a story of a female jihad fighter in its Ramadan issue). Similarly, the groups display the suicide attackers on their websites and of course publish videos of their last wills. To a great extent this death culture has succeeded in rooting itself in Palestinian society. According to Palestinian Center for Policy and Survey Research (PSR) surveys, by 1995 48.6 percent of the population supported suicide attacks. Later on, this figure rose to around 70 percent.

Hezbollah also developed cultural practices to glorify suicide attacks, making extensive use of the propaganda tools at its disposal to turn the suicide attackers in its service into admirable role models by glorifying them and their actions. Thus, for example, Hezbollah turned the image of Ahmed Qassir, the suicide attacker who blew up the headquarters of the Israeli Defense Forces in Tyre in 1982, into a mega-celebrity in the Arab world by putting up posters of him in many public places, establishing a memorial site for him in Tehran, and holding annual memorial ceremonies for him on the anniversary of his suicide. In addition, Hezbollah's spiritual leaders have provided suicide attacks with a strong spiritual-religious context, imbuing them with an ideological rationale while at the same time dehumanizing the Israeli enemy.

Still, the death culture is also marketed by purely secular groups. The Tamils, for example, glorify and reinforce social traditions which are relayed from generation to generation and which extol the value of self-sacrifice. Their main emphasis is on Hindu values such as heroic self-sacrifice, self-abnegation, and commitment, which are imprinted in the consciousness of Tamil society. All these have undergone a type of transformation and have been adopted in the context of suicide attacks. Various practices are used in order to promote this type of process. Every year on July 5, for example, Black Tigers Day is celebrated to commemorate the suicide attacks and honor the suicide attackers who sacrificed themselves for the group. Hundreds of shrines throughout the Jaffna region have been built in memory of the suicide attackers, and ceremonies are held similar to those conducted for the gods in the regular religious temples. The shrines are decorated with flowers and oil is offered on the altars. In addition, on that day the Tamil radio station broadcasts the stories of the suicide attacks. Another ceremony is held on November 25 – Heroes' Night – for those who gave their lives for the liberation of their people (that day is also part of a whole week at the end of November – Martyrs' Week). The funerals of Tamil suicide attackers are similar to those of Palestinian suicide attackers, being turned into national events, including extensive publicity.

As part of the discussion of the community dimension it is worth noting that in the model presented, religion is not the primary or central explanation for the appearance of suicide attacks. It is rather one more tool to aid the terror groups in reinforcing a culture of death via practices and in contexts familiar to the public they represent, and from whom they are interested in recruiting suicide attackers.

In conclusion, two main community components support the emergence of suicide attackers in a specific community. The first is a long-standing sense of deprivation, hopelessness, and despair, while the second is the harnessing of these feelings in order to instill a culture of death in the community. The success of a group in establishing a death culture in the community will help it acquire legitimacy from the public it represents, garner support, and of course recruit candidates for carrying out suicide attacks.

The Rational Organizational Generation

Like other political organizations (such as interest groups, political parties, and social movements) terror groups seek first and foremost to achieve long-term and short-term political goals, and to secure a dominant status in the political or community arena; they are constantly preoccupied with ensuring the group's survival over time and maintaining its cohesion. Terror groups, however, are unique in that the design of their structure and methods of operation are a direct result of their systematic use of violence. It is important to note that the nature of the violence used is not crucial as long as it aids the group in realizing the goals it has set for itself.

In addressing the organizational generation, there are three distinct facets that account for when a terror group resorts to suicide attacks. First, a campaign of suicide attacks will be carried out by groups that are in a prolonged, violent conflict against a considerably stronger opponent. In many cases, the use of suicide attackers is the last military option of a group under heavy military pressure. This was the situation in the early 1990s in Sri Lanka, when the LTTE felt compelled by the heavy military pressure exerted against it by the Sinhalese army to resort to suicide attacks in order to reduce its losses (which were much higher during its direct clashes with the local army). Similarly, the PKK in Turkey and the Chechen separatists in Chechnya began using suicide attacks largely in response to their own need to continue proving they were still operative despite the heavy military pressure exerted against them. Finally, the Palestinian case also demonstrates terror groups' use of the weapon of suicide attack as a tool for achieving a strategic balance in the face of a stronger enemy. This balance is largely the result of the impressive operational effectiveness of suicide attacks (suicide attacks in Israel over the last ten years caused an average of 43.59 casualties a year, compared to an average of 8.37 in remote-controlled bombings and 3.7 in shooting attacks). Unlike "regular" terror attacks, the suicide attacker is a smart bomb who can choose the optimal place and timing in order to produce as many casualties as possible. In addition, suicide attackers can more easily penetrate urban civilian areas and have a particularly strong psychological effect on the victimized population, because of the impression they make by their determination and willingness to lose their lives for the sake of their goals.

Second, at the local level, the groups that initiate waves of suicide attacks use them to recruit support from the public they claim to represent. Thus, when the leader of a group senses that the use of a suicide attack campaign strengthens public support for his group, he will continue to initiate suicide attacks. In the Palestinian arena it is possible to observe how the Islamic groups viewed suicide attacks as a central tool in competing with the PLO and the Palestinian Authority. This fact was quite prominent in talks with Hamas activists, who revealed that the suicide attack campaign stemmed, among other things, from their desire to control the Palestinian street. They believed that they could use the suicide attack campaign to raise the morale of the Palestinian population and thus win its admiration and loyalty toward the group and its goals.

Indeed, to a great extent the Islamic Palestinian groups did succeed in gaining more public support through the suicide attack campaigns. For example, the monthly surveys conducted by PSR during 1993, before the large-scale use of the suicide attack tactic, showed that support for Hamas among the Palestinian public stood at around 12–13 percent. By November of the following year, however (after the initiation of the suicide attack campaign), this support had climbed to 18 percent, and the combined support for Hamas and Islamic Jihad, their partner in the suicide attack campaign, was over 21 percent. This increase in the numbers of supporters of Hamas, and the increase of over 15 percent in the numbers supporting Islamic Jihad, indicates a certain success by the suicide attack campaign in attracting support for these groups. During the al-Aqsa intifada the Islamic groups even managed to gain popularity to equal that enjoyed by the Fatah.

Another group that hoped to use its activities to gain broad popular support was Hezbollah, which launched a suicide attack campaign in order to compete with Amal and to strengthen its support among the Shiite population in southern Lebanon. During the years in which Hezbollah initiated suicide attacks, it actually did manage to expand its popularity among the Shiites in the Beirut region (beyond the support it enjoyed from the Shiite population in southern Lebanon), while exploiting the fact that the Shiite population was enchanted by and admired the group's acts of self-sacrifice. In conclusion, it can be stated that Hezbollah's suicide attacks both raised the status and power of the Shiite community, and pushed that community, which suffered from the Israeli occupation, into the group's arms. Furthermore, the heroic image attached to Hezbollah quite surprisingly resulted in a spread of support for this group far beyond the boundaries of the country's Shiite population. Incidentally, Hezbollah's success in garnering support via suicide attacks prompted the rival Shiite group, Amal, to implement suicide attacks as well.

Finally, the LTTE also used suicide attacks to gain support from the Tamil population for their struggle, by strengthening the affinity of the Tamil population with the group and its goals. To this end, the group presented the suicide attacks as a positive measure that was necessary in order to guarantee the national and ethnic goals of the Tamil people in the future, stating: "You have to be ready to sacrifice your life today in order to ensure a better future."

In concluding the presentation of the rational-organizational generation, it is worth noting an additional facet typical of this generation. This is the fact that sometimes the suicide attack is used as a weapon for waging internal disputes within the group, or to fulfill other needs of the group. Sometimes we see militant factions in the groups expressing their dissatisfaction with their leadership by initiating a suicide attack campaign, and sometimes the leadership itself will implement suicide attacks in order to suppress the militant factions within it. There is evidence, for example, that the September 11 attacks were part of an attempt to consolidate the ranks of al-Qaeda and to reduce tensions that had developed between the leadership in Kabul and the al-Qaeda cells scattered in various places around the world.

In relation to the Chechen groups and the LTTE in Sri Lanka, suicide attacks served as an effective tool for increasing support beyond the countries in which these groups operated. The Chechen groups gained external economic support and volunteers. Suicide attacks against Russian forces in Chechnya and in Russia itself led to an infusion of funds to the separatists from international terror groups, including from al-Qaeda. The LTTE also benefited from suicide attacks, in the exposure and aura they created, making it easier for the group to develop operative networks throughout the world and increasing the funding sent to the group from external sources, thus encouraging the large Tamil population living outside Sri Lanka to rally to the group's cause.

Finally, there is evidence that during Hamas's first suicide campaign, there were many instances when the internal leadership sought not to implement suicide attacks, in order to prevent a direct confrontation with the Palestinian Authority and harm to the group's civilian infrastructure. At the same time, the external leadership, which wanted to emphasize its superiority, created networks of suicide attackers anyway, and initiated attacks. Thus there were many instances when suicide attacks were an expression of the will of the external leadership to demonstrate its superiority and control over the group.

Third Generation: the Network Perspective for Explaining Suicide Attacks

In the preceding sections we have presented the first two generations in the study of suicide attacks. In this section we will present a new generation of approaches in this field: the networks generation. The theories developed in this generation assume that the approaches of the two previous generations were effective in explaining the use of suicide attacks by the terror groups that operated until the 2000s. Starting in 2000, however, most of the terror groups that served as case studies for an explanation of suicide attacks via organizational models almost completely ceased their attacks. At the same time, however, not only did suicide attacks not disappear, they actually increased – there have been at least 2.7 times as many suicide attacks since the beginning of 2000 as there were from the early 1980s until the end of 1999.

This increase can be explained by the fact that while there was a decline in suicide attacks by established groups, there has been a rise in suicide attacks by groups with a network structure, different in character from the veteran, established groups. Furthermore, even among other illegal groups, such as international crime groups, there has been a marked transition from an organizational activity pattern to network behavior patterns.

It is therefore difficult to apply the research methods used in studying those earlier groups in order to comprehend the suicide attacks of recent years. A prominent example of this difficulty is al-Qaeda, which is fundamentally different from the groups mentioned previously. Most of the studies that focused on al-Qaeda stressed the fact that this is not a group with a clear leadership echelon or an orderly structure. Furthermore, even the Palestinian terror groups changed during the al-Aqsa intifada and became more similar to al-Qaeda in their structure and way of operating.

The change in the characteristics of the structure and operative patterns of the groups that now initiate suicide attacks leads to the conclusion that in order to understand the motives and characteristics of the suicide attacks of recent years, this phenomenon must also be examined using the social network analysis approach – a sociological approach that probes how network characteristics influence and mold the functions of the network's members. This is in addition to the application of existing theories concerning the study of suicide attacks. To this end, we will first explain the main characteristics of networks compared to those of organizations, and then present initial findings from the research on suicide networks.

Even though the results of the suicide attacks perpetrated by networks are identical to those of attacks carried out by organizations, there are a number of significant differences between them in other respects. Unlike an organization, which is characterized by a clear leadership echelon, the network has a nonhierarchical structure that is made up of connections between its members and is not based on formal rankings of positions. Instead of a leader, a network has a "hub," who is a player situated at the center of the network by virtue of having the largest number of connections with members of the network, and by virtue of his location at its geographical center. Contrary to the organizational concept, in which the leader is at the top of the organizational hierarchy, the hub is usually a local activist who is frequently replaced and sometimes shares his influence over the network with other hubs; his importance stems from his ability to connect the various elements required to carry out a suicide attack. In some of the networks the hubs are local representatives of an organization, who receive funding and orders, usually indirectly, from the organizational leadership, which is located quite far away.

Another difference between the organization and the network concerns the functioning of the network structure compared with the organizational structure. In most cases, organizations are characterized by a strict hierarchy, like that in a military unit, while the network structure is usually informal and fluid. A structure of the latter type is not hierarchical and lacks distinctions between the leadership echelon and the activists. Thus a network can be set up in one day, change its structure, and disappear after a short period. The networks themselves have varied structures, from chain networks, in which the flow of information must go through all the members of the network to reach a particular member; to star networks, in which all the network's members are connected to one another via the hub; to networks in which there are maximum connections between all the members, meaning that each member is connected to all the others.

The difference between the network and the organization is also manifest in the process for recruiting new members. Organizations recruit new members via recruitment programs, in which new members are persuaded or compelled to join various operations, including suicide attacks. Networks, on the other hand, are frequently established on the basis of existing ties, such as friendship or family relations, and in most cases new members are recruited using the "friend brings a friend" method. The connections in a network can be loose, linking a large, widely spread network that is inside its own community, or they can be very strong, if the network is small and in a foreign environment, as happened in the case of the suicide networks involved in the September 11 attacks in the United States. Even the weak ties are quite important, however, because they are used for bringing in new members, which is not possible in a network consisting of close ties between small numbers of members.

As for the training of new members, organizations have quasi-military training frameworks in which new members are trained, and such frameworks are cut off from the community in which the organizations operate. The training process in networks is extremely short, and in most cases the trainer is also the recruiter.

In certain cases, members of a network can create a social "bubble," in which they are cut off from their surroundings, but in other cases they can be influenced by the attitude of the environment that surrounds them, with respect to the idea of self-sacrifice as a component of terror.

These differences between organizations and networks indicate that in order to understand the factors that motivate the network to carry out suicide attacks, research must focus on the hubs and their motivations for perpetrating suicide attacks. A number of interests can be identified among the hubs, some of them personal, some ideological, and some local political, but all are motivators for suicide attacks. In the case of the Palestinian suicide terror networks, for example, the hubs were motivated by competition for local public opinion.

One of the first researchers to use the network approach was Marc Sageman, who employed this method to describe the "Global Salafi Jihad," which al-Qaeda represents nowadays. He views al-Qaeda as composed of a few regional clusters, which are built around "hubs." These clusters in turn are all related to the Central Staff cluster. Sageman stresses that these networks are not motivated by inadequacy, shame, or vulnerability, but rather by feelings of friendship, kinship, discipleship, and worship, with friendship playing the key part. The main weaknesses of these networks are their hubs. The hub can become a point of attack on a network because most of its communications take place through it. The elimination of a hub breaks the network down into an isolated, noncommunicating group of nodes and essentially paralyzes it.[2]

Pedahzur and Perliger also used the network approach to analyze Palestinian suicide actions. One of their main findings was the peripheral nature of suicide attackers in their network. Another important finding dealt with decision-making in the networks. Decisions were actually made, to a great extent, by local activists, and the struggles between local and family groups proved to be the most important motivating factor for the initiation of suicide attacks.[3]

Finally, it can be stated that in recent years there has been a change in the activity patterns of terror groups, requiring researchers to use different approaches and techniques to add to the understanding of the motivations behind today's suicide attacks.

Conclusions

In this chapter we have sought to present a three-generational explanatory model of suicide attacks, including the various facets of this complex phenomenon. It is clear that this phenomenon has undergone far-reaching changes in recent years. Groups that previously used this tactic have ceased using suicide attacks, and they have been replaced by new groups that do use them. Furthermore, even the existing groups have undergone a transformation and have adjusted themselves to the changing environment of the twenty-first century. Today there are mainly local cells of terror networks, receiving general direction and support from the organizational leadership, and operating on their own when executing a suicide attack. In this type of situation, the organizational leadership is not involved at all in the operational process of dispatching the suicide attacker, and this is handled by the local cell. Similarly, the environment beyond the terror cell is less important and there is a greater emphasis on the network's internal processes and the determination of its members.

An effective campaign against this phenomenon must therefore focus on damaging the networks and mainly on their hubs, while at the same time striving to neutralize the effects of suicide attacks. Israel's success in reducing the intensity of suicide attacks against it by using this combination of tactics is an example of such a campaign. During 2006 Israel arrested and killed a number of prominent terrorist leaders. During January 2006 the Israeli Security Service arrested members of another Hamas terror network from Hebron, whose members were responsible for a number of shooting attacks. In June, Israel assassinated Jamal Abu Samhadana, the leader and the founder of the Popular Resistance Committees in Gaza. In addition, Israel arrested Ibrahim Hamed, the leader of Hamas's military wing in the West Bank. At the same time, a number of terrorist networks were uncovered, such as the Hamas network from the Hebron area in December 2006, whose members conspired to kidnap soldiers and transfer them to Gaza, in order to negotiate the release of Palestinian prisoners from Israeli jails. These activities show the scope of Israeli military and intelligence counterterrorist activity against Palestinian terror networks in Gaza and West Bank during the year 2006. As is evident from the events of the past few years, Israel managed to crush much of the leadership of the terror networks, while at the same time quashing some of the elite leadership of the Islamic organizations. This neutralizing of the side-effects of suicide attacks was supplemented by the establishment of a comprehensive defense system in the urban Israeli civilian environment, and the toughening of the treatment of the Palestinian population. Still, despite this success, it must be remembered that no strong-arm model for coping with terror has proved effective in the long term. Suicide attacks have almost always subsided only after the country coping with them has managed to reduce the support for such attacks among the population represented by the organization perpetrating them.

Notes

This chapter is based on an earlier chapter published in Hebrew in a book entitled *Ticking Bombs* (2005).

1   The Minority at Risk (MAR) database tracks 284 politically active ethnic groups. It was initiated by Ted Robert Gurr in 1986 and is based at the Center for International Development and Conflict Management (CIDCM) at the University of Maryland.
2   Marc Sageman, *Understanding Terror Networks* (Philadelphia: University of Pennsylvania Press, 2004), pp. 152–8, 178.
3   Ami Pedahzur and Arie Perliger, "The Changing Nature of Suicide Attacks: A Social Network Perspective," *Social Forces*, 84.4 (2006): 1987–2008.

4

The Imperial Republic in an Age of War: The United States from September 11 to Iraq

Michael Cox

Introduction: Rome on the Potomac?

Modern America is strangely fascinated by imperial Rome. Our
Capitol, and our best train stations look Roman. Roman and classical images surface in popular culture at regular but not chance
intervals: the big films of the 1950s and 1960s, from *Ben Hur*
(1959), *Spartacus* (1960) and *Cleopatra* (1964), and *Fall of the
Roman Empire* (1964) were also films of the Cold War, in which
the imperial analogy looked very attractive. The classical block-
busters then stopped quite suddenly, however, with Vietnam-era
doubts. The idea revived with *Gladiators* (2000) or *Troy* (2004)
and *Alexander* (2004). Classical empires literally speak to us – but
they require some interpretation.[1]

Intellectual constructs tell us a great deal about how we try to
make sense of the world, even if they sometimes they tell us less
about the real world itself. The Cold War produced many such,
from the notion of "the free world" itself through to the always
dubious idea that the Soviet Union sought world domination.
Indeed, during the last decade of the Cold War, much was made

of the Soviet threat and what many academics regarded as the almost inevitable decline of the United States, when in fact the former was in headlong retreat and the latter about to experience a decade-long renaissance. All this of course came to a quite unexpected end between 1989 and 1991, leaving many intellectuals confused and for the most part concerned about the shape of the future world order. Some took refuge in liberal nostrums (some would argue banalities) like the "end of history"; others (invariably realists) predicted that we were about to go back to a more dangerous past. The majority however tended to bank on what seemed a far more relevant and dynamic idea: globalization. The notion was not without its appeal. In fact, for a while, there seemed to be no other academic label that more accurately defined the nature of the post–Cold War era. Once again though there was a gap between what at least some writers assumed was unfolding – no less than the withering away of states and the disappearance of geography – and what in fact was taking place on the ground. The idea thus lost some, if not all, of its sparkle among a whole host of increasingly disenchanted analysts. Indeed, according to one of the more critical, by the end of the 1990s globalization and with it the theories it had spawned was now quite dead, reduced to conceptual rubble by the idea's contact with reality.[2]

Intellectuals, like nature, it seems, abhor a vacuum, and no sooner had the globalization debate been consigned into that proverbial dustbin of history than yet another great idea began to be discussed in earnest: namely, what kind of conceptual creature was this vast, sprawling entity, known as the American system of power? It was none too clear. But brute facts this time actually looked like brute facts, and after having seen off its main enemy in 1991 and then experiencing what could only be described as a most rejuvenating ten years, it did begin to look as if the world was confronted with a unique situation: a superpower that was more than just a superpower.[3] This may have meant the world was seriously out of balance. But few intellectuals seemed willing to challenge the proposition that no other nation in history had enjoyed such formidable advantages. Even one-time pessimists began to think the unthinkable – none more so than Paul Kennedy, for several years the English prophet of American doom. Kennedy, recall, made his reputation in the late 1980s by predicting the longer term "relative" decline of America as a great power.[4] Now he began to sing from a very different hymn-sheet. After a decade of economic growth, he noted, with the American military in the ascendancy, and its popular culture sweeping all before it, it was no longer possible to talk (as he had done only a few years before) of the US as if it were just some normal great power.[5] America was different, exceptional even, and the sooner we all recognized the fact the better.[6]

In the midst of these musings two things occurred which converted a fairly easy-going debate into a deadly serious one. The first was 9/11 and with it the fear of more attacks on the United States to come. The second was the revolution this then produced in US foreign policy and what followed in the shape of the Iraq War. The combination of fear on the one hand and opportunity on the other not only seemed to render more traditional foreign policy notions irrelevant, but called forth a flurry of debate about how to rethink the role of the United States in a new international system. In the process, an important, challenging, and for some deeply disturbing idea began to gain some influential adherents: that not only was the United States an empire in all but name but had better begin behaving like one. Long thought buried by most academics,[7] the notion of empire in particular rapidly started making a most dramatic intellectual comeback.[8] As Charles Maier was to observe, "a decade ago, certainly two," the very idea of empire would have caused "righteous indignation" among most American observers. But not any longer, it seemed.[9] As Ronald Wright noted, "how recently we believed the age of empire was dead," but how popular the idea was now becoming in certain American circles.[10] And what many now appeared to be suggesting was quite startling: that we should start calling things by their right name, drop the pretence that America was different to other great powers,[11] and accept that if the world was going to remain a stable place, the US had to act in much the same imperial fashion as the British and Romans had done several centuries before. One of the new gurus – a Scot – was more explicit still. America he noted had always been an empire, remained one, and now had to behave like one.[12] Indeed, according to some analysts, it was precisely because the United States had been insufficiently assertive in the 1990s – now referred to in some conservative circles as that "decade of neglect" – that 9/11 happened in the first place. Such inertia was no longer an option. In a fragmenting postmodern world, where small bands of fanatics could cause havoc and mayhem, there was only one possible solution. Politicians might want to call it something else, and no doubt President Bush would deny that "America" had "an empire to extend."[13] But that is precisely what the United States would have to do. Other existing methods had been tried and found wanting. Now, in a new era, where old forms of deterrence and traditional assumptions about threats no longer held, it was up to America to impose its own form of order on a disorderly world: to fight the savage war of peace (to quote one of the new gurus) so as to protect and enlarge the empire of liberty.[14]

The intellectual turn to empire raises a whole raft of questions, and in what follows I want to explain how and why an idea that had "dared not speak its name" for at least a generation was suddenly thrust back on to the agenda during the first few years of the twenty-first century.[15] I make three broad points. The first is that in many ways the idea of a specifically American empire is not really new at all. Indeed, it has a long and distinguished pedigree that stretches back over 200 years. Furthermore, while the more modern version of the discussion about empire only really began in earnest at the turn of our new century, the debate in one form or another had been developing for many years – and it is important to look at this debate to put the contemporary discussion into some context. This in turn leads to a second issue: about the appropriateness of the term itself. Here I concede at least one point: the notion of a specifically American empire does have its problems.[16] However, as I try to show, these problems are in my view outweighed by its utility as a comparative tool of analysis, one which has not been fully exploited in the past, largely because it has for so long been associated with a radical critique of American foreign policy.[17] Finally, I want to explore the future of the American Empire. Here I take issue with those who have argued – and with more passion than ever since the imbroglio in Iraq – that the United States has already become the "first failed empire of the twenty-first century."[18] There is no doubt that the US is facing serious problems as a result of Iraq. These should not be underestimated. Blunders though are one thing. To talk of a failing empire however is something else altogether. Indeed, as I will attempt to argue by way of a conclusion, we would be most unwise to write the United States off. It might be hubristic to talk of yet another American century.[19] Nonetheless, the US not only retains extraordinary powers of recuperation – recall how quickly it recovered from Vietnam; for good reason and for the foreseeable future it is bound to remain the central player at the heart of the world order.[20] We should not be writing an obituary for the American Empire just yet.

An Empire of Liberty?

One of the central themes of American historiography is that there is no American Empire.[21]

It is an empire without a consciousness of itself as such, constantly shocked that its good intentions arouse resentment abroad. But that does not make it any the less of an empire, with a conviction that it alone, in Herman Melville's words, bears "the ark of liberties of the world."[22]

The concept of empire in the United States was of course first employed by the "Founding Fathers" to describe a political mission linked to a geographical aspiration in which liberty and continental expansion were intimately connected.[23] One in effect could not exist without the other. Thus the conquest of America required a people yearning to be free, while freedom, as Frederick Jackson Turner later noted in one of the more important essays ever written on American history, demanded an ever expanding frontier.[24] This influential, and very American notion combined in turn with another equally powerful set of ideas about American exceptionalism, a condition which described the obvious fact (at least obvious to most Americans) that the United States was both distinctive and superior to all other nations. This not only rendered it immune to criticism from abroad – always useful for a nation with global ambitions; it also meant it had the God-given duty to spread the dream and promise of America beyond its own shores. Indeed, as many Americans readily admitted, if the American way was good enough for the United States then it was certainly good enough for the rest of the world.[25] But in no way should this be confused with imperialism of the more traditional kind. After all, even though the US might have used force outside of its borders on no less than 101 occasions between 1801 and 1904, its mission – at least in its own mind – was not to conquer other peoples but to liberate them from despotism, in much the same way as it had liberated itself from British rule in the late eighteenth century. In this fashion, the US managed to carve out a special position for itself in the long history of aspiring world powers. Not for it the ideological embarrassment of trying to defend the institution of colonialism, or the costs involved in occupying other countries, but the more noble purpose of bringing a better way of life to others less fortunate than itself. Naturally, such an outlook inevitably infused US foreign policy with a particularly moralistic and idealistic tone, much to the great chagrin of later realist critics like Morgenthau and Kennan. But it also permitted it the rare privilege of pursuing policies designed to advance its own interests while all the time believing, or at least claiming, that it was doing so for the benefit of mankind. J. R. Seeley once wrote that the British acquired an empire in a fit of absent-mindedness. When the United States acquired one of its own it would be in a state of "deep denial."[26]

The rise of the United States as a world power by 1898, and its more complete emergence as a superpower in two stages at the end of the First and then the Second World War, is one of the great American stories with its assortment of European deadbeats, perfidious but heroic Brits, internationalist paragons, and isolationist villains, all playing their various walk-on parts in a play of epic proportions that in the end left only one serious actor standing on the stage of history. Yet to read many of the less reflective tales told about this spectacular but deeply uneven process, one could easily come away thinking the United States never really wanted to become a major international player in the first place. It was, to use that most useful of phrases, a most "reluctant superpower," one that feared "entangling alliances," which was only enticed out of its natural state of self-imposed isolationism by the threat posed by others. It is all very comforting. But brute facts still remain brute facts – as Chris Brown has rather nicely put it – and the fact of the matter is that by 1945 this most innocent of countries, with apparently little liking for the idea of power, and even less for running the world, happened to be in charge of most of the world's economic resources, the majority of its military capabilities and a network of bases stretching across two oceans and four continents. No doubt it was helped in this endeavour by the foibles of others; moreover, there were many Americans who actively strove to keep the United States at home. Nonetheless, when the guns fell silent, this retiring wallflower with apparently few ambitions of its own found itself in a position of influence unparalleled in history. Little wonder that Washington now came to be known by some as the new Rome, and its Chief Executive spoken of more often than not as the "Imperial" President.[27]

Nor did the Cold War do much to halt America's upward mobility. If anything, this often dangerous and costly conflict afforded the United States many important opportunities; and in this, ironically, it was much helped by the activities of its chief rival, the Soviet Union. The Soviet threat was real enough. That much is obvious from any reading of the new primary sources.[28] Yet the USSR's often brutal and sometimes ill-judged actions not only did little to weaken the West but in many vital respects helped shape and define it.[29] As President Harry Truman readily conceded, Stalin was in his own way as much a Western asset as he was an American enemy. Indeed, Soviet actions not only helped US leaders mobilize America's vastly superior capabilities against what turned out to be a most incomplete superpower rival, but over time provided them with almost the most perfect of all imperial ideologies. For if the Soviet Union was a menace to the whole of the free world – as cold warriors claimed – then this demanded nothing less than a global response. Moreover, if the menace took several forms, then the US would have to develop the capabilities and policies needed to counter this, from building extensive international alliances and extending military aid to the far corners of the globe, to reconstructing the global economy and taking the lead role in those various multilateral institutions that would ensure its healthy development. In these various overlapping ways, the United States managed to extend its reach to every part of the free world. Of course, Pax Americana did not manage to penetrate everywhere. Nor did its economic position go unchallenged. In fact, for most of the 1970s and 1980s, many pundits assumed it was rapidly falling behind its more competitive allies in Europe and Japan.[30] No matter. By the time the edifice of the Cold War came tumbling down, the United States – and the United States alone – still possessed what others lacked: a series of embedded assets that gave it true global reach.[31] As one of the more celebrated (liberal) theorists of the new American Empire later remarked, what word other than empire could fully encompass the awesome thing that had become the American international order with its host of dependent allies, its vast intelligence networks, its "five global military commands," its more than one million men and women "at arms on five continents," and its "carrier battle groups on watch in every ocean"? None at least that he could think of.[32]

It was at this precise point in time that we can begin to trace the sources of what is now referred to as the "new" American Empire. It is an act in two parts. Part 1 was played out in the 1990s, a period according to the conventional wisdom that was marked by drift, indecision, and a lack of grand strategy. But as has been recently shown, the more we look at the so-called lost decade, the more we discover the opposite of what many pessimists claimed at the time and what some pundits have argued since.[33] Thus, far from retreating as some assumed it would, the US actually did the opposite (especially in the realm of international economics); and instead of losing direction as some predicted it might, by the end of the 1990s it had become far more self-confident – in part because of the collapse of Soviet power, in part because Europe and Japan failed to mount any serious challenge, in part because the US maintained relatively high levels of military spending while others did not, in part because of a dramatic surge in its own economic fortunes, and in part because of its continued integration into a set of powerful regional alliances in Europe, Asia, and Latin America in which it was the leading actor. Little wonder that by the end of the century we find a whole raft of writers, from the radical left to the liberal middle, beginning to argue, with some gusto, that previous talk about American decline had been so much hot air. The United States, it was now argued, had never been in such good shape. Certainly, as one century gave way to another, the American mood had never seemed so buoyant.[34]

Yet in spite of this, there were some who still felt the US could do much better, or more precisely, could do far more to exploit all these various assets and turn them to American advantage.[35] Reaganite by background, hegemonist by inclination, and keenly aware that there existed a growing gap between US military capabilities and America's ever expanding global role, the new cohort were determined to remove all the constraints which they felt had been imposed on the last remaining superpower by the "international community" in the post–Cold War period.[36] Primacy was the name of the game and a new American century the prize.[37] However, the former would mean nothing and the latter remain a pipe-dream without a much greater projection of US hard power. As Charles Krauthammer put it, "after a decade of Prometheus playing pygmy" the United States now had to act.[38] Some even drew lessons from the late nineteenth century to make their case for them. By the end of the 1880s the US, they argued, was economically powerful but internationally irrelevant. Something therefore had to be done, and in the end it was, first by more resolute state intervention, and then by some very determined presidential leadership. The lesson was clear: decisive political action was essential again if the United States wanted to realize its full potential. This in the end is why Clinton was such a disaster. He may have talked about US leadership but at heart he was a born-again multilateralist who was prepared to stake all on the ability of international institutions to achieve world order.

This was a road to nowhere. Indeed, in the neoconservative vision of an America unchained, even such bodies as NATO could no longer be regarded as being unambiguously useful assets. There was also the difficult problem of Europe. With a Europe unwilling and incapable of building a serious military capacity of its own, America – it was argued by the new right – had for too long been far too sensitive to the continent's needs. Not any more. In a world where the key threats to global security emanated from outside of Europe, and in which the Europeans were more often than not likely to get things wrong than right (note here their collective failure in Bosnia), there was no need to buy into the shibboleth known as the transatlantic security community. And to be blunt, there were very good reasons for not doing so given the European inclination to resolve problems in just the sorts of ways – through recourse to international law and global regulation – that were bound to tie the American Gulliver down.[39]

Long before 9/11 therefore the intellectual ground was already shifting on the right. However, it took the quite unexpected election of a particular kind of president, followed by the even more unexpected tragedy of September 2001, for the balance of the argument to shift decisively toward those who had for some time being arguing for a more expansive foreign policy. Naturally, forging what amounted to a neo-Reaganite foreign policy for a postcommunist world would be no easy task.[40] And as we now know, during its first few months in office, the Bush team ran into a barrage of international opposition to its policies.[41] This is why 9/11 was so important, not because it reduced criticism from abroad (though for a brief moment it did) but because it created an acute sense of crisis which made previously controversial policies now seem far more acceptable at home. If nothing else, 9/11 certainly proved in the most dramatic fashion possible that the world was still a very dangerous place, and that unless decisive action was taken things could easily get much worse. Indeed, the so-called "war against terror" – which soon metamorphosed into something much wider – provided the neoconservatives, as they readily conceded, with an opportunity of unparalleled importance. For if, as it was now claimed, America was threatened by a transnational and undeterrable enemy with hidden cells here and shadowy allies there who were prepared to use weapons of mass destruction to achieve their theological ends, then Washington quite literally had no alternative but to intervene robustly and ruthlessly abroad. The fact that this might cause resentment in other countries was unfortunate. But this was of much less concern to certain Americans than achieving results. Ultimately, the new right took a quite philosophical view of all this foreign noise. In the end, they reasoned, what would shape international attitudes would not be weasel words but decisive action backed up by overwhelming military power. Situations of strength not diplomatic niceties would determine how friends and enemies responded to new Bush Doctrine.[42]

What Is an Empire?

Over the last two millennia the word "empire" has meant many different things to different people from different countries at different times.[43]

September 11 therefore not only marked a significant watershed in its own right, but was successfully used by those who had earlier "spotted" what one British admirer of American neoconservatism referred to later as "an historic opportunity" to exploit the possibilities already present in a post–Cold War world.[44] This does not mean the Bush team did not view the threat of terrorism as being real. Nor is it meant to imply that every member of the Bush administration was now won over to the idea of empire, or that it then pursued a wise course of action. This is not the point. All we are pointing to here is a connection – between a very real trauma on the one hand and a larger game-plan on the other – that led many to conclude that a more assertive course of action was not only feasible but essential too. It would certainly not be the first time in history (nor possibly the last) that a great power was to be driven by that heady combination of fear and opportunity to pursue what others later, or at the time, perceived to be good old-fashioned imperialism.[45]

But even if we accept this, and even agree with the judgment that the real issue now was "not whether the United States has become an imperial power" but "what sort of empire [Americans] intends theirs to be,"[46] this still does not answer the question as to whether or not we should really be employing the term empire at all. As a notion it might be suggestive. It might even have much to recommend it as a metaphor. But none of this addresses the important issue of appropriateness: and there have always been and remain some very serious intellectual objections to the idea.[47] One concerns the very obvious fact that the United States controls very little territory itself; another is that if America were an empire then why has it championed the principle of self-determination; and a third is that if it had the kind of power some now claim it does, then why does it sometimes appear to have less influence over world affairs than one would imagine? A number of critics would also argue that it makes little sense to talk of an American empire under what Anthony Giddens has termed modern "runaway" conditions; and if it did, then how do we account for the fact that the United States not only seems unable to control financial markets but cannot even "extend democracy to other regions, to impose its own system on the rest of the world"?[48] These are all fair-minded questions, and cannot be dismissed, as some of the more conspiratorially minded might like to do, by accusing those who advance them of supping with the devil.

Let us deal firstly with the issue of territory. It is obviously the case that most empires in the past, from the Greek to the Spanish, the Ottoman to the Russian, have been defined as such because they brought vast swathes of land belonging to other people under their control. It is equally true that the United States in the main has not practiced such forms of annexation beyond its current boundaries. And to some, therefore, this is proof that the United States is not an empire in any meaningful sense of that word. This is a fair point even though it might be considered a rather narrow definitional base upon which to discuss and compare all empires. But even if we were prepared to – just for the moment – this still ignores one rather important historical fact: that America has indeed done more than its fair share of land grabbing. In fact, those who would claim that the United States is not an empire because it has never acquired other people's territory seem to forget that the nation we now call the United States of America only became the United States of America because it annexed a great deal during the nineteenth century: from France and Russia (through purchase), Spain and Mexico (by military conquest), from Britain (by agreement) and, most savagely, from those 3 million native Americans who were nearly all eliminated in the process. Admittedly, this tells us little about how it then used its massive geographical power base in the global arena. Nor can we assume that what it did in the process of conquering the American interior, it would do, or would want to do, to the rest of the world. But it does at least hint at the possibility that ruthlessness and ambition in the pursuit of power and the American experience are not quite so alien to each other as some would have us believe.[49]

Then there is the small matter of Latin and Central America. Admittedly, neither was ever formally colonized by the US. But should that preclude us from thinking of the US relationship with its immediate south in imperial terms? Perhaps so, if you are an American from the United States. But that is not the way most Latin Americans look upon their own problematic connection with their very large and extraordinarily powerful neighbour to the north. Nor to be blunt do many North Americans. As even the more uncritical of them would readily concede, the whole purpose of the famous Monroe Doctrine was not to limit American influence in the region but to embed it. Moreover, the story thereafter is not one of US disengagement from the region but the latter's more complete integration into an American-led system – one which presupposed a definite hierarchy of power, was sometimes brutally exploitative in character, and was constructed around some fairly typical racial stereotypes of the "other." More than that. It was built on the good old-fashioned ideology – much beloved by European colonials – which assumed that certain areas should, of right, fall within the sphere of influence of one of the great powers. In fact, it was precisely because the Americans thought in such terms that policy-makers in Washington (even more liberal ones) rarely felt any compunction in intervening in the region whenever and wherever they saw fit. If this was not imperialism by any other name, then it is difficult to think what might be.[50]

However, there still remains the more general question about territory and the degree to which America's overall lack of territorial ambition means we should either not use the term or only do so in the most qualified fashion possible. There is no unambiguously straightforward answer. In the end it very much depends on whether or not territory, and territory alone, constitutes the basis of empire. Many would insist that it does. Dominic Lieven, for example, has argued that "there has to be some sort of direct rule over the dominion for a power to be classified as an empire."[51] Others however would point to the complex forms which all empires have taken through time; indeed, a study of the most developed would indicate that they have invariably combined different forms of rule, none more successfully than America's presumed predecessor, Great Britain. As the famous Gallagher and Robinson team showed in their justly celebrated work, British imperialism entertained both formal annexation and informal domination, direct political rule and indirect economic control. The real issue for the British therefore was not the means they employed to secure the outcomes they wanted, but the outcomes themselves.[52] Thus if one could create a system overall that guaranteed the right results – which for Britain meant a stable international space within which its goods could find a market and its capital a profitable home – then that was perfectly fine. And what was fine for the British, it could be argued, has been equally fine for the Americans. In fact, not only did they adopt a similar set of criteria after 1945 by which to measure success, many of its more able leaders like Dean Acheson were great admirers of the British Empire. The British, he felt, had done a very good job in the nineteenth century defending the world trade system by pumping their surplus capital into other countries; and there was no reason why the United States with its vast wealth and enormous power after the Second World War should not do the same. In many ways, it had no real alternative in his view. For as he argued at the time, global order presupposed power, power resided with states, and it was up to the strongest state – the hegemon, to use the jargon – to pay the bills and enforce the rules of the game. And if it did not do so (as it had failed to do in the interwar period), then the international system was doomed.[53]

Of course, nobody would be so foolish as to suggest that the United States achieved total control of the whole world as a result. Nor did it always get its own way, even with the most dependent of its allies.[54] Nonetheless, it still achieved a very great deal and did so in a quite conscious fashion. Indeed, in a relatively short space of time, following what amounted to a 30-year crisis, it managed to construct the basis for a new international order within which others – old enemies and traditional rivals alike – could successfully operate. But not only did they manage to operate; the international economy as a whole flourished, to such an extent that between 1947 and 2000 there was a 20-fold increase in the volume of world trade and a 700 percent rise in gross world product. And the US achieved all this under the most testing of political conditions, with all sorts of ideological "barbarians" constantly trying to pull down what it was attempting to build.[55] So successful was it, in fact, that after several years of costly standoff it even began to push its various rivals back – initially in the contested and unstable Third World, then in Eastern Europe, and finally in the enemy's heartland itself. Not for it therefore the Roman fate of being overrun by the Mongol hordes, or the British experience of lowering the flag in one costly dependency after another. On the contrary, by the beginning of the 1990s the American Empire faced neither disintegration nor imperial overstretch, but found itself gazing forth upon a more open, seemingly less dangerous world in which nearly all the main actors (with the exception of a few rogue states) were now prepared to accept its terms and come under its umbrella. Clearly, there was to be no "fall" for this particular empire.[56]

But this still leaves open the problem of how we can legitimately talk of an American empire when one of the United States's primary objectives in the twentieth century has involved support for the right of self-determination. The objection is a perfectly reasonable one and obviously points to a very different kind of empire to those which have existed in the past. But there is a legitimate answer to this particular question – that if and when the US did support the creation of new nations in the twentieth century, it did not do so out of pure idealism but because it realistically calculated that the breakup of other empires was likely to decrease the power of rivals while increasing its own weight in a reformed world system. As the great American historian William Appleman Williams noted many years ago, when and where the US has combated colonialism – both traditional and communist – it did so for the highest possible motive. But the fact remains that it only acted in this fashion (and then not always consistently) in the full knowledge that it would win a host of new and potentially dependent allies as a result.[57] Imperialism, as others have pointed out, can sometimes wear a grimace and sometimes a smile; and in the American case nothing was more likely to bring a smile to its face than the thought that while it was winning friends among the new states, it was doing so at the expense firstly of its European rivals (which is why so many of Europe's leaders disliked Wilson and feared FDR) and then, after 1989, of the USSR.[58]

This brings us then to the issue of influence and the capacity of the United States to fashion outcomes to its own liking under contemporary conditions. The problem revolves as much around our understanding of what empires have managed to do in the past as it does around what we mean by influence now. Let us deal with both issues briefly – beginning with the first question about influence.

As any historian of previous empires knows, no empire worth the name has ever been able to determine all outcomes at all times within its own *imperium*. All empires in other words have had their limits. Even the Roman Empire, to take the most cited example, was based on the recognition that there were certain things it could and could not do, including by the way pushing the outer boundaries of its rule too far.[59] Britain too was well aware that if it wanted to maintain influence it had to make concessions here and compromises there in order not to provoke what some analysts would now refer to as "blowback."[60] How otherwise could it have run India for the better part of 200 years with only 50 thousand soldiers and a few thousand administrators? Much the same could be said about the way in which the United States has generally preferred to rule its empire. Thus, like the British, it has not always imposed its own form of government on other countries; it has often tolerated a good deal of acceptable dissent; and it has been careful, though not always, not to undermine the authority of friendly local elites. In fact, the more formally independent they were, the more legitimate its own hegemony was perceived to be. There was only one thing the United States asked in return: that those who were members of the club and wished to benefit from membership had to abide by the club's rules and behave like gentlemen. A little unruliness here and some disagreement there was fine; so long as it was within accepted bounds. In fact, the argument could be made – and has been – that the United States was at its most influential abroad not when it shouted loudest or tried to impose its will on others, but when it permitted others a good deal of slack. It has been more secure still when it has been invited in by those whose fate ultimately lay in its hands. Indeed, in much the same way as the wiser Roman governors and the more successful of the British viceroys conceded when concessions were necessary, so too have the great American empire-builders of the postwar era. Far easier, they reasoned, to cut bargains and do deals with those over whom they ultimately had huge leverage than to upset local sensitivities. It was only when the locals transgressed, as they did on occasion by acting badly abroad or outside the bounds of acceptable behaviour at home, that the US put its foot down firmly to show who was really in charge.[61]

Yet the skeptics still make a good point. Under modern conditions, it is extraordinarily difficult for any single state to exercise preponderant influence at all times, a point made with great force in both a recent radical attempt to theorize the notion of empire[62] and a liberal effort to rubbish it.[63] The argument is well made. In fact it is obvious: under conditions of globalization where money moves with extraordinary speed in an apparently borderless world, it is very difficult indeed for any state – even one as powerful as the United States – to exercise complete control over all international relations. There is also the question of its own economic capabilities. The United States might have a huge military capacity. However, in the purely material realm it is far less powerful than it was say 20 years ago – before Europe and China became more serious economic actors – or immediately after the war, when it controlled 70 percent of the world's financial resources. All this much is self-evident and any honest analysis of the "new" American empire would have to take this on board. But one should not push the point too far. After all, the US economy continues to account for nearly 30 percent of world product, it is roughly 40 percent bigger than any of its nearest rivals, the dollar still remains mighty, and Wall Street is still located at the heart of the international financial system. Furthermore, as the better literature on modern globalization shows, the world economic system is not completely out of control; governments still have a key role to play; and the enormous resources at the American government's disposal not only give it a very large role in shaping the material environment within which we all happen live, but also provide it with huge influence within those bodies whose function it is to manage the world economy. America's control of these might not be complete, and the outcomes might not always be to its liking. But they get their way more often than not. As one insider rather bluntly put it, "[International Monetary Fund] programmes are typically dictated from Washington."[64] Furthermore, as Robert Wade has convincingly shown, by mere virtue of its ability to regulate the sources and supply routes of the vital energy and raw material needs of even its most successful economic competitors, the US quite literally holds the fate of the world in its hands.

Finally, any assessment as to whether or not the United States is or is not an empire has to address the problem of perception, or more concretely of how US leaders view America's role and how the world in turn looks upon the United States. It is difficult to make easy generalizations. Nonetheless, it would not be a million miles away from the truth to suggest that most members of the Washington foreign policy elite do tend to see themselves as masters of a larger universe in which the United States has a very special part to play by virtue of its unique history, its huge capabilities, and its accumulated experience in running the world for the last 50 years. At times they may tire of performing this onerous task. Occasionally they falter. However, if it was ever suggested that they give up that role, they would no doubt throw up their hands in horror. Being number one does have its advantages after all. It also generates its own kind of imperial outlook in which other states are invariably regarded as problems to be managed, while the United States is perceived as having an indispensable role to perform, one of such vital importance that there is no reason why it should always be subject to the same rules of the international game as everybody else. This is why the United States, like all great imperial powers in the past, is frequently accused of being "unilateral." The charge might be just, but basically it is irrelevant. Indeed, as Americans frequently argue (in much the same way as the British and the Romans might have argued before them), the responsibilities of leadership and the reality of power mean that the strong have to do what they must – even if this is sometimes deemed to be unfair – while the weak are compelled to accept their fate. So it was in the past; so it has been, and will continue to be, with the United States.

The Future of the American Empire – after Iraq

Not since Rome has one nation loomed so large above the others.[65]

The American era appears to be alive and well. That encapsulates the conventional wisdom – and it is woefully off the mark.[66]

Recognizing the utility of the idea of empire however is one thing; speculating about the future of empires is quite a different matter, especially in the American case where so much of this in the past appears to have been so wide of the mark with its predictions of imminent demise, long-term decay, and absolute or even relative decline. But it is still something we need to do, in large part because the nature of the debate has shifted so dramatically within the United States itself since the initial burst of hubristic euphoria in the immediate aftermath of 9/11. Indeed, following the initial

party when it seemed the heady brew called American power
could never run out, a very large hangover appears to have
descended on the United States – and many are even beginning to
wonder what all the imperial fuss was about in the first place.
With the neoconservatives in headlong retreat in Washington, and
the costs in terms of blood and treasure going up in Iraq, some can
hardly recall the time when the US could talk in bold terms about
punishing enemies and rewarding allies, while using its vast military power to make and break regimes it happened not to like.
Some even think it is time – once again – to revisit the notion of
decline.[67] The bubble they argue has burst (or is just about to).
The Bush project has failed. And like Nero all he can do is fiddle
while the new Rome burns. The American era is over.[68]

There are at least three reason to question this overly simplistic, short-term prognosis based primarily – though not only – on
what has been happening in Baghdad and the streets of Basra
over the past three years. The first and most obvious is the realist
one: that at the end of the day, no other power has the military
capabilities or the economic wherewithal to seriously challenge
the United States. Europe may have once been seen as a major
future contender by some analysts. But that was long ago. Japan
is only now coming out of a ten-year depression; moreover, it
remains very firmly within the American camp while showing
not the slightest interest in abandoning it. Russia of course has
been in decline for over ten years; and if it has staged something
of a comeback of late it has only done so because of the high
price of oil. And finally, even though China appears to be almost
permanently on the rise – much to the alarm of some people in
Washington – it has made it abundantly clear that it does not
seek to challenge the United States. Indeed, if Chinese international behaviour is anything to go by, then it is clear that contemporary states – however upwardly mobile they may be – see
every advantage in working with and alongside the United States
and not against it.

Secondly, we should not forget what some now seem to be
forgetting in the shadow of Iraq: namely what Susan Strange
identified long ago as America's many structural advantages,
ranging from its several alliance systems (still intact), to the dollar

(under challenge but still hegemonic), its vast military (still vast), and of course its financial and commercial clout. Indeed, a rereading of the iconoclastic Strange on the many strengths of what she quite openly referred to as the American Empire would serve to remind modern pessimists why it is not about to fall off its proverbial perch. As she wisely pointed out, intellectuals have always been fascinated by the idea of imperial decline. It all began with Gibbon, and the decline and fall of the Roman Empire, at the end of the eighteenth century, and ended up with Paul Kennedy reflecting magnificently but wrongly about the United States almost 200 years later. But as she also noted, what might have been true for Rome was not necessarily true for America. We should thus beware historians bearing false analogies.[69]

Finally, we should take care not to identify the United States with either one unpopular president or one set of controversial policies. America is more than just George W. Bush, and his administration more than just a group of blinkered ideologues who dislike foreigners, hate the United Nations, and assume the best form of diplomacy is to bomb countries you don't like first and then ask questions later. In other words, we should not judge the long-term future of the United States through the failings of one man or the ideas of those who may once have had this particular president's ear. Bush in the end will go. America will get out of Iraq. And the world and America's place in it are then likely to look very different. It is of course impossible to know how history will treat Bush. However, some will no doubt reflect on the central paradox of his term in office: that policies largely undertaken to defend and extend US imperial influence probably did more damage to the American Empire than those pursued by his less abrasive predecessor. From this perspective, it may well take the election of another American liberal to make the American liberal Empire safe for posterity.[70]

Notes

This chapter is based on a preliminary presentation given at Goodenough College in November 2002. It was later published in *Millennium* and elsewhere (see below), and has been significantly revised for this collection.

For earlier versions of this essay see "The Empire's Back in Town: Or America's Imperial Temptation – Again," *Millennium*, 32.1 (2003): 1–27, "Empire, Imperialism and the Bush Doctrine," *Review of International Studies*, 30.4 (2004): 585–605, and "Empire by Denial: The Strange Case of the United States," *International Affairs*, 81.1 (Jan. 2005): 15–30. See also the debate around my thesis on empire in *Security Dialogue*, 35.2 (2004): 228–61.

1 Harold James, *The Roman Predicament: How the Rules of International Order Create the Politics of Empire* (Princeton: Princeton University Press, 2006), p. 1.
2 Justin Rosenberg, "Globalization Theory: A Post Mortem," *International Politics*, 42.1 (Mar. 2005): 2–73.
3 G. John Ikenberry (ed), *America Unrivaled: The Future of the Balance of Power* (Ithaca: Cornell University Press, 2002).
4 See Paul Kennedy, *The Rise and Fall of Great Powers* (New York: Random House, 1988).
5 This issue is addressed in Barry Buzan, *The United States and Great Powers* (Cambridge: Polity, 2004).
6 I discuss Paul Kennedy's late conversion to the cause of US hegemony in my "American Power Before and After the Towers," in Ken Booth and Tim Dunne (eds), *Worlds in Collision* (Basingstoke: Palgrave, 2002), pp. 152–61.
7 Jack Snyder, *Myths of Empire: Domestic Politics and International Relations* (Ithaca: Cornell University Press, 1991).
8 Max Boot, "The Case for American Empire," *Weekly Standard*, Oct. 15, 2001.
9 Charles S. Maier, "An American Empire? The Problems of Frontiers and Peace in Twenty-First Century World Politics," in Lloyd Gardner and Marilyn Young (eds), *The New American Empire* (New York: New Press, 2005), p. xi.
10 Ronald Wright, "For a Wild Surmise," *Times Literary Supplement*, Dec. 20, 2002, p. 3.
11 See Andrew J. Bacevich, *The Imperial Tense: Prospects and Problems of American Empire* (Chicago: Ivan R. Dee, 2003).
12 Niall Ferguson, *Colossus: The Rise and Fall of the American Empire* (London: Penguin, 2004).
13 For example, see the speeches by Bush to cadets at West Point June 1, 2002, and to veterans at the White House November 11, 2002.

14 Max Boot, *The Savage Wars of Peace: Small Wars and the Rise of American Power* (New York: Basic Books, 2002).

15 See Niall Ferguson, "The Empire that Dares Not Speak its Name," *Sunday Times*, Apr. 13, 2003.

16 See for example Martin Shaw, "Post-Imperial and Quasi-Imperial: State and Empire in the Global Era," *Millennium*, 31.2 (2002): 327–36.

17 "Those who by virtue of age and sobriety can remember the 1960s may recall the term 'American empire' as a bit of left-wing cant," Wright, "For a Wild Surmise."

18 Michael Mann, *Incoherent Empire* (London: Verso, 2003).

19 Alfredo Valladao, *The Twenty First Century Will Be American* (London: Verso, 1996).

20 See Thanh Duong, *Hegemonic Globalisation: US Centrality and Global Strategy in the Emerging World Order* (Aldershot: Ashgate, 2003).

21 William Appleman Williams, "The Frontier Thesis and American Foreign Policy," *Pacific Historical Review* (1955), also in Henry W. Berger (ed.), *A William Appleman Williams Reader* (Chicago: Ivor R. Dee, 1992), p. 89.

22 Michael Ignatieff, "Empire Lite," *Prospect*, 83 (Feb. 2003): 36.

23 See Walter A. McDougall, *Promised Land: Crusader State; The American Encounter with the World* (Boston: Houghton Mifflin, 1997).

24 Frederick Jackson Turner, "The Significance of the Frontier in American History," published in 1893.

25 See Pierre Hassner, *The United States: The Empire of Force or the Force of Empire?* Chaillot Papers 54 (Paris: European Union Institute for Security Studies, 2002), p. 14.

26 Ignatieff, "Empire Lite"; Ferguson, "The Empire that Dares Not Speak its Name."

27 The best short description of the US power position in 1945 is by Donald W. White, 'The Nature of World Power in American History: An Evaluation at the End of World War Two', *Diplomatic History*, 11.3 (1987): 181–202.

28 See the 13 bulletins of the important Cold War International History Project based at the Woodrow Wilson Center, Washington DC.

29 A point made often by George F. Kennan, the architect of containment; see my "George F. Kennan: Requiem for a Cold War Critic, 1945–1950", *Irish Slavonic Studies* (1990).

30 See my "Whatever Happened to American Decline? International Relations and the New United States Hegemony," *New Political Economy*, 6.3 (2001): 311–40.

31 See, for example, Susan Strange, "The Future of the American Empire," *Journal of International Affairs*, 42.1 (1988): 1–18, and Stephen Gill, *American Hegemony and the Trilateral Commission* (Cambridge: Cambridge University Press, 1990).

32 Ignatieff, "Empire Lite," p. 36.

33 Andrew J. Bacevich, *American Empire: The Realities and Consequences of US Diplomacy* (Cambridge: Harvard University Press, 2002).

34 Bruce Cumings, "Still the American Century," in Michael Cox, Ken Booth and Tim Dunne (eds), *The Interregnum: Controversies in World Politics, 1989–1999* (Cambridge: Cambridge University Press, 1999), pp. 271–99.

35 This section draws heavily from the excellent first-hand description provided by Nicholas Lemann, "The Next World Order: The Bush Administration May Have a Brand-New Doctrine of Power," *New Yorker*, Apr. 4, 2002.

36 See the publications of the Project for a New American Century at www.newamericancentury.org. Key conservative figures associated with this very important pressure group included Max Boot, Frank Carlucci, Midge Decter, Elliot Abrams, Robert Kagan, Donald Kagan, R. James Woolsey, William Kristol, William J. Bennett, Aaron Friedberg, Dick Cheney, Donald Rumsfeld, Dan Quayle, Lewis Libby, Paul Wolfowitz, Fred C. Ikle, Jeb Bush, Peter W. Rodman, and Norman Podhoretz.

37 See in particular Fareed Zakaria, *From Wealth to Power* (Princeton: Princeton University Press, 1999).

38 Charles Krauthammer, "The New Unilateralism," *Washington Post*, June 8, 2001, p. 29.

39 See Robert Kagan, *Paradise and Power: America and Europe in the New World Order* (London: Atlantic Books, 2003).

40 William Kristol and Robert Kagan, "Toward a Neo-Reaganite Foreign Policy," *Foreign Affairs* (July–Aug. 1996).

41 I discuss European criticism of the early Bush policies in my "Europe and the New American Challenge after September 11: Crisis – What Crisis?" *Journal of Transatlantic Studies*, 1.1 (2003): 37–55.

42 As Secretary of Defense Donald Rumsfeld put it following the war with Iraq: "Being on the terrorist list" of states "is not some place I'd want to be"; quoted in *The Times*, Apr. 14, 2003.

43 Dominic Lieven, *Empire: The Russian Empire and its Rivals* (London: Pimlico, 2003), p. 3.

44 Andrew Roberts, "Americans Are on the March," *The Times*, Apr. 12, 2003.

45 Interestingly, the American historian John Lewis Gaddis, now court historian to the Bush administration, saw the immediate postwar years (when the US was at the height of its power in world historic terms) as being one marked by "a return of fear"; see his *The Cold War* (London: Allen Lane, 2005), pp. 5–47.

46 Quote from Andrew Bacevich cited in Ferguson, "The Empire that Dares Not Speak its Name."

47 See for example the critique of empire in the name of hegemony in John Agnew, *Hegemony: The New Shape of Global Power* (Philadelphia: Temple University Press, 2005).

48 Mary Kaldor, "American Power: from 'Compellance' to Cosmopolitanism," *International Affairs*, 79.1 (Jan. 2003): 1–2.

49 I discuss this in my "America and the World," in Robert Singh (ed.), *Governing America: The Politics of a Divided Democracy* (Oxford: Oxford University Press, 2003), pp. 13–31.

50 The presidential champion of self-determination, Woodrow Wilson, sanctioned the use of military force to the "South" on nearly ten occasions during his period in the White House.

51 Dominic Lieven, "The Concept of Empire," *Fathom: The Source for Online Learning*, at www.fathom.com/feature/122086.

52 See John Gallagher and Ronald Robinson, "The Imperialism of Free Trade," *Economic History Review*, 2nd ser., 6.1 (1953): 1–25.

53 This point is outlined in terms of International Relations theory by Robert Gilpin, *Global Political Economy: Understanding the International Economic Order* (Princeton: Princeton University Press, 2001), pp. 97–102.

54 See G. John Ikenberry, "Rethinking the Origins of American Hegemony," *Political Science Quarterly*, no. 104 (1989): 375–400.

55 Figures from Martin Wolf, "American and Europe Share the Responsibility for World Trade," *Financial Times*, Apr. 23, 2003.

56 See the chapter on "Imperial Anticolonialism" in William Appleman Williams, *The Tragedy of American Diplomacy* (Cleveland: World Publishing, 1959).

57 On the uses of self-determination as a means of advancing US influence see Michael Cox, G. John Ikenberry and Takashi Inoguchi (eds), *American Democracy Promotion: Impulses, Strategies, Impacts* (Oxford: Oxford University Press, 2000).

58 On British suspicion of Wilson and Roosevelt see Niall Ferguson, *Empire: How Britain Made the World* (London: Allen Lane, 2003).

59 See John Wacher (ed.), *The Roman World* (2 vols, London: Routledge, 1990), p. 139.

60 A term recently coined by Chalmers Johnson in his *Blowback: The Costs and Consequences of American Empire* (New York: Metropolitan Books, 2000).

61 "Empire is the rule exercised by one nation over others both to regulate their external behavior and to ensure minimally accept-able forms of internal behavior within the subordinate states"; quoted in Stephen Peter Rosen, "An Empire, If You Can Keep It," *National Interest*, no. 71 (Spring 2003): 51.

62 "The US does not and indeed no nation-state can today form the centre of an imperialist project"; cited in Michael Hardt and Antonio Negri, *Empire* (Cambridge: Harvard University Press, 2000), pp. xiii–xiv.

63 Joseph Nye Jr, *The Paradox of American Power: Why the World's Only Superpower Can't Go It Alone* (New York: Oxford University Press, 2002).

64 Joseph Stiglitz, *Globalization and its Discontents* (London: Penguin, 2002), p. 24.

65 Nye, *The Paradox of American Power*, p. 1.

66 Charles A. Kupchan, "The End of the West," *Atlantic Online*, Apr. 18, 2003, at www.theatlantic.com.

67 Emmanuel Todd, *Après l'empire. Essai sur la decomposition du système américain* (Paris: Gallimard, 2002).

68 Charles Kupchan, *The End of the American Era* (New York: Vintage, 2002).

69 See Susan Strange, "The Persistent Myth of Lost Hegemony: Reply to Milner and Snyder," *International Organization*, 42.4 (1988): 751–2, and Strange, "The Future of the American Empire."

70 This is at least implicit in Bacevich, *The American Empire*.

5

Europe and the War on Terror

William Wallace

The world did change for the United States on September 11. It did not change for Europe. The social construction of the threat to America that we've seen played out across the United States in the years since September 11 has exaggerated the sense of an existential threat to America. It was impressive to visit New Orleans after September 11 and see the banners on the churches and the schools, the sense in which everyone rallied around the flag and felt themselves to be under attack across the United States – even though the attack had happened a thousand miles away in New York. The overwhelming majority of the population in the United States remained entirely safe. If you live in Madison, Wisconsin, or in Sandpoint, Idaho, or most other places across the USA, the idea that the terrorists would come within a thousand miles is out of this world. Nevertheless, suddenly you feel threatened.

In Europe all of us who have lived in major cities have learned gradually over the last 30 or 40 years to tolerate a certain level of insecurity. When I was a junior researcher I can remember cycling in from where I was lodging in London, down into Downing Street, padlocking my bike to the railing outside the Prime Minister's office and residence at Number 10 and walking in; that is now totally beyond the bounds of possibility. Slowly we have accepted regimes that limit our

security. We recognized over a long period in London that if
you traveled on the Underground it was quite possible you might
be blown up. But the odds were you would not be, so we nevertheless got on the tube and, partly because the whole of the
campaign of the Irish Republican Army (IRA) crept up on us,
we got used to it, accepted it and say to our American friends,
"Actually London is still safer than Cincinnati – the likelihood
of being shot in an American city is still far higher than the
likelihood of being blown up in a terrorist incident in the
United Kingdom."

But that is not what it feels like, because of this immense
effort put into what one has to call the social construction of
America as globally threatened. I have a very vivid memory
of going to a meeting in Washington in November of 2001 of
the Association of Professional Schools of International Affairs
(the Kennedy School, the Woodrow Wilson School, etc.). We
had the deans of all these schools and they had invited a number
of us from Europe. After a while they asked us to comment
on how we saw the implications of September 11, and one by
one we all started to make comparisons with our own societies
and how we had responded to terrorist problems of the previous
30 years. What really shook me was the dean of the Maxwell
School saying, supported by others: "There **is** no comparison."
Their point of view was: "What has happened in the United
States is different from what you've been experiencing." Now
as a political scientist I have to say you must always compare.
If the top public policy analysts in the United States think
that they are in a different drama existentially from us, as
they clearly did at that point, then we are in a world which is
extremely difficult for the Americans and the Europeans to agree
about. And that is very much a part of our problem. We have
after all been dealing with terrorists in Europe for a very long
period.

Chris Brown in his opening chapter rightly talked about the
new terrorism as a novel form of fascism. The splendid book by
Karen Armstrong[1] on fundamentalism is particularly valuable
not only because it compares Jewish, Christian, and Muslim
fundamentalism but also because it puts them in the context

of modernity: the disconnections of modernity and the response of traditional religions to the threat of modernity, which, after all, is what fascism, and communism, and anarchism in late nineteenth-century Europe were also about. And we had Fenians in Ireland – the Special Branch in Britain owes its origins to police efforts to contain and infiltrate these original Irish rebels. They spoke a foreign language, they had priests of a foreign religion, Roman Catholicism (as we thought of it in those days), and they cooked, quoting the Huddersfield examiner of around 1890, "disgustingly" . . . thus constructing the Irish as a real threat to Huddersfield. On the Continent there were terrorist organizations among the Serbs, and the Bulgarians, and the Macedonians; the Macedonians were a particularly fearsome bunch of international terrorists. The origins of Interpol came out of the Austro-Hungarian intelligence service and its response to Serbian, Bulgarian, and Macedonian terrorist threats. When Interpol was set up after the First World War it inherited the Austro-Hungarian files on these terrorist movements. So, in a sense, we Europeans have been living with terrorism for a long time.

But, as our American friends always say, "You always look backwards; we look forwards." There is a real tendency for Europeans, therefore, to insist that "this is not that different from where we were before: let's look at the historical parallels." I regret to say that American political analysts almost always reply, "That's not relevant," just as the problem we have in discussing the Middle East with our American friends is that most of us start with the assumption that American hegemony over the last 50 years provides the context for how one has to approach the Middle East now. I am often shocked to discover how American policy-makers with whom I discuss the Middle East seem unaware that the United States has been the hegemon in the Middle East since the early 1950s, since, indeed, it demolished Iranian democracy in the coup of 1954.

In the last 30 years, Europeans have lived under a number of limited threats of transnational terrorism. Limited, I stress, because they are not of the global sort we now face. Take the IRA, with Czech-supplied Semtex paid for by Libya, shipped through France; the Red Army Faction in Germany using France as a safe haven, funded, as we now know from the Stasi files, by the East Germans; or the Red Brigade in Italy – a whole range of transnational threats of one sort or another.

Again, I have been staggered in Washington since 2001 to discover that Americans are unaware that over the last 30 years part of the threat Europeans have faced has been one of terrorism against American targets on European soil. I have actually listened to Americans say, "You Europeans don't understand: they will start attacking you in Europe." To which one has to say, "Well, actually that's what they've been doing since the Munich Olympic Games, and even earlier than that." In response to that threat the Europeans have developed a whole network of collaboration. If you look at the growth of what is now the third pillar of the European Union, justice and home affairs – or, since we actually prefer euphemisms, the area of "Freedom, Security, and Justice" – it began in the 1970s with two groups, group Pompidou, which was concerned with the international smuggling of drugs, and group Trevi, which was concerned with international terrorist threats, including the transnational Palestinian and Arab terrorist threat against Israel and United States targets in Europe. Out of that has grown a remarkably sophisticated European network which includes Europol, a European police network: it's not yet a European FBI, although Helmut Kohl famously made a speech calling for a European FBI as early as 1987. When I asked a German official why he had done so, I remember one laughing. . . . "He just read the file on the Italian mafia infiltration of the restaurant trade in Germany." So there are many types of transnational crime and protection rackets, some of which overlap with terrorist networks. There are four European transnational databases on which some of you may well indeed appear without knowing it. There is a fingerprint database, a database on immigrants who should be stopped coming through, there's a customs database, and a Schengen information system with access for the police forces of a range of different countries.

I find it quite remarkable that this has grown up without most governments – or civil liberty groups – being very interested. Statewatch is the only body in Britain which has attempted to monitor this, to call attention to the civil liberties implications of the growth of, not exactly a police state, but, certainly, a security apparatus in Europe. Statewatch is badly underfunded; very few people pay attention to it. I spent three years as the chair of the House of Lords Sub-Committee which was looking at the Justice and Home Affairs Process: we produced report after report on all of this, and could not interest a single newspaper in paying attention to the growth of this very large apparatus.

This apparatus has grown up partly because of the growth of transnational crime, people smuggling, drug smuggling, but also because of the realization that drug smuggling, people smuggling, etc., all overlap with terrorism. The KLA, the Albanian forces that operated in Kosovo, funded themselves through people smuggling, and through drug smuggling, and through shaking down legitimate Albanian businesses across the rest of Europe. It even extended, I was told by one of my students, to trying to shake down Albanian students in London and elsewhere. And that, therefore, is one of the things that have led European police forces to learn to collaborate, and they now collaborate to a remarkably high degree. I was in Warsaw about three years ago, and met the liaison officers from European Union member states who represent national police forces from the EU in collaboration with the Poles. That network has been growing very rapidly, again hardly reported in national parliaments, hardly understood in the West. Networks like these we find deal with Sikhs, with Tamils, as exile groups promoting revolution in their states at home, and attacks on emissaries abroad. We have Kurdish minorities, extremely well organized, and in London we have Saudi, Algerian, and other exile groups who are plotting regime change in their own countries.

Is that legitimate? London has traditionally been a base for exile groups, plotting regime change in authoritarian regimes. But are we happy with the extent to which in the modern world that still continues? The French government five years ago was already attacking the British, saying that London was the focus for Arab terrorism: meaning, in part, terror against the authoritarian Algerian regime. The Saudi government has also said the same about the British government. We come to the point here in which the principles of an open liberal society and a democracy come up against the principles of security and stability. And that's a problem that we cannot resolve.

I'd like to say a little bit about the European and American divide – about how we interpret what we now face. Europeans do understand that it is not business as usual, partly because the American reaction has been so strong, partly also because the threat of Muslim terrorism appears to be so widespread – it has spread through Indonesia, even Singapore, Malaysia, the Philippines. So we are facing a thing that is not purely an Arab problem but is the problem of the attraction of a new creed for disaffected youth in the Third World. I am going to have to put it in those terms. Communism was the creed of the disaffected 20 to 30 years ago and provided justification for youth and disaffected radicals across the Third World. They went to Lumumba University in Moscow and came back and fomented revolution within their societies. Communism has failed. Islamic fundamentalism is now the creed which disaffected radicals follow. It is a religious creed, not a secular creed, but we should make the comparison.

European societies fear they are now in the middle of a clash of civilizations in which the United States wishes to construct a total war. Americans I talk to call it the Fourth World War – the Third World War was the Cold War. They say this is the Fourth World War. And they see it in these global terms, and they also see it in Manichean terms. For it is good versus evil: you are on one side or the other, you are either Western and civilized and stand up for freedom, or you're an enemy of freedom. European societies are trying to find a way around this presentation of absolutist choices and to preserve a sense of liberty, which is extremely difficult to do when insecurity grows.

I say this as a liberal Christian who belongs to a Church, the Anglican Church, in which the idea of liberal religion is itself very strongly under threat. The whole purpose of the Church of England, as I understand it, is the idea that if you are human, you don't know in the absolute sense of certainty: that, as St Paul says, "for now we see, as through a glass, darkly" – dimly, without being sure of what we believe we see. It's only God that knows. And who are we to say that we understand what God is saying? The essence of fundamentalism is to say, "I do understand what God is saying, and what's more I'm going to kill you if you disagree."

So we have a different analysis from that of the United States. We have a different interpretation of Christianity from the United States: we are a much more secular collection of societies than the United States. It is very striking that the only Church in Europe which really relates to the Southern Baptists who have dominated the Republican Party recently is Ian Paisley's Free Presbyterian Church in Ireland. Indeed, Ian Paisley's doctorate comes from Bob Jones University at which President Bush as a candidate famously spoke, and for which he got into trouble since it still has rules against interracial dating.

I find myself more and more uncomfortable with the question that we all stand for the same values, because the Christian right in the United States is actually standing for a very different interpretation of Western values from those for which the Rooseveltian coalition that won the Second World War stood. Indeed, part of what we see in the United States is a revolt against the legacy of Franklin Delano Roosevelt in favour of a much more fundamentalist approach to politics. We don't share the American approach to the Middle East, we don't share the American approach to Likud in Israel, we are critical of the American approach to Iran. We have been critical of the dismissal of nation-building in Afghanistan and elsewhere, where European governments find themselves uncomfortable bouncing along behind the United States, often under American command, attempting to moderate American policy. In 2003 alone, there were over a hundred thousand troops of European Union states in operations outside the European Union: in Afghanistan, Iraq, Bosnia, Kosovo, eastern Congo, Sierra Leone, Ivory Coast, and elsewhere. In most of these, except in central and west Africa, they've been operating under American influence, attempting to introduce a European approach to dealing with the problems of reconstructing societies: nation-building, as we regard it, as the British forces regard it, policing, as the Italian *carabinieri* and others regard it, as an important semi-military role. European contingents have been very unhappy with American troops who have not been trained in these functions, who do not have a sense of how you mix with the local population. The level of contempt you sometimes meet within the British armed forces about the American armed forces reflects their perceived lack of understanding, indeed, their training which resists any idea that you mix with the local population – that you have to build trust as part of the way you behave post-conflict. Nonetheless, we have dispatched troops. So, Europe is uncomfortable alongside the United States.

And we try to explain to the Americans that some of our experience is relevant. We are all ex-imperial powers. We have made the same mistakes, often several times. We tried to run Iraq in the 1920s and we made an awful mess of it. We even tried to use airpower to control Iraq. A young officer called Harris, who later as the Air Marshall in charge of RAF Bomber Command became a great enthusiast for bombing Germany in the Second World War, was in charge of the Royal Air Force in Iraq at that time. They did their best to bomb tribes into submission, but it didn't work very well.

We're also very painfully aware that there is a link with immigration and with the ethnic minorities we have in Europe. That's another major preoccupation for European countries. There are 15 million Muslims living in Europe. They are part of our society. But often, I think, we are no longer quite so sure how much they are *all* part of our society. They are a more recognized part of our society than in the United States. The United States also has a substantial Muslim minority but, by and large, they are invisible. The extent to which in the United States Muslims are regarded as foreign – whereas here we have come, whether we like it or not, to regard Muslims as part of our society – came home to me when I happened to have written an article for *Foreign Affairs* in the spring of 2001 which referred to the extent to which younger generations in European cities grow up knowing necessarily about Ramadan and Eid and having Muslim friends, as my own children do because they went to a school that is 25 percent Muslim. After September 11, I had phone calls from two people – one from the *New York Times* and one from the *Washington Post* – asking, "Would you like to amend that paragraph in your *Foreign Affairs* article, in the light of what you've seen?" The Muslim community in Europe is highly diverse and well embedded. Some are very successful, but the community contains, nevertheless, as we saw with the young Yemeni from Sheffield, who, to the amazement of his friends and family, went out and became a suicide bomber, some alienated youth, who feel that there may be other loyalties. So, suddenly we're having to ask how much are these Muslim communities integrated into our societies – "What is being said in our mosques, what is being taught in our Muslim Friday and Saturday schools?" – in a way in which we were not asking three or four years ago. That is another very major problem for us.

In Britain, we have on the whole, again, been more relaxed than in some other countries. The Germans have been much more uptight, partly because Germany remains a more explicitly Christian society. Until quite recently it has been difficult for second or third generation people of Turkish origin to become German citizens and so to become fully integrated into Germany. In the Netherlands there's been a quite remarkable transformation of attitudes in the last four or five years. It's what one has to call the Pim Fortuyn phenomenon: his campaign argued that the fundamentalist values about gays and about women held by Muslims in the Netherlands, 35 percent of the population of Amsterdam, likely to be the majority in Amsterdam in 20 years, are seen to be threatening the secular values of the Netherlands as a whole. Therefore there is the very strong demand for assimilation and for thinking hard

about how you educate the younger Muslim generation. Much
the same in Denmark: the introduction of a law that wives
brought in from abroad can only be brought into Denmark
when they have learned the language, learned something about
culture – a much greater restriction on out-marriage, people
coming in from a third country. In France, the secular state
has pinned its principles to resisting headscarves: something
which we have been traditionally very relaxed about in this
country but in France this is seen as a symbol of the threat
to French secularism. It is the Third World living within the
First World. And it is something that the Europeans are very
confused about. We all now recognize that whether we like it
or nor immigrants will continue to come into Europe in large
numbers over the next 20 years. I listened to the Greek prime
minister's advisor on immigration giving us a talk a few months
ago on what percentage of the Greek population they expect
to be of non-Greek ethnic stock over the next ten years, and
it is pretty striking. They already have a half million Muslim
Albanians living in the country. Most of the immigrants coming
into Europe will be Muslims. They will come from North
Africa and from the Middle East because if one looks at the
population pressures, one knows where the pressure to migrate
is going to be most strongly felt. While we disagree with the
current American interpretation of the Middle East, we are
also uncomfortably aware of those excellent studies conducted
by the UN Development Programme in the last few years.
These are studies involving Arab economists and Arab sociolo-
gists which draw attention to the failures of economic and political development in the Middle East, and to what is wrong with
the entire educational structure of the Arab and, indeed, to some
extent of the entire Muslim world, which inhibits political and
economic development, inhibiting, in turn, the transition from
premodern societies through to modernity with the recognition
that liberalism and an open society is better. So we are highly
conflicted.

Finally, there are some real dilemmas about how European
societies see themselves – how our deep belief in civil liberties,
in an open society in which the legitimacy of dissent is recognized

and in which asylum-seekers can be accepted, is compatible with this much more diffuse threat from an increasing population pushing to come in and getting in whether we try to stop them or not. The majority of immigrants who enter Europe now enter illegally – one way or another – or else enter Europe legally and then stay on after their visas have expired. We find ourselves therefore also conflicted about our transatlantic links – with the United States asking for access to all these European databases, asking for us to contribute to American security, but rejecting that this should be on a mutual basis. There are to be American inspectors for containers in Rotterdam, but not European inspectors in New York – of course that may not be necessary. There are American demands for personal data on passengers going across the Atlantic, but of course we cannot have access to American data in return. One of the most delicate issues within European–American relations at the present moment is precisely this security agenda – with a sense that the United States is asking for a one-way traffic in security exchanges with the Europeans.

Lastly, European states are also deeply uncertain about the extent to which the Russians and others are exploiting the war on terrorism for their own ends. Authoritarian societies, not just in Russia but across Central Asia, are saying, "We are good allies of the United States in the war on terror, and by the way we just locked up another 2,000 people." And the contradictions in American policy toward the Middle East, in which the United States is determined to bring democracy, and toward Central Asia, where the United States is now in bed with some deeply corrupt authoritarian regimes, are part of what we are uncomfortable with about American policy, just as we are uncomfortable with American policy toward President Putin because our interpretation of the conflict in Chechnya is different from the Americans'. So the difficulties which the Europeans face boil down to these: first, how do we protect the European model of an open society in the face of this new and diffuse threat; and, second, how do we persuade our American allies to construct the world rather differently from the Manichean way they have followed since 2001.

Notes

This chapter is based on a presentation given at Goodenough College in November 2002.

1   Karen Armstrong, *The Battle for God* (New York: Ballantine, 2000).

6

Russia and the War on Terrorism

Margot Light

Ever since he became Russia's president in 2000, Vladimir Putin has been arguing that Russia is fighting international terrorism in Chechnya. After the attack on the World Trade Center and the Pentagon on September 11, 2001, he was among the first foreign leaders to telephone President George W. Bush. He also sent a telegram in which he decried the "barbaric terrorist acts, directed against innocent people" and expressed Russia's "most sincere condolences to the relatives of the victims of this tragedy, as well as to all those injured, the whole American people." He added that "we well understand your grief and pain. The Russians have themselves experienced the horror of terror."[1] In what appears to have been spontaneous individual gestures, ordinary people brought bunches of flowers which they left outside the American Embassy. The four national television channels took the unprecedented step of replacing planned programs and advertising with nonstop coverage of the situation in the United States. Many Muscovites believed that Americans now understood what they had suffered in 1999 when two apartment blocks in Moscow were blown up. Russian officials linked the threat to Russia from Chechnya to the international terrorists who had perpetrated the acts in the United States.

Within a couple of weeks, Russia had joined the coalition against terror, promising to share intelligence and offering political support to the US President. President Putin promised to increase the supply of weapons to the Northern Alliance in Afghanistan, which had been ousted by the Taliban in 1996 and had been fighting against it ever since (this was the first public admission that Russia had been supplying the Northern Alliance with arms). He also offered to open Russian airspace to US airplanes for humanitarian flights, and to participate in search and rescue operations. When the leaders of the Central Asian states offered bases to the coalition for the attack against Afghanistan, Putin announced that he had approved the offer. Since September 11, he has consistently insisted that Russia and the United States are fighting the same war on terrorism.

In fact, despite Putin's insistence that America and Russia are fighting the same war, Russia's war is very different from America's war on terrorism. There *are* similarities, but the differences between their wars are greater than the similarities. Moreover, the manner in which Russia fights its war against terrorism affects Russia's relations with the West, and US policy in the pursuit of its war against terrorism often conflicts with what Russia perceives as its vital national interests. In order to demonstrate this, I shall begin by pointing out the similarities and differences between the two wars against terrorism. In the second section, I will examine the use of terrorism in the wars in Chechnya and Russia's response. I will argue that Putin's policies are ill-designed to win the war and have serious consequences for Russia's internal and external development. I shall then explain how America's pursuit of its war on terrorism infringes Russia's perceived national interests. I shall conclude by contending that Russia's war on terrorism is likely to continue because the war suits a number of "players."

Similarities and Differences between Russia's War and America's War against Terrorism

Insofar as the "war against terrorism" is a war against al-Qaeda that began in earnest on 9/11, and insofar as Afghanistan was the first battlefield on which it was fought, the war against terrorism clearly has its origins in the Cold War, and Russia (as the legal heir to the Soviet Union) and the United States share the blame. But the terrorist threat did not begin on 9/11 and al-Qaeda existed before 2001. To quote Fred Halliday, "Al-Qaeda did not arise from the subconscious of Islamic or Arab minds, but from the Cold War, in particular the financing, training and arming of tens of thousands of jihadi militants by the US, Saudi Arabia and Pakistan for the war against the PDPA and the Soviet army in Afghanistan in the 1980s."[2] And the civil war that finally resulted in the Taliban taking power in Afghanistan in 1996, while not caused by the Soviet Union, was certainly greatly exacerbated by the invasion in 1979 and the participation of the Soviet army in the war.

Halliday argues that another legacy of the Cold War is "the arrogance, ignorance and instinctive resort to force" that accompanies the exercise of power over other peoples. He refers not so much to the conduct of the war itself – though I would include the conduct – but to the exercise of power afterwards, and there is a similarity in this between Russia and the United States. The difference is that whereas the perpetrators of ill treatment at Abu Ghraib prison and Camp Bread Basket are brought to trial, Russian forces who are responsible for similar and worse actions in Chechnya are not. And in the Russian case, I would add to the catalog of examples of "arrogance, ignorance and instinctive resort to force" the callous treatment of the victims and survivors of terrorism, as witnessed during and after the Dubrovka theatre and Beslan sieges, although carelessness with human life and disregard for human dignity are, perhaps, more a legacy of Stalinism than of the Cold War per se.

Another similarity between Russia and the United States is their attitudes to terrorism, particularly the way in which the emotions aroused by terrorist acts against their respective homelands narrow the possibility of rational discourse about causes – and thus the ability to canvas potential alternative responses. Any attempt after 9/11 to understand why al-Qaeda had undertaken the attacks on the World Trade Center and the Pentagon was regarded by most Americans (and many people in Britain) as anti-American, just as after Beslan using the term "rebel" rather than "terrorist" to describe Chechen secessionists, or depicting their actions as "resistance" instead of "terrorism," is regarded by Russians as grossly anti-Russian. And surely this binary, black and white, "if you are not with us, you are against us" categorization has its origins in the communist/anticommunist thinking of the Cold War.

The final similarity worth noticing between Russia's war and the West's war against terrorism is the extent to which governments in the United States (and Britain) and Russia have responded to terrorism by reducing civil liberties in the name of defending democracy – and how little protest this has aroused from those whose freedoms are affected. I would argue that the apparent acquiescence of the vast majority of people to the curtailment of their civil liberties is motivated not just by a genuine fear of terrorism but also by the desire not to be thought to be "soft on terrorism." Here, too, there are echoes of the Cold War when many people's attitudes to the policies of their own governments on both sides of the ideological divide were tempered by fear of being seen as "soft" on communism or imperialism.

However striking these similarities, the differences between the wars Russia and America are fighting against terrorism are great. Whereas the strength of the US causes terrorism, in the case of Russia the origins of the terrorist threat lie in the weakness of the state. Political instability, poverty, and inequality in Russia in the 1990s provided a fertile climate for radical groups to attract followers and for foreign Islamic networks to penetrate the country.[3]

A second difference is that Russia and the United States are dealing with different enemies. America's chief enemy in the war against terrorism is al-Qaeda (even if implicating al-Qaeda in the pressing danger represented by Saddam Hussein was scarcely credible). In Russia, however, the terrorist threat originates primarily in Chechnya. However many foreigners there are in Chechnya now, there can be little doubt that the terrorism that threatens Russia originated in the two wars to prevent Chechen secession – and the very notion of terrorism has become synonymous with Chechnya. That means that although it is unclear

what political goals al-Qaeda is pursuing in relation to America
– and therefore it is virtually impossible to imagine what kind of
political solution could bring an end to terrorism directed against
the United States – Chechen separatists have, or at least had,
clear political goals. It is feasible to imagine (though almost
impossible to bring about) a political solution which would
remove the rationale for Chechen terrorism.

Despite the local causes of terrorism in Russia, well before
9/11 the Russian leadership had frequently argued that Chechen
terrorists were trained and funded by Osama bin Laden. After
the Taliban took power in Afghanistan in 1996, Russians
complained that militants and mercenaries from the Balkans
and the Middle East who had been trained in Afghanistan –
they usually called them Wahhabis then – were active in
Chechnya. Throughout 2000, Putin used the term "international
terrorism" to describe the enemy against whom Russia was
fighting a second war in Chechnya.[4] Since September 11, he
has made an explicit link between fighters in Chechnya and al-
Qaeda. When President Putin declared Russia to be a member
of the coalition against terror, Russia's war against terrorism
became part of *the* war against terrorism. A brief examination of
Russia's war in Chechnya will establish whether this reflects
reality.

Russia's War on Terror

Russia is a federation, consisting of 89 federal units, some
of which are based on eponymous national groups and are
called national republics, others of which are simply administrative regions. Chechnya is one of the national republics. It is
a small mountainous area in the North Caucasus, enclosed by
the Russian Federation, except for one short external frontier
in the south that borders Georgia. Its population was about
1 million in 1989 of whom 75 per cent were Chechen and
25 per cent Russian. This is unusual in the Russian Federation, where Russians form the majority even in most national
republics.

Russia had expanded into North Caucasus in the late eighteenth century, and Chechens have fought them intermittently ever since. In 1944 Stalin deported almost the entire nation (half a million people) to Siberia and Central Asia, accusing them of collaborating with the Germans, and Chechnya disappeared from the map of the Soviet Union. They were rehabilitated in 1957 during Khrushchev's destalinization campaign and permitted to return to Chechnya, which reappeared on the Soviet map as Chechen-Ingushetia. In 1991, before the disintegration of the USSR, a nationalist movement came to power in Chechnya and declared the republic independent and separate from Ingushetia. Chechens neither participated in the 1993 referendum, nor voted in the elections for the new parliament.

Russian military intervention in 1994 led to a war that lasted until 1996 and ended in the defeat of Russia.[5] It is estimated that the first war led to 80,000 deaths and 415,000 displaced persons. Prior to the war, Chechnya had been a largely secular society. As casualties rose during the war, and Chechnya's economic, political, and social problems deepened, disaffected Muslim groups became increasingly radicalized. Moreover, the conflict attracted religious volunteers recruited and funded from abroad. The war of secession was gradually transformed into a jihad – fought by means of guerrilla warfare and terrorism – against Russia.

Chechnya was reduced to ruins by the first war, and Russian funds promised for reconstruction in the Khasavyurt Accord which brought the war to an end either failed to arrive or were embezzled. General Aslan Maskhadov, who had been elected president in 1997, had limited control over the country and could neither prevent crime and kidnapping, nor rein in the warlords who had begun to operate independently during the war. In August 1999 Chechen fighters crossed into the neighboring North Caucasus Republic of Dagestan to support a declaration by an Islamic body based there of an independent Islamic state in parts of Dagestan and Chechnya. They were beaten back by local forces and the Russian army.[6]

A series of massive bombings of apartment blocks in Moscow, Volgodonsk, and Bunaisk in September 1999 which claimed more than 300 lives was blamed on Chechen rebels. In response to the terrorist attacks and the events in Dagestan, Russia launched a second intervention into Chechnya which led to the second Chechen war that still continues today – although Moscow declares that it has been over since 2002.[7] In March 2003 Russia held a referendum in Chechnya and claimed an overwhelming majority in favour of a new constitution stipulating that the republic is part of the Russian Federation. Later that year elections were held and a pro-Moscow local government was put in place with Ahmed Kadyrov as president.

The distinction that is usually made between terrorism and guerrilla warfare is that the latter is directed against combatants, while terrorism is directed against civilians. That distinction is blurred in Chechnya: guerrilla warfare and terrorism are organized by the same leaders, financed from the same sources, and they have the same aims. Terrorist tactics such as suicide bombing are used against Russian forces and local pro-Moscow officials as well as against civilians. But there is also, in Chechnya, ordinary banditry, frequently including kidnapping for financial gain.[8] The cases most publicized have involved foreigners kidnapped for ransom, but Russian forces are also alleged to kidnap Chechens for the same reason.

Terrorist tactics have been a feature of the war since 1995, used both in Chechnya and in the rest of Russia. Examples include the holding hostage of an entire hospital in Budennovsk in June 1995. When Russian forces tried to storm the hospital, more than 100 Russian civilians were killed. Six months later another hospital was taken hostage in Dagestan and 28 Russian civilians lost their lives, many of them killed by Russian forces. In both cases, the Chechens appear to have aimed initially at military targets. In 1998 four engineers from Britain and New Zealand were kidnapped and murdered in Chechnya. In 1998 and 1999, Russian presidential representatives, Valentin Vlasov and General Gennady Shpigun, were kidnapped in Chechnya. Just over three years after the 1999 apartment block bombings, Chechen terrorists seized the Dubrovka theatre in Moscow in October 2002 and held about 800 people hostage. Most of the rebels and some 120 hostages were killed when Russian forces stormed the building. In May 2004 President Kadyrov was killed by a suicide bomber in Grozny, the capital of Chechnya. In late August that year, suicide bombers brought down two planes in Russia, which was followed within a few days by the siege of the Beslan school in North Ossetia.

In short, there is no doubt that terrorism has emerged as the major threat to Russian security. But it is also true that there has been a cycle of Russian repression, Chechen revenge, and Russian retaliation. Human rights abuses by Russian forces are commonplace. The Russian government, and Russians more generally, consider that Chechens are terrorists and this appears to be accepted as sufficient justification for violence perpetrated by Russian forces against ordinary Chechens. To say that Russia's brutality has, inevitably, radicalized the Chechen population is not to excuse terrorism, but to question the effectiveness of the responses that Russia, like most other governments faced with terrorism, has undertaken.

Russia's conduct of the first war in Chechnya was the subject of much criticism by the Council of Europe, the Organization for Security and Cooperation in Europe (OSCE), the UN Commissioner for Human Rights, the European Union, and the governments of the United States and of most of Europe. Until 9/11 the second war in Chechnya was also criticized. There have also been critical reports published by nongovernmental organizations (NGOs).[9] After 9/11 the criticism became muted, but in the last couple of years it has again become one of the contentious issues in Russia's relations with much of the outside world.

The Russian response to terrorism has not been confined to Chechnya. There has been constant pressure on Georgia for harboring Chechen terrorists in the Pankisi Gorge, across the Chechen–Georgian border. After the Beslan siege, in a statement reminiscent of President Bush's Doctrine of Preemption, President Putin threatened preemptive action against terrorist bases abroad.[10] There was little doubt that Georgia was intended to heed the warning. In early 2002 the US had sent military advisors to Georgia to train its forces for antiterrorist operations and to help address the increasing lawlessness in the region. Perhaps for this reason, Russia's threat has not been implemented, but nor has it been retracted.

Putin has also used Beslan as a pretext to continue the programme of strengthening the Russian state that he had launched when he was first elected president in 2000. Putin did not regard the 1990s as a period of emerging democracy but as a decade during which the Russian state was allowed to become fatally weak. From Putin's point of view, the decentralization that Yeltsin had encouraged had served to fragment the Federation and had led to the kind of regional separatism of which Chechnya was simply an extreme example. As a result, he had long been convinced that restoring a firm grip over Russia's regions was necessary to preserve an integrated country and defend national security from the threat of secessionism and terrorism. The tragedy of Beslan – both the siege itself and the ineffective response of the local authorities – made him even more certain that centralization was necessary. He saw it as the remedy for ineffectual local government, and for the corruption that had permitted terrorists to bribe their way into the school in Beslan and on to the two planes that were brought down shortly before the siege.

Putin's programme had been launched well before the Beslan tragedy. Early in his first term he had, for example, strengthened state control of the media, in part in order to control information about the Chechen war. He had also attempted to increase the authority of the federal government by establishing a "power vertical" staffed predominantly by people from the security organs. One aspect of his power vertical was the creation of seven federal regions, each presided over by a governor-general who is responsible to the presidential administration. In addition, in the name of separating legislative and executive powers, he had removed the regional governors from the Federal Council, the upper chamber of the Russian parliament, replacing them with representatives appointed by the governors.[11]

Since Beslan, Putin has repealed the popular election of regional governors, replacing it with a system whereby he nominates them and the regional legislature is restricted to approving his nomination. He has also passed a law so that the next Duma will be

elected entirely on the basis of proportional representation based
on party lists (previously half the deputies were elected from
single-member constituencies). In short, he has moved away
from the idea of a federation "from the bottom up," arguing that
unless federalism in Russia is a top-down process, the state will
remain fatally weak.[12] As mutual agreements between the federal
centre and the subjects of the federation are replaced by the
delegation of power from the top, the Russian Federation is
gradually reverting to the Soviet formula of "federal in form but
unitary in practice."

The problem is that by removing local participation in
decision-making through the electoral process, these reforms are
more likely to make it more difficult for Moscow to govern the
Russian Federation effectively than they are to strengthen the
state. They will also serve to depoliticize an already apolitical
population. They will increase the distance between the people
and those who govern them, and undermine the fragile pluralism
and democracy that Russia achieved in its first decade. This is
not the way to build civil society. And nor is it at all clear how
these measure will reduce the threat from terrorism. Indeed,
absent an end to the war in Chechnya, it is difficult to see what
could eradicate terrorism in Russia.

What *is* clear is that Putin's political changes have been the
subject of much criticism from Russia's partners in the coalition
against terrorism, notably in the run-up to the Bush–Putin summit
in February 2005, when Bush threatened to take Putin to task
for backsliding on Russian democracy. In short, the manner in
which Putin is fighting his war against terrorism adds to the tensions in Russia's relations with the United States that have arisen
as a result of America's war against terror.

America's War on Terror

As long as the coalition against terrorism was concentrated on
the war in Afghanistan, American aims were compatible with
those of Russia. But as soon as President Bush claimed in
2002 that there was an "axis of evil" consisting of countries that

harbored terrorists and aimed to produce weapons of mass destruction, it became clear not only that America and Russia did not have identical enemies, but that America's pursuit of the members of the axis of evil would soon infringe Russian interests.

Historically, the Soviet Union had good relations with North Korea and Iraq, and, for most of its history, neighbourly relations with Iran. In the mid-1990s, in an attempt to diversify Russian foreign policy, relations with North Korea and Iraq had been revived. Russia also has strong commercial relations with Iran, in particular supplying both the know-how and the wherewithal for a nuclear power station at Bushehr. In 2000, Putin also appeared to launch a particular form of what might be called "niche diplomacy," devising for Russia the role of intermediary to assist these "rogue states" reintegrate into the international political system.

Russian leaders do not believe that their enemies are in Iraq, Iran, and North Korea. Although they thought that Saddam Hussein represented a threat, they argued that the threat could be contained. They did not accept that the Iranian government sponsored terrorism, and were adamant that they were not assisting Iran to produce nuclear weapons. And although they disapproved of Kim Jong Il's nuclear ambitions, they did not perceive North Korea as a military threat. As soon as President Bush turned his attention from Afghanistan to the "axis of evil," Russian and American purposes began to diverge.

Russia's opposition to the war against Iraq is well known and I shall not dwell on it here.[13] Instead I shall turn briefly to the Commonwealth of Independent States (CIS) because it is here that Russia perceives not just divergent purposes, but that US policy infringes on Russia's vital national interests.

Since 1991, there has been a revival of religion in Central Asia. The revival of Islam was a potentially stabilizing factor, since it filled the void that the collapse of the communist belief system had left. Shortly after independence, however, a civil war broke out in Tajikistan between the former communist elite and an opposition force that contained Islamic groups. As a result of the Tajik civil war, the four other Central Asian states banned most

opposition parties and movements, and prevented the emergence
of legitimate political opposition. The defeated Tajik rebels took
refuge in Afghanistan, as did the outlawed Islamic Movement of
Uzbekistan (IMU). Russia intervened in the Tajik war and its
troops still guard the border between Tajikistan and Afghanistan.
Aiming to establish an Islamic state in the Ferghana Valley, the
IMU launched military actions in 1999 and 2000 from Afghanistan through Tajikistan into Kyrghyzia and Uzbekistan. Russia
established a CIS Counterterrorism Center in response to the
activities of the IMU but had neither the capabilities nor the
political will to intervene.[14]

The war against terrorism in Central Asia changed radically
after 9/11, when the United States decided to use airbases in
Uzbekistan, Kyrgyzstan, and Tajikistan. President Putin, despite
opposition from his military advisors, rapidly gave his consent.[15]
In late November 2001 it was widely reported that the IMU's
military leader, Juma Namangani, had died from wounds received
during the US bombing of Afghanistan. It seems unlikely that
any IMU infrastructure has survived the bombing campaign.[16]

Despite Russia's public support for the war on terrorism in
Central Asia, there is considerable anxiety about the continued
involvement of the United States in Central Asia, an area which
Russians regard as unambiguously within their legitimate sphere
of interest. It seems unlikely that the United States will withdraw
from Uzbekistan or Kyrgyzstan in the near future, not only
because the situation in Afghanistan is far from stable, but also
because of American interests in the energy resources of the
Caspian Sea. American military advisors have been in Georgia
since 2002 to train local forces in antiterrorist operations. Russia,
therefore, no longer exercises sole influence in either Central Asia
or the Caucasus.

It is in the context of the continued US presence in the CIS
in its pursuit of its war against terrorism that the differences
between Russia's and America's war against terrorism threaten
to become, in Russian perceptions, an infringement of Russia's
vital national interests. Western objections to the manner in
which Russia fights its counterterrorism campaigns (objections
which Russians reject and deeply resent) exacerbate Russian sus-

picions that US strategy in the region is aimed at weakening Russia's legitimate interests.

Conclusion

There are contradictions in Russian views about the war against terrorism. Moscow depicts its war in Chechnya as part of the global war against terrorism, thus internationalizing it. Yet it also insists that the war is its "internal affair," resists advice about how it should be prosecuted, and rejects any suggestion that international intervention might assist in resolving the Chechen conflict. America, too, rejects advice about what policy it should follow against terrorism. The consequence for Russia, as for America, is that its war against terrorism has a negative effect on its relations with other states.

The fact that neither the war against Chechnya nor the war against Afghanistan have eliminated terrorism has not persuaded either Putin or Bush that a war against terror is absurd. To quote Martin Wolf, "one cannot fight abstract nouns."[17] If terrorism could be defeated by military means, al-Qaeda would have been destroyed in Afghanistan, given the immense military power of the United States. And Russia's war against Chechen terrorists would have succeeded, because, for all Russia's weakness, there is no doubt that in conventional military terms it is immeasurably stronger than Chechnya.

This does not mean that there are easy political means by which to defeat terrorism. In the case of Russia, three groups are said to be resistant to a political solution because they have an interest in perpetuating the war in Chechnya.[18] Russian federal forces have strong incentives to remain in Chechnya, such as higher pay and the financial benefits they enjoy from black-market trading and extortion. The second group that has an interest in sustaining the conflict are the Kadyrovtsy, that is, the followers of the assassinated pro-Russian president of Chechnya, Ahmed Kadyrov, and the forces controlled by his son Ramzan. They too are responsible for extrajudicial killings, torture, and abductions for profit.[19] The third group that needs the war are the warlords and terrorists themselves. No longer are they rebels whose sole political agenda is independence for Chechnya. The war in Chechnya has become a self-fulfilling prophecy. Since 1997–8 Islamic groups have become predominant in the region, yet, as de Waal points out, al-Qaeda is a parallel, and not the central, movement. He argues that the presence of two Arabs among the 31 terrorists who carried out the hostage-taking in Beslan accurately reflects the proportion of international to home-grown rebel forces in Chechnya today.[20]

There is one school of thought that argues that there is a fourth group in Moscow that fuels the conflict – President Putin and his presidential administration. The explanation is that "Russia's war against terrorism is not about winning, it is about having it."[21] The reason is that Vladimir Putin arrived in the Kremlin with a clear perception that Russia's very existence was threatened and that the only way to save it was to recentralize the state through firm administrative control. He needed a lever to do this and the war against terrorism provided, and continues to provide, just that. Moreover, the war against terrorism contributes significantly to bolstering Putin's popular support. Paradoxically, while the only way Yeltsin could win a second term as Russian president in 1996 was by ending the war against Chechnya, in 2000 the second war against Chechnya gave Putin an unprecedented first-round victory in the presidential election. His support has barely fallen since then. According to this school of thought, it is only when Putin believes that he has succeeded in recentralizing the state, or when his public support begins to wane, that he will begin to seek a political means to end the war.

When that time comes, he will have to look to the silent majority of Chechens who suffer violence both at the hands of the Russian forces and from the Kadyrovtsy. If he really wants to eradicate terrorism, these are the people he will need to court, rather than the people he appoints from Moscow and allows to perpetrate atrocities in his name. For the war against terrorism in Russia can ultimately only be won by ending the war in Chechnya, and that requires persuading ordinary Chechens that the terrorists represent the greater, not the lesser of two evils.

Notes

This chapter was commissioned especially for this collection.

1 At http://usinfo.state.gov/is/international_security/terrorism/sept_11/sept_11_archive/Leaders_Worldwide_Condemn_Terrorist_Attacks.html.
2 *The Observer*, Jan. 30, 2005.
3 Fiona Hill, "Putin and Bush in Common Cause? Russia's View of the Terrorist Threat after September 11," *Brookings Review*, 20.3 (Summer 2002): 33.
4 See, for example, his annual address to the Federal Assembly in June 2000, at http://president.kremlin.ru/appears/2000/07/08/0000_type63372_28782.shtml (accessed Mar. 12, 2005).
5 For a discussion of the various reasons that have been suggested to explain why, after tolerating de facto Chechen independence since 1991, the Russian government went to war in 1994, see James Hughes, "Chechnya: The Causes of a Protracted Post-Soviet Conflict," *Civil Wars*, 4 (Winter 2001): 11–48; Matthew Evangelista, *The Chechen Wars* (Washington, DC: Brookings Institution Press, 2002).
6 Evangelista, *The Chechen Wars*, pp. 63–4.
7 For an account of the two wars, see ibid., Chs 2 and 4. Anna Politkovskaya, *A Dirty War* (London: Harvill, 2001), gives one of the few accounts of the second war by a Russian reporter.
8 Dmitri Trenin, "The Forgotten War: Chechnya and Russia's Future," Policy Brief 28, Carnegie Moscow Center, Nov. 2003, p. 2.
9 See, for example, "Endless Brutality: Ongoing Human Rights Violations in Chechnya," A Report by Physicians for Human Rights, Jan. 2001, at www.phrusa.org/research/chechnya/chech_rep.html (accessed Mar. 14, 2005).
10 The Bush Doctrine of Preemption was announced in a speech at West Point in 2002. For the text of the speech, see www.whitehouse.gov/news/releases/2002/06/20020601-3.html (accessed Mar. 13, 2005). For a recent reiteration of Russia's right to strike terrorist bases outside of its territory and to do so without any warning, see Russian Defense Minister Sergei Ivanov's response to journalists, reported in www.rferl.org/newsline/2005/03/070305.asp (accessed Mar. 14, 2005).
11 For an assessment of these measures, see Pavel K. Baev, "Instrumentalizing Counterterrorism for Regime Consolidation in Putin's Russia," Studies in Conflict and Terrorism, 27 (2004): 337–52.

12 Fiona Hill, "Putin and Bush in Common Cause?" p. 6.
13 For an analysis of the effect of the war on Russian–American relations, see A. Belkin, "US-Russian Relations and the Global Counter-Terrorist Campaign," *Journal of Slavic Military Studies*, 17.1 (Mar. 2004): 13–28.
14 Svante E. Cornell and Regine A. Spector, "Central Asia: More than Islamic Extremists," *Washington Quarterly*, 25.1 (2002): 193–206.
15 Since the Central Asian states were sovereign and independent, they did not, of course, require Putin's permission. His "consent" can be interpreted, therefore, as a face-saving response to the loss of Russia's perceived role as the sole guarantor of Central Asian security.
16 "The IMU and the Hizb-ut-Tahrir: Implications of the Afghanistan Campaign," Central Asia Briefing, International Crisis Group, Jan. 2002.
17 *The Financial Times*, Sept. 22, 2004.
18 I draw heavily in this section from a report of an event at the Carnegie Endowment for International Peace on October 28, 2004 on Chechnya, and in particular on Tom de Waal's speech. See "Chechnya: What Can Be Done?" Carnegie Endowment for International Peace, at www.carnegieendowment.org/events/index.cfm?fa=eventDetailandid=729 (accessed Mar. 14, 2005).
19 Fiona Hill, Anatol Lieven, and Thomas de Waal, "A Spreading Danger: Time for a New Policy toward Chechnya," Policy Brief, 35, Carnegie Endowment for International Peace, Mar. 2005.
20 "De Waal, Chechnya: What Can Be Done?"
21 Baev, "Instrumentalizing Counterterrorism," p. 338.

7

Southeast Asia and Global Terror

Kerry Lynn Nankivell and James Boutilier

Observations to the effect that the world was changed irrevers-
ibly by the tragic events of September 11, 2001 have become so
pedestrian as to be unhelpful to those who try to understand
international relations. Overwhelmed by the scale and audacity
of attacks on the World Trade Center and the Pentagon, scholars
and practitioners have tended to take for granted that global
politics has been subsumed by the US-led War on Terror. This
is especially true of geostrategic analyses since the attacks. While
it is undeniable that 9/11 represents a seminal event in the
post–Cold War global environment, much academic scholarship
and policy analysis since then has made Washington the subject
of virtually all strategic development. The rest of the world, in
all its diversity, has become a mere object of Washington's post-
9/11 security strategy. This analysis breaks with this trend, demonstrating the ways in which the events of 9/11 have been
exploited by governments in Southeast Asia to further their
national interests, relegating the purpose and priorities of US
policy-makers to the periphery of strategic developments in the
region.

The Southeast Asian context has refracted, rather than
reflected, Washington's policies and priorities in the War on
Terror. Contrary to the presumptions of conventional neorealist paradigms that usually inform strategic scholarship, the

governments of Southeast Asia have neither unequivocally "band-wagoned" nor "balanced" Washington in the War on Terror.[1] We will use the scientific term "refraction" as an analogy of geostrategic behavior that lies somewhere on the spectrum between Waltz's bandwagoning (in which the policies of a stronger state are adopted by a weaker state as a means to enhance the weaker state's security) and balancing (when weaker states come together to balance the preponderant power of an existing or aspiring hegemon).[2] Refraction refers to the distortion of great power (or hyperpower, in this case) policy as it is contextualized in a particular region or state. In terms of the analysis offered here, the concept of refraction is meant to highlight independent policy-making by Southeast Asian governments in their own prosecution of the War on Terror. Their strategies are not necessarily reflective of Washington's priorities for Southeast Asia, a region that is thick with national agendas, ambitions, and historical legacies. The concept is meant to accord due weight to Southeast Asian governments' capacity for policy-making, and dispel common perceptions of the region as a reflective surface on to which Washington's priorities in the War on Terror have been projected. This does not suggest that these governments are necessarily duplicitous in their dealings with, or that they present a danger to, Washington. Rather it highlights that if and when their policies dovetail with those of the United States it is because of compatible national interests, and not because of Washington's irresistible pull as the center of gravity for international relations.

Having introduced this exploration in terms of what it will offer, we believe that it is important, at this juncture, to clarify what it will not. This analysis will not describe the detailed structure and machinations of particular terrorist organizations, such as Jemaah Islamiyah (believed to be responsible for the Bali bombing of October 12, 2002 and the subsequent Marriott bombing in Jakarta of August 5, 2003). Nor will we explore the dense network that links these extremist groups together across Southeast Asia. Instead, we will look specifically at the ways in which governments have incorporated the US-led

War on Terror in their respective security strategies in the pursuit of their national interests. Generally, we hope to draw some inferences about the nature of statecraft and governmental cooperation in international relations.

In a discussion meant to highlight the diversity of interest at work in strategic policy-making in Southeast Asia, it would be remiss not to make one further qualification. Any treatment of the behavior of Southeast Asian states as a single unit is bound to run into difficulty. There are ways in which the entity "Southeast Asia" exists only on a map; it often seems the case that the countries in question are related only by an accident of geography and not by convergence of interest. By virtue of its complex diversity, there are very few characterizations that one can make about the subregion that do not overlook some anomalous feature or another. This analysis is no exception, and is, in fact, further complicated by the limited analytical space available. Thus, rather than saddle the reader with empirical facts demonstrating policy divergence between Washington and Southeast Asian capitals, we will explore only the post-9/11 dynamic between the United States and the Philippines and the United States and Malaysia, as the most pronounced examples of policy refraction in the War on Terror in Southeast Asia.

We will see, for example, how Manila's cooperation with Washington, which culminated in the Philippines being designated a Major Non-NATO Ally in October 2003, cannot be explained in terms of the simple dynamic of dominance. The relationship is as indelibly marked by the preexisting and ongoing national security interests of President Arroyo's administration as it is by the priorities of the White House. Next, we will consider Malaysia's role in the War on Terror, occupying as it does the middle ground between ally and adversary of the United States. We will explore why the occupation of this political space is central to Malaysia's successful prosecution of the War on Terror. Finally, we will complement these case studies by analyzing the lessons that practitioners and scholars of international relations can draw from them.

The War on Terror as Civil Strife:
The Case of the Philippines

A crystalline example of the ways in which the US-led War on Terror has been refracted in Southeast Asia is offered by the policy dynamic in the Philippines, one that brings together the governments in Washington and Manila as well as two indigenous insurgent organizations, the Moro Islamic Liberation Front (MILF) and the Abu Sayyaf Group (ASG). While the ASG's connections to international terror have drawn Washington's attention, the group constitutes only a peripheral threat to the government in Manila. President Arroyo's primary strategic concern is, arguably, the decades-old insurgency waged by the MILF. Prior to 9/11, it looked as if the insurgency would only be concluded through painful political negotiations. After 9/11, however, renewed US interest in the Philippines provided President Arroyo's administration with a unique opportunity to gain material and ideological support in its struggle against the MILF, tilting the balance between adversaries that had been largely stalemated. The dynamic created by Washington's prosecution of the War on Terror in the Philippines is more nuanced than simple Waltzian "bandwagoning," though the coincidental and complementary strategic interests of Manila and Washington tempt analysts to oversimplify the strategic relationship. A fuller understanding can only be achieved by appreciating how these actors and their priorities intersect to inform Manila's strategy in the War on Terror and contribute to the pursuit of its national interest.

The Moros of Mindanao

Arguably, Moro separatism has presented the largest obstacle to governance in the Philippines over the last several decades. The Moro community is a Muslim minority concentrated largely in the southern portions of Mindanao. Distanced from Manila by history and culture,[3] and distanced from other Islamic societies by the local idiosyncrasies of Moro Islam,[4] the Moros fought to create an independent Moro state, answerable neither to the government in

Manila, nor the wider Southeast Asian Muslim community. The most successful campaign for Moro liberation was waged by the Moro National Liberation Front in the 1970s.

Today's Moro Islamic Liberation Front (MILF) was created in 1977 as a splinter group that broke away from well-established Moro National Liberation Front (MNLF). The MILF was born of alienated insurgents dissatisfied with the MNLF leadership's negotiations with the Philippine government at the time. Exhausted by years of fighting, and encouraged by their international sponsor, Libyan dictator Colonel Qaddafi, to reach a compromise with the government, the MNLF agreed at the end of the decade to relinquish their demand for an independent Moro homeland in return for greater autonomy within the Philippine nation. The autonomy agreement provided senior government and military posts for some MNLF fighters, and, thus, was perceived by many as the leadership's betrayal of the Moro people in return for material gain.

Hashim Salamat, a MNLF fighter, exploited this dissatisfaction and broke off to establish the MILF in 1977. Since then, the MILF has waged war against Manila and has engaged recently in off-again, on-again negotiations for greater autonomy or independence in Mindanao. The Moro cause has been legitimized by other Muslim states, especially Malaysia, and has been equated by Southeast Asian Muslims with the Palestinian cause in the Middle East. They see it as a struggle by a Muslim community oppressed by non-Muslim rule. Today the MILF enjoys an intermittent ceasefire (begun in 2001) with the government of President Arroyo, and is engaged in negotiations brokered alternately by Malaysia and, recently, Norway.

Prior to the World Trade Center attacks, conflict with the MILF had led only to stalemate and, subsequently, to negotiations. While the MILF appeared unable to win independence from Manila, Manila was never successful in asserting its control over their region of Mindanao. The conflict was deadlocked, and it is fair to say that negotiations were the orphan of military exhaustion rather than the fruit of real compromise by either side. Post-9/11, and within this strained dynamic, Washington's renewed interest in Muslim insurgency in Southeast Asia provided strategic and normative leverage to the Arroyo government. Thus the Philippine government has taken up Washington's cause against Islamist violence, but skillfully refracted it in such a way that it serves Manila's interests vis-à-vis their long-time rivals, the MILF. A fuller appreciation of this dynamic requires an understanding of the nature of Washington's interest in the Philippines as part of its War on Terror.

Washington's war: US priorities in the Philippines

The Abu Sayyaf Group (ASG), literally "Bearer" or "Father of the Sword," is a small cadre of militants that splintered from the Moro Islamic Liberation Front in 1991. The ASG looks to establish an Iranian-style theocracy on Mindanao, and enjoys the support of international jihadists, including al-Qaeda and Jemaah Islamiyah, in this endeavour. The group has become well known, not for its military victories against the Armed Forces of the Philippines (AFP), but for its kidnappings for ransom. It uses these operations to fund low-level attacks that are more than a nuisance but fall short of constituting a serious challenge to the Arroyo government. However, Abu Sayyaf's links to international terror, as well as its successful kidnapping of US citizens, and connections to Ramzi Yousef (who was convicted for his role in the attempted bombing of the World Trade Center in 1993), place the group squarely on US policy-makers' radar screens as a threat to US security.

The association between the Abu Sayyaf Group and international jihadists like Osama bin Laden and Ramzi Yousef is undeniable. The group's founder, Abduragak Abubakar Janjalani, was a student of jihad in Afghanistan under bin Laden and was one of many jihadist missionaries who returned to Southeast Asia after the Soviet–Afghan war with a view to exporting jihad from Afghanistan to other parts of the Muslim world. Accordingly, the United States has played an active part in aiding the government of the Philippines in its fight against the Abu Sayyaf Group as part of Washington's campaign against international terror.

US military involvement in the Philippines since September 11, 2001 represents the most notable expansion of American operations abroad after Afghanistan and Iraq. Beginning in 2002, the United States deployed 660 Special Forces personnel to the Philippines to act as military advisors to the AFP in their fight against organizations on Washington's terror watch list, such as the Abu Sayyaf Group. To that end, the Philippines Forces received 30 million US dollars earmarked for training and equipment procurement in counterinsurgency, 30 UH-1H combat helicopters, including spare parts for maintenance, up to 25 million US dollars toward the establishment of a Philippine Combat Engineering Unit and up to 10 million dollars in Presidential Drawdown Authority for equipment, spare parts, and maintenance (above and beyond what is specifically provided for in other components of the military assistance package). Most controversially, the 660 military advisors continue to be deployed with Philippine forces on missions into combat zones, though they are not authorized to fire unless fired upon. In an effort to underpin the package and ensure its longevity, US military advisors have also undertaken a Comprehensive Security Review of the Philippines security infrastructure in order to better understand "Philippine security needs and how the United States can best support Philippine military modernization and reform."[5] To legitimize American involvement in the Filipino security infrastructure, the Philippines was granted Major Non-NATO Ally status (MNNA) officially on October 7, 2003. Though mainly symbolic, this designation grants the Philippines priority for arms procurement and allows Manila access to defense items that are normally restricted so far as export from the United States is concerned, such as depleted uranium antitank ammunition. The military aid and involvement have been substantial, and reflect the importance that Washington attaches to the campaign against the Abu Sayyaf Group as part of the larger, global campaign against terror.

A fuller account: the War on Terror refracted

Though menacing in terms of its ability to network with other groups of international terrorists, the Abu Sayyaf Group consists of no more than a few hundred insurgents (buttressed by a few thousand supporters) out of a national population of 84.5 million. Since its creation in 1991, Abu Sayyaf has not presented enough of a threat to the government in Manila to bring it to the negotiation table, unlike its more moderate counterpart, the Moro Islamic Liberation Front. Though President Arroyo's government has consistently petitioned Washington to include the MILF on its terror watch list, thereby bringing US military might to bear on the MILF in the same way that it has been focused on the Abu Sayyaf, Washington remains reluctant to do so. In the immediate aftermath of President Arroyo's trip to Washington in May 2003, during which she reportedly requested that the Bush administration designate the MILF a terrorist organization, the MILF publicly renounced the use of Islamist terror as a means of furthering its political ends. Washington maintains that so long as MILF commanders distance themselves from the worldwide network of Islamist terror that is targeting the United States, it will receive the support and encouragement of the United States in its peaceful negotiations with Manila.

Whatever the case, President Arroyo has made a substantial gamble in opening her country's security infrastructure so widely to the United States. As a former imperial power in the Philippines, and long-time regional hegemon, the United States does not enjoy a high profile in Filipino society. Only a decade ago, the United States was asked to leave the military bases that it had maintained on the islands since its defeat of the Spanish in 1898. In 1991, the Senate of the Philippines passed a constitutional ban on foreign troops in Filipino territory, a clause that speaks directly to the threat that US military hegemony was thought to represent to Philippine sovereignty. Since President Arroyo's increased post-9/11 cooperation with the Bush administration, she has faced mounting criticism from her own administration. Most significantly, her vice president, Teofista Guingona, resigned his cabinet post in the foreign ministry because of policy differences regarding the US military presence in the country.[6] The political risks that President Arroyo has assumed by virtue of her cooperation with the United States in the War on Terror have been considerable, and not commensurate with the national security benefits that she will reap vis-à-vis the Abu Sayyaf Group.

Thus the development of US–Filipino relations in the post-9/11 period cannot be interpreted merely as President Arroyo's complacent reflection of Washington's priorities and policies in the War on Terror. This kind of analysis is simply not convincing because it does not explain President Arroyo's willingness to bear the very real political costs associated with cooperation with Washington. However, if one takes into account the strategic and normative advantages that President Arroyo has gained vis-à-vis the Moro Islamic Liberation Front as a result of her alliance with Washington in the War on Terror, the political risks that she has taken appear rational. Despite public protests over a renewed US military presence in the Philippines, President Arroyo has exploited the opportunity to weaken the Moro insurgency, one that involves thousands of insurgents and enjoys some measure of political legitimacy at home and abroad. Arguably, added training and equipment in counterinsurgency, ostensibly directed at defeating the Abu Sayyaf, cannot help but be useful to the government in their campaign against the MILF. Further, most analysts agree that it remains a priority of the Arroyo administration to discredit the MILF and guarantee its total military defeat by continuing to lobby for its inclusion on Washington's list of international terror groups.[7]

Whether or not the government's ambition of strategic victory is realized, President Arroyo has already, through the War on Terror, gained considerable normative advantage over her MILF opponents. The general discrediting of Islamic movements around the world since September 11 has removed an important pillar from the MILF's political platform and placed it on the normative defensive. After several decades of robust military campaigning, the MILF has been underwritten by Islamic states that espouse its cause in terms of Islamic solidarity in the face of colonial exploitation by non-Islamic societies. The War on Terror threatens to demote the MILF from the rank accorded a resistance organization with legitimate political goals, to the status of a third-rate al-Qaeda franchise, bent on terrorism for its own sake. The normative difference is significant: the former is legitimate and can find support among the international community, the latter is the enemy, by definition, of all states concerned with international peace and order.

Thus Washington's War on Terror is refracted in the Philippines, not reflected. Manila's relationship with Washington is far more complex than simple co-optation allows. President Arroyo's administration maintains distinct policy goals and priorities and its leveraging of US support in order to achieve those goals should not be confused with pursuing Washington's strategic interests for the purposes of courting favor. In fact, the pursuit of Washington's support with respect to the MILF arguably diverts US efforts to a military contest that sits outside of Washington's strategic priorities.

President Arroyo has accepted considerable political risk in her alliance with Washington. However, in return, she gains strategic and normative advantage over the MILF, her administration's greatest national security problem. The defeat of the 25,000-strong MILF, which has waged an insurgency for over a quarter of a century, would be a significant political coup that would hand her a victory that eluded her predecessors. President Arroyo's relationship with Washington is complex and nuanced; the Philippines remains the center of a national security complex which cannot be fully understood when it is viewed simply as a satellite of Washington's War on Terror.

The War on Terror as Identity Formation: The Case of Malaysia

Malaysia's prosecution of the War on Terror since the Bali bombing on October 12, 2002 provides another classic and easily identifiable example of the ways in which Washington's War on Terror has been refracted. Malaysia's government has traditionally been intolerant of extremism and insurgency. Consequently, it has managed to remain relatively free to pursue economic development while its neighbours have been preoccupied with concerns about internal security and national unity. Thus, when the United States embarked upon its own war against Islamist extremism after 9/11, Kuala Lumpur immediately sought to distinguish its own battle against jihadists from the one waged by Washington. The refraction of the War on Terror in Malaysia has been an exercise in socialization; it has been an occasion for Malaysia to consolidate its identity as the leading voice of strong but moderate Islamic states, neither subservient to the West nor "hijacked" by reactionary, extremist groups. This consolidation process has brought Malaysia into frequent conflict with policy-makers in the United States, at the very time that Malaysia's effectiveness in investigating and detaining suspected terrorists has placed the two countries on a similar policy path. In this way, and much to Washington's frustration, Malaysia is neither "with" the United States nor "against" it, but pursues its own national interest, constructed around the need for a strong Malay Islamic identity.

The Malay dilemma

At the forefront of development in the region,[8] Malaysia offers one of the most globalized economies in the world,[9] and boasts education, literacy, and health indicators characteristic of the developed rather than the developing world. As one American journalist notes:

> Forty-three years ago, Malaysia lagged behind Haiti in *per capita* income; since then it has grown an average of 7 percent annually and would rank third in *per capita* wealth in the Western Hemisphere. By almost any standard, its growth is outstanding. Given what the country was able to overcome – the deadly Malay–Chinese race riots in 1969, continued muted ethnic divisions, the lack of a democratic tradition, a prior dependence on extractive industries – Malaysia is one of the great international success stories of the past generation.[10]

The miracle of Malaysia's economic and governmental rebirth from a history of colonialism and underdevelopment is attributable, in large part, to the strong leadership of Dr Mahathir bin Mohammad and the United Malays National Organization (UMNO). The party remains the country's governing party and, along with the recently retired prime minister, the guiding voice in national development. Though supplemented by sound economic and social policies, UMNO's success has been built on a foundation that is as much about the rejection of a colonial past as it is about the renaissance of the Malay Muslim identity. As a country whose Muslim Malays (approximately 58 percent of the population) have been dominated economically by (alternately) Christian European colonialists and ethnic Chinese Malaysians, Malaysia's emergence as a force in global politics and economics has depended heavily on the creation of a strong Muslim Malay community that can take its rightful place in Malaysian and international society. Dr Mahathir and his party have always constructed the Malaysian interest around a defiant Malay Islamic identity: his book *The Malay Dilemma* (1970) calls for a resurgence of Malaysian ingenuity and hard work to restore Malays to their rightful position at all levels of the Malaysian government and economy.[11] Though harsh in its criticisms of Muslim Malay complacency, its message formed the basis upon which the new nation was built.

Initially, the War on Terror presented some policy challenges for Kuala Lumpur. Though Dr Mahathir's government fought its own battles with Islamist militants on Malaysian territory even before terrorism came to dominate the global security agenda, it could ill afford to dance *sans chagrin* to Washington's tune. In order to maintain its standing as a government of and for Muslim Malays, and a model nation with a strong, positive Islamic identity in international politics, Kuala Lumpur was forced to stake out a middle ground and diverge from Washington's foreign policy without betraying its own opposition to fundamentalism and terror.

Terrorism in Malaysia

Despite Kuala Lumpur's efforts (before the events of September 11, 2001 and October 12, 2002), Malaysia's government, like the others in the region, was painfully unaware of the strength and scope of terrorist networks in Southeast Asia. Though Kuala Lumpur realized the threat to its own national security by the Islamist Kumpulan Mujahideen Malaysia (KMM), it is not clear that officials appreciated the extent of the networked capabilities that KMM could draw upon throughout Southeast Asia, or the nature of the group's ties to international terrorist groups, such as al-Qaeda and Jemaah Islamiyah. Before international terror literally hit close to home with the Bali bombing in October 2002, Malaysia's government investigated KMM insurgents and held hundreds of suspects under its Internal Security Act; an Act which effectively allows the government to detain suspects indefinitely without charge. This national approach, however, was soon deemed inadequate when the Malaysian government came to understand the scope of the threat facing the region as a whole, after the Bali massacre rallied Southeast Asia's governments against the common threat of extremist violence.

The United States and Malaysia have long enjoyed friendly relations and little publicized military cooperation. US and Malaysian forces engage in annual joint exercises, US naval vessels routinely make ship visits to the country, and Malaysian training sites are used by US Navy SEALs and US Army personnel. Since September 11 brought US strategic interests closer to Southeast Asia, cooperation has deepened to include US overflight rights and privileged access to Malaysian intelligence.[12] However, as the importance of Southeast Asia as a "second front" in the War on Terror became evident to policy-makers in Washington, the United States quickly become interested in a different kind of relationship with Malaysia's defense sector. Following the Bali bombing, which violently exposed the density of jihadist networks throughout Southeast Asia, Washington offered combat troops to the Malaysian government in order to help it rid the country of Islamist extremists. The offer was unceremoniously rejected, although relatively little was said about it in the press.[13]

This should not be taken to mean that Malaysia does not cooperate with the US military if and when Washington's interests are seen as supportive of Malaysia's strategy in prosecuting the War on Terror. Kuala Lumpur continues to receive military aid from Washington, and continues to acquire a significant amount of training and equipment from United States forces.[14] The two nations, along with other states in Southeast Asia, planned to set up a regional antiterrorism center in Kuala Lumpur, though Washington withdrew its financial support following policy differences over the US-led invasion of Iraq. This does, however, confirm that Malaysia's prosecution of the War on Terror is formulated very much on its own terms, and not necessarily with reference to Washington's priorities and policies.

Thus the Kuala Lumpur–Washington relationship with respect to combating international terrorism demonstrates policy cooperation and divergence. On the one hand, Kuala Lumpur is willing to share intelligence with Washington and its Southeast Asian neighbours in order to better track, monitor, and arrest those who belong to terrorist organizations and use violence against legitimate governments and their civilian populations. On the other hand, Kuala Lumpur has approached the War as an opportunity to restate and reinforce its legitimate Islamic identity in national and global terms. This policy has been two-pronged: at home, the UMNO-dominated government, first under Prime Minister Mahathir and now under Prime Minister Abdullah Badawi, has staked out the contours of acceptable Islamic practice by condemning terror in the region and remaining intolerant of sedition and terror. In this vein, Malaysia has regulated Islamic schools in order to control the content of religious teachings and prevent their use by extremists to indoctrinate children and youth in violent, extremist Islam.[15] In the foreign policy realm, the government has remained critical of "the West" (led by the United States), the War on Terror as a War on Islam, and Israel's conduct in the Middle East. Most famously, at the October 2003 meeting of the Organization of the Islamic Conference (OIC) in Kuala Lumpur, Prime Minster Mahathir alleged the existence of an international Jewish conspiracy, "ruling the world by proxy."[16] His comments prompted loud protests from the US Congress and a subsequent threat to cut off military aid to the country that has been, in many ways, Washington's most reliable and vital ally in the "second front" of the War on Terror.

The War on Terror refracted

Thus, Malaysia occupies an uncomfortable place in Washington's strategic environment, as neither ally nor adversary in the War on Terror. In fact, having refused to be easily co-opted by Washington's strategy, Kuala Lumpur is frequently an ideological thorn in Washington's side. However, Mahathir and Badawi have not allowed their ideological opposition to America's prosecution of the War on Terror[17] to interfere with their shared interest in a more robust security infrastructure in Southeast Asia. The bilateral interaction between Washington and Kuala Lumpur, like the dynamic between Washington and Manila, is more complex than the balancing–bandwagoning dichotomy allows. Simply put, such a binary categorization does not adequately account for the limits to and opportunities for cooperation between the United States and Malaysia. Furthermore, a balancing–bandwagoning analysis ignores the fact that the relationship is actively defined by the contours of Malaysia's national interest, grounded as it is in the construction of a strong Malay and Muslim identity, and not in reaction to Washington's priorities.

Thinking about International Relations

The central argument in this discussion, induced from empirical evidence of the development of policy by the governments in Manila and Kuala Lumpur in the post-9/11 era, is that Southeast Asian governments have refracted, and not simply reflected the foundational policies of the US-led War on Terror. The aim of this investigation is modest: to engage in limited discussion, demonstrating the calibrated policy divergence between Washington and Southeast Asian governments in the War on Terror. Obviously, the extent to which policy divergence occurs and the causes of that divergence deserve fuller treatment than is accorded here. Similarly, existing scholarship on the matter would be enhanced by a more comprehensive investigation of the particular ways in which other Southeast Asian states, most interestingly Indonesia and Thailand, have also refracted

Washington's preferences in their pursuit of national interests in the War on Terror. The preceding investigation is self-consciously limited, but hopefully raises important questions about the nature of our understanding of developments in international security.

The thesis presented is, in some ways, obvious and predictable: states pursue their national interests first and foremost in the formulation of their strategic policies. It is all the more striking, then, that this simple and self-evident truth is frequently set aside in scholarly and policy-making accounts. These case studies highlight the need for an appreciation of contextuality in defense and foreign policy formulation. It is certainly difficult for the policy-maker to resist the temptation to put the interests and pursuits of his or her own government at the conceptual center of international relations. This is even more the case for the policy-maker in a relatively strong state compared to a relatively weak one. However, policy-making that assumes that the world is a blank slate upon which priorities can be inscribed without a consideration of local context is policy-making that risks, at best, unexpected consequences, and at worst, failure to achieve its objectives. In contrast, policy-making that is sensitive to local intricacies is policy-making that can foresee challenges and maximize opportunities. Sound policy-making requires an appreciation of the simple reality that all states pursue their own national interest, and will do so in their own way.

For the scholar of international relations, the preceding discussion problematizes the neorealist perspective common in most strategic analyses. First, it uncovers one way in which the basic structuralism of neorealist thought is not subtle enough to explain international relations. Neorealist thought cannot account for the behavior of states when that behavior falls somewhere between "balancing" and "bandwagoning." This kind of binary construction of state behavior is simply not appreciative of the complexity of the world in which we live. Second, the analysis demonstrates the need in strategic studies (as a subset of International Relations) for an inductive model, rather than a deductive one. Though our models are meant to be just that (generalized patterns of international relations extrapolated and not reiterations of particular histories), the preceding case studies suggest that there is much room for improvement in the models currently used by theorists of strategic development in International Relations. Our models should be able to lend explanatory power to real world examples. If our theorizing about international relations cannot explain or acknowledge the social fact of state behavior, it risks becoming both fruitless and frivolous.

Most of us have a long way to go in understanding policy-making in Southeast Asia. It is a region that has been geostrategically vital throughout the twentieth century and beyond, but remains little understood. If this investigation has shed light on the way that Southeast Asia fits into the US-led War on Terror, and the obstacles that stand between us and contextualized knowledge of the region, it has more than achieved its objective.

Notes

This chapter was commissioned especially for this collection.

The views expressed in this article are those of the authors, and do not reflect the official policy of Canada's Department of National Defence.

1 Terms that will be familiar to International Relations scholars, most often attributed to Kenneth Waltz, *Theory of International Politics* (New York: McGraw-Hill, 1979); Stephen M. Walt, *The Origins of Alliances* (Ithaca: Cornell University Press, 1987).

2 This analysis does not claim to be the first, or even the most comprehensive critique of "balancing" and "bandwagoning" in neorealist theory. For example, a theoretical investigation of alternatives to the balancing–bandwagoning paradigm is offered in Chong Ja Ian, "Revisiting Responses to Power Preponderance: Going beyond the Balancing–Bandwagoning Dichotomy," Working Paper 54, Institute of Defence and Strategic Studies, Singapore, Nov. 2003. This analysis is the first treatment, that we are aware of, that makes use of such case studies in the Asian context.

3 The Moros of the Philippines were never fully conquered by either Spanish or American colonizers. Insurgency became the natural state on Mindanao for almost a century, which meant that the

region could not be administered or developed in conjunction with the rest of the islands.

4 Traditionally, Moro Islam incorporates pre-Islam religious practice, such as animism and spirit worship. Since the 1980s, as more and more Moro Muslims have enjoyed interaction with Muslims from Central Asia and the Middle East, these local idiosyncrasies have become less pronounced among some groups.

5 US State Department, "Fact Sheet: US to Provide Anti-Terrorism Aid to the Philippines," 19 May 2003. Full text available at http://usinfo.state.gov/regional/ea/easec/arroyofact.htm.

6 "Philippine Vice President resigns as Foreign Minister," *Japan Today*, July 2, 2003, at www. japantoday.com/gidx/news221329.html.

7 Indeed, during the short-lived mutiny of the Philippine military in July 2003, mutineers alleged that members of the Philippine forces continue to sell weapons to the MILF and even stage attacks in order to encourage increased violence against Philippine civilians, to the end of discrediting the rebels in Washington.

8 Malaysia trails only the city-state Singapore and the oil-rich sultanate of Brunei in terms of GDP per capita.

9 Malaysia is ranked the fourth most globalized economy worldwide, using the traditional measure of exports of goods and services as a percentage of GDP. Malaysia's exports of goods and services accounted for 81.3 percent of its GDP in 2002; Economist Intelligence Unit, "Country Briefings: Malaysia," *The Economist*, Jan. 1, 2003; full text available at www.economist.com/countries/Malaysia/profile.cfm? folder=Profile-Economic%20Structure.

10 Scott McConnell, "The Malay Dilemma: A Newly Prosperous Nation Faces Islamic Fundamentalism," *American Conservative*, Sept. 8, 2003.

11 Mahathir bin Mohamad, *The Malay Dilemma* (Singapore: D. Moore for Asia-Pacific Press, 1970).

12 Detailed in a speech by Malaysia's defense minister Najib Razak to the US-based Heritage Foundation and the Center for Strategic and International Studies: Najib Razak, "US–Malaysia Defense Cooperation: A Solid Success Story," May 3, 2002, at www.heritage.org/Research/Asiaandthe Pacific/HL742.cfm.

13 Barry Desker and Kumar Ramakrishna, "Forging an Indirect Strategy in Southeast Asia," *Washington Quarterly*, 25.2 (Spring 2002): 161–76.

14 Most recently, the US Senate approved 1.2 million US dollars in military aid to Malaysia, though it was tied to Kuala Lumpur's continued support of religious freedom in the country.

15 Michael Richardson, "Asians Take a Closer Look at Islamic Schools," *International Herald Tribune*, Feb. 12, 2002, at www.iht.com/articles/47803.html.

16 Thalif Deen, "US Aid Threat Fails to Faze Malaysia," *Asia Times*, Oct. 30, 2003, at www.atimes.com/atimes/Southeast_Asia/EJ30Ae02.html.

17 Most notable in Malaysia's cautious approach to the coalition invasion of Afghanistan in 2001 (opposed by many Malays), and its vocal opposition to the subsequent operation in Iraq in 2003.

8

From Terrorism to Human Security in Africa

Timothy M. Shaw

The horrific logic of contemporary "terrorism," especially the ultimate "fundamentalism"[1] of the "suicide bomber," stands in contrast to the mercenary logic of those impoverished communities who seek to profit from informal/illegal extractive industries. This chapter seeks to interrogate and contrast both contemporary genres; together they challenge the assumptions and prescriptions of much international relations/political economy, as indicated at the end. As Pliny cautioned centuries ago: ex Africa semper aliquid novi.[2]

"Terrorism" comes in multiple shapes and sizes, many of which are all too familiar in Africa. The continent has been relatively marginal in current conflicts around the Middle East, but it may yet be dragged into such tensions, in part as its own diverse yet coexisting cultures may be "infected" by religious-based "fundamentalisms" elsewhere. Human development/rights/security are more threatened today than for many decades, despite some incremental development just before and just after formal independence, postponed by the intransigence (i.e. state violence) of white minorities which generated distinctive forms of "terrorism" (also known as "liberation movements") in southern Africa into the 1980s. In a revisionist mood, we need to revisit these ten years after the first majority-rule democratic election in South Africa, as their promises have not always been realized and some of the romanticism around them was clearly misplaced.

Unhappily, the anticipated "peace dividend" of the end of the Cold War never materialized in Africa. Instead, the myriad conflicts which the superpowers and their allies had fostered on the continent, often leading to weak or corrupt regimes, were transformed into battles over resources, which enabled the basic needs of some citizens to be met while facilitating the importation of arms to sustain access to coltan, diamonds, gold, timber, etc.[3]

In turn, some of these post-bipolar exchanges or supply chains[4] have been penetrated and exploited by al-Qaeda and other "terrorist" networks[5] seeking to launder resources to pay for their demand for guns and other lethal equipment. So the connection with 9/11, which I suggested in a review of Africa in 2002[6] was particularly present around the Sudan and the Horn of Africa, can also be traced to the alluvial, informal extraction of diamonds in Sierra Leone. Indeed, while the Khartoum regime now seems to seek to be seen to be signed up to the "antiterrorism coalition" as part of a broader multilevel negotiation over its "separatist" south, at least until very recently that in Liberia continued its multifarious activities in association with a global network of Lebanese, al-Qaeda and Hezbollah groups: "The campaign against terrorism and the emerging links between the RUF [Revolutionary United Front], Liberia and terror networks has had an important impact on Liberia's ability to conduct business as usual."[7]

Both the UN and nongovernmental organizations like Global Witness have produced persuasive analyses of the illegal networks which have developed around the mineral and other resources of Angola, Congo, Liberia and Sierra Leone, which lead to arms imports, largely from the former Soviet Union.[8] These exposés in turn have led to the "Kimberley Process" to attempt to contain the production and transportation of "conflict diamonds," whether used in exchange for materiel or for nonlethal goods.[9] I deal further with such "new multilateralisms" below.

The apparent imperative of the "war on terrorism," at least for the world's sole superpower – the US – constitutes a "mixed message" when democracy and good governance also remain as conditionalities to secure development finance and aid. The South is constrained and confused by contradictory conditionalities: economic liberalization under structural adjustment programs (SAPs) and schemes for heavily indebted poor countries (HIPCs), on the one hand, and on the other hand, political liberalization of post-bipolar democratization, now both compounded by the seeming irrefutability of the US-led coalition against rogue states. Yet the return to more arbitrary rule contrasts with the claims of greater accountability, democracy, participation, and transparency expressed by the good governance advocates. Moreover, if fundamentalisms have something to do with alienation, then strategies which retard progress toward multiculturalism/ multiracialism in the new century are surely both unfortunate and untimely. The underlying causes of terrorisms need to be recognized and addressed, not just their symptoms. Similarly, for the US itself, Homeland Defense may reduce progress toward globalization as it complicates cross-border trade in goods and services, let alone skills and peoples. So Africa's not insignificant economic achievements under the African Growth and Opportunity Act (AGOA) passed in the US may be eroded by the Patriot Act.

I turn in the rest of this chapter to two regional cases drawn from contemporary Africa, along with attention to major themes concerning Africa as one part of the non-Western world, notwithstanding its myriad forms of interdependence with the West such as migrations and diasporas. And I conclude with some preliminary reflections on the implications of such analysis for established disciplines and genres in the social sciences.

Weak States and Strong Mafias?

The long process of state formation (and decline) in the post-colonial world is connected to transnational networks in complex ways, just as in the era of colonization trading companies and religions aided and abetted the expansion of the states system from its European core to the world beyond its frontiers. In this sense,

9/11 and the global war on terror have not fundamentally altered
the dynamic interplay of territoriality and transnationalism.[10]

At the end of the twentieth century, as underlined at the end of
this section, the academy, particularly the established world of
"International Relations," failed the world of policy as it paid
insufficient attention to the proliferation of weak and poor new
states in the 1990s, especially in Eastern Europe and Central
Asia, unlike its (still scant?) attention to such states in Africa in
the late 1960s and early 1970s. But in the early period of formal
decolonization, weakness meant lack of development and visibil-
ity. Today the costs of weakness are much higher and have a
wider effect as assorted transnational gangs are willing and able
to subvert, even hijack, regimes. The mixture of weak regimes
and strong mafias/militias was a destabilizing one, as Afghanistan
reveals.

Conversely, post-bipolarity and after 9/11, the West, especially
the US, may come to appreciate that states cannot be endlessly
shrunk, since the security let alone the "external" economic costs
are cumulative. So it may welcome the opportunity afforded by
the framework of the New Partnership for Africa's Development
(NEPAD), as indicated in recent G8 summits,[11] to revise and
revive its connections with African regimes, in part for reasons of
the so-called "war on terrorism" in which US Special Forces seemingly operate globally, including Africa, almost at will. On the
other hand, its ominous, unilateral notion of "preemptive intervention" challenges established norms of international law and
may continue to destabilize any lingering "world order."

There are multiple forms of globalizations, rather than a sin-
gular phenomenon, generating a mixture of results, including
varieties of antiglobalization. The latter "movement" is also highly
heterogeneous and was riding the crest of the wave after the
"battle of Seattle" of protestors at the ministerial meeting of the
World Trade Organization (WTO) at the end of 1999. The terrorist attacks on the Twin Towers stopped it in its tracks for a
while, but opposition to wars in Afghanistan and Iraq along with
continuing organizing against the WTO has led to its revival and
rejuvenation.[12]

Conversely, globalizations and their related logistics or supply chains need to recognize the informal and illegal activities – "black" or "underground" economies of blood diamonds, drugs, gangs, mafias, money laundering, new slavery,[13] people smuggling, small arms, etc. – as well as more familiar formal and legal activities as the former may constitute 10–25 percent of today's global economy.

Symptomatic of myriad new security challenges was Britain's decision to stop British Airways flying to Nairobi in mid-May 2003 for several weeks because of intelligence that one of the al-Qaeda masterminds of the US embassy attacks of five years earlier – Fazul Abdullah Mohamed – was back in the country from Somalia and was planning to launch a missile attack on a UK airliner. The impact on Kenya's tourist and related industries (for instance, supply chains around fresh produce: flowers, fruit, and vegetables) was considerable because the ban lasted almost a month, though it did not spread to other global airlines. Similarly, Kenya experienced a pre-9/11 attack, on the US embassy in Nairobi in mid-1998, and then subsequent attacks on an Israeli hotel and airliner in Mombasa in November 2002.

As Martin Shaw laments, the established "discipline" apparently closest to such shifts – "International Relations" – has been among those least willing to change their assumptions, analyses, and projections:

International relations plays a particular role in the development of global social science. It is the field that superficially most resembles an arena for new global understanding . . . the transformation of international relations is, however, very problematic. The international and the global are not two ways of expressing more or less the same idea . . . Ultimately . . . the disciplinary definition of the international is limiting . . . an increasingly important role is played by interdisciplinary fields – such as environmental, communications and cultural studies as well as IPE [International Political Economy] – which have often seen the most radical posing of global transformation. An early example, of course, was development studies . . .[14]

Greed and/or Grievance: Toward a "Real" Political Economy of Cojnflict?

The increasingly influential "political economy of conflict" perspective suggests that "greed" has now become more important than "grievance" as an explanation for violence, notwithstanding the persistence of much of the latter. Certainly, state-sanctioned militaries in many parts of the South have learned to take care of themselves as their states provide decreasingly sufficient revenues.[15] And the profitability of such natural resources leads to "protection" by mafias and militias, with their own associations with drugs and guns. In turn, in Africa and elsewhere in the South, street children have proliferated, leading to the ready recruitment of child soldiers, another horrific aspect of underdevelopment, alienation, and manipulation.

For both global and local reasons, then, after more than a decade of the political economy of conflict in Africa, there are growing, interrelated internal and global pressures to negotiate so that the spoils of war do not completely spoil the continent. Notwithstanding the resilience of some regional wars,[16] by 2004 there seemed to be a new atmosphere emerging in which conflict was becoming less acceptable and accepted. Rather, a new set of relations appeared to be in gestation among states, civil societies, and companies, which is the conceptual framework adopted and developed in a recent comparative collection by Tony Addison which treats five problematic cases.[17] An African Renaissance, as aspired to by the New Partnership for Africa's Development? To be sure, any such process is problematic and unpredictable, involving a heterogeneous and changeable set of national, regional, and global actors and interests.

The scale of the challenge to weak regimes from mafias in Africa (as in Central Europe and Central Asia) is apparent from the *Small Arms Survey*:[18] over 100,000 active insurgents (over 50 percent of the global total) and another 50,000 semiactive or inactive, plus over 50,000 militia. On the other hand, the illicit rewards are likewise huge, especially when the alternative forms of accumulation are so minimal: the UNITA rebel movement in Angola received over 4 billion US dollars from diamond sales after the end of the Cold War and before the turn of the century and its leader's demise; Charles Taylor's regime pocketed 400 million US dollars annually in the mid-1990s from timber, diamonds, and iron ore, and then some 200 million dollars annually from diamonds alone; in Sierra Leone, the RUF received 30–125 million dollars annually for its blood diamonds; in 18 months at the turn of the century, the Rwandan government received 250 million dollars for DR Congo coltan; and finally, the Khartoum regime now nets some 400 million dollars annually for oil from the south.[19]

The G8 summit in Canada in mid-2002 might mark a turning point not just in the character of conflict on the continent but also in Africa's relations with the North. Unlike earlier African development strategies, such as the Lagos Plan of Action in the early 1980s, NEPAD was conceived and formulated in collaboration with the North, especially the G8 but also the Global Coalition for Africa and the World Economic Forum. And while the initial African formulation was silent on "security," the G8 statement from Kananskis concentrated on issues such as multiple types of conflict, from shorter-term HIV/AIDS to longer-term ecology/water, as well as the imperative of an effective peer review mechanism through which to recognize and reward regimes which are aspiring to good governance.[20]

Meanwhile, given the dramatic transformation in the nature and frequency of "peacekeeping," novel divisions of labor are emerging, with NATO-related coalitions of the willing superseding more familiar UN blue-beret operations in salient troublespots like Central Europe and Central Asia. In parallel, in the remaining, less central UN operations, especially those in Africa, other divisions of labor are apparent among peacekeepers (more from the South, including the continent, than ever, including the reemergence of "middle power" roles, such as those of Nigeria and South Africa in their respective regions) and between them and nonstate agencies, both NGOs and multinational corporations (MNCs).

The political economy of conflict perspective challenges/ undermines/weakens more optimistic/idealistic notions of human security. It likewise complicates peacekeeping operations if mafias/militias have to be contained. Hence the refocus on new, flexible forms of "multilateralisms" including nonstate as well as state coalitions.

"New" Multilateralisms: On to Nonstate Actors in Global Coalitions?

State sovereignty implies responsibility, and the primary responsibility for the protection of its people lies with the state itself. Where a population is suffering serious harm, as a result of internal war, insurgency, repression or state failure, and the state in question is unwilling or unable to halt or avert it, the principle of non-intervention yields to the international responsibility to protect.[21]

US unilateralism, ostensibly in part a response to terrorist threats to its "national security," threatens multilateralism everywhere. So "new" forms of multilateralism, if necessary without the global hegemon, are becoming more imperative in order to achieve some balance and some residual internationalism. This creative multilateralist response to the unilateralism of the Bush II administration becomes ever more imperative if multiculturalism/multiracialism are considered essential weapons in the execution of any longer-term war on terrorism.

Similarly, notwithstanding 9/11, the erosion, even disappearance, of basic needs being met, let alone human security in territories like Congo, Liberia and Somalia, triggers the global "responsibility to protect" citizens who otherwise lack human security because of state failure or neglect.[22] The report of the International Commission on Intervention and State Sovereignty suggests that such protection entails the responsibilities to prevent, react, and rebuild: a considerable contrast with the more dramatic yet not necessarily sustainable new US doctrine of "preemptive intervention."

The particular pressures for peace talks vary between regions and over time, within as well as around Africa. But all involve some mix of global to local/state to nonstate actors; that is, tracks 2 and 3 as well as traditional track 1 intergovernmental diplomacy.

The contemporary Ottawa[23] and Kimberley[24] processes themselves involve a flexible mix of tracks 1 to 3.[25] Yet despite pressures for the success of negotiations around the containment of conflict diamonds, major NGOs involved remain sceptical because the Kimberley Process Certification Scheme is not yet overly effective; monitoring remains problematic, which is of concern to some companies, unions, cities, communities, and consumers, as well as NGOs.[26] Such innovative forms of mixed actor multilateralisms may pick up some support from both pro- and antiglobalization forces, along with advocates of democratic/ good governance. And some elements in global and local civil society and media, etc., may also encourage them. Such forms of new multilateralism[27] do go some way to balancing US unilateralism and the threat of sclerosis if not paralysis of the UN system.[28]

The diversity of outcomes from often protracted peace processes is quite apparent in the trio of territories which used to be Somalia, even although in theory they are one state, and despite the Arta Peace Conference in neighboring Djibouti in 2000 and the ensuing IGAD process (IGAD was formerly the Intergovernmental Authority on Drought and Development). In Somalia, around Mogadishu, anarchy and conflict reign still. And in Puntland some semblance of statehood is emerging. By contrast, in the old British Somaliland, national and presidential elections were held in 2002–3, and basic facilities like banking and cell-phone networks are back in operation. Yet Hargeisa has yet to be recognized as an independent state.

Despite images and stereotypes to the contrary, not all conflict on the continent involves nonstate/nontraditional actors or direct economic causes. The classic war between Ethiopia and Eritrea in the early months of the new millennium was between two standing armies and led to an orthodox UN peacekeeping force, landmine clearance, border demarcation, etc.[29]

Yet, as Breytenbach has argued, echoing William Reno, most of the continent's contemporary conflicts "... happen in weak states, non-state actors such as rebels are prominent, and the privatization of interstate relations is relevant. We conceptualize this as a triangle of interrelated forces with three types of role-players: weak state rulers, rebels and mercantilists who capitalize on the profits of scarce resources."[30]

Such a distinctive triangle, by contrast to those in stronger, more stable states, leads on to concern about new civil–military relations, as (1) the former now includes civil society not just parliaments and parties; and (2) the latter now extends to private military or security operatives, both legal and illegal.

The rest of this African overview focuses on the tension between the continuing economic imperatives of conflict and growing pressures from a variety of sources and for a variety of reasons for more active and sustainable peace processes. It suggests that there may be more than one "Africa," as the continent presents ever more diversity: from "African democratic developmental states" like Botswana, Mauritius, and Uganda, to stereotypical "anarchy" like Congo, Liberia, and Somalia.[31] This also entails some revisionist rethinking of the impacts of "liberation movements" on the continent, not just northern and southern but also including the overthrow of Amin/Obote in Uganda, etc., in which Tanzania played such a central, expensive, and disregarded role. Such reflections parallel those already mentioned about emerging divisions of labor in peacekeeping operations on and off the continent among national armies, NATO and non-NATO, and a variety of nonstate actors.

From Sun City to Congo's Killing Forests

A number of long-running conflicts have been resolved and brought close to resolution. In a sign of greater determination amongst regional countries to solve their own security problems, the NEPAD . . . has security elements . . .[32]

Following decades of traumas in and around the Congo (formerly Zaire), a series of roundtable talks were held in October 2001 and early 2002 in the rural but glitzy Sun City resort in South Africa, hosted by that government as an aspect of its commitment to NEPAD/regional peace and development. This led to a formal peace agreement in April 2003, but few expect this to be the authoritative last word – merely a basis for continued pressure and jockeying among "internal" factions and "external" allies.

The Congo constitutes a massive human tragedy, especially given its cornucopia of raw resources: some 3.5 million deaths due to war over 15 years, including mass murders in the east in early 2003.[33] In theory, in early 2003, the remaining troops from Rwanda and Uganda were to be withdrawn in the footsteps of earlier exits in the first half of 2002 of Angolan, Namibian, and Zimbabwean soldiers. But these diplomatic, tactical "retreats" may merely lead toward "proxy" extraction and a series of intense battles encouraged by neighbors and other interested parties, both economic and political, ethnic and strategic. Such an off-budget, supplementary revenue stream may be essential for regime survival in Harare, Kampala, Kigali, and elsewhere.[34]

Endless Traumas in West Africa?

Wars over resources and identities have continued to erupt in West Africa at the start of the new century despite considerable progress toward renewed human security and maybe human development in Sierra Leone. But, as the latter was pacified, battles over diamonds and timber moved into Guinea and back into Liberia at immense human cost. The so-called "balloon effect" means that when conflict is contained in one part of such a region it pops up elsewhere.[35]

Until his diplomatic extradition to Calabar in Nigeria in 2003, the regime of Liberia's Charles Taylor remained the regional "spoiler" despite him being under considerable censure/pressure, including declining support from his mentors in Burkina Faso and Libya. The UN and NGO exposés of the blood diamond nexus diminished his credibility and legitimacy, with the Kimberley Process and related strategies leading to the demise of his RUF in Freetown. Meanwhile, at home, Liberians United for Reconciliation and Democracy (LURD), assumed to be supported by

Guinea, marched on Monrovia in early 2002, resulting in another 60,000 refugees, some fleeing into Côte d'Ivoire.

According to the International Crisis Group (ICG) and other observers, the seemingly unstoppable conflict in Liberia was a function of interests in the original post-bipolar Mano River Union regional wars of the 1990s. In particular, Liberian antago-nists have actively supported contending sides in the neighboring civil strife. Thus ICG accuses Taylor of fighting LURD in the Côte d'Ivoire and of employing Ivorian rebels from the country's western region to combat opposing Liberians. Meanwhile, the embattled Ivorian president, Laurent Gbagbo, supported a break-away faction of LURD – the Movement for Democracy in Liberia – that was fighting Taylor in eastern Liberia. ICG called for support for the International Contact Group on Liberia of major regional and global states, the African Union, the European Union, the Economic Community of West African States (ECOWAS) and the United Nations:

> ECOWAS and the wider international community must deal with the growing tendency of leaders in West Africa to sponsor rebel-lions abroad to protect their positions at home. Burkina Faso, Guinea, Liberia and Côte d'Ivoire have all employed rebel groups either to get rid of their domestic enemies or to remove neighbor-ing leaders they do not like.

The terrible violence in Sierra Leone largely concluded in January 2002 with a mix of continuing orthodox interventions by ECOMOG (the armed Monitoring Group set up by ECOWAS) and the UN and novel robust British interventions: a distinctive, pragmatic coalition. The decade-long conflict left some 43,000 dead and many more physically and psychologically wounded. Successful elections in Sierra Leone in May 2002 led to the defeat of RUF and the installation of a (relatively!) legitimate regime with (somewhat) enhanced prospects of stability and reconstruc-tion. UNAMSIL's 20,000 peacekeepers constituted the largest UN force ever assembled on the continent, and after the elections it was augmented by some 2,000 police as well. Donor sup-port for reconstruction has been rather generous and the new government has been given HIPC status and terms: some 40,000 ex-combatants are receiving demobilization payments. But the new regime needs the Kimberley Process to work well enough for its criminalized diamond industry to be restructured and revived. And the continuing regional conflict – now centered in Côte d'Ivoire – could yet undo any advance toward human development and security in Sierra Leone.

A new but not unrelated conflict arose at the century's end in the hitherto peaceful and relatively prosperous Côte d'Ivoire, with profound consequences for the region and continent, as well as for its French associates. This is inseparable from ongoing wars in neighboring states in which successive Ivorian regimes, including the extended families of the ruling administrations, have been involved/implicated.[36] Meanwhile, the post-Rawlings government in Accra stands to benefit, especially as the instability in Côte d'Ivoire means higher prices for cocoa, etc.

Battles over Oil in Angola, Nigeria, and Sudan

The high price of oil between the wars in Kuwait and Iraq at the start of the new century exacerbated tensions in major oil producers on the continent, especially as the North, particularly the US, came to favor sourcing energy from outside the Middle East. Although there were peace talks in both Angola and Sudan in 2002, with the latter's continuing into 2004, ethnic, regional, and religious conflict intensified in Nigeria ahead of and after the mid-2003 elections, with profound implications not only for development in Nigeria but also for major oil companies, particularly Shell. Because of dramatic hijackings of oil rigs and their staffs, occasional shutdowns of its Nigerian wells have had an impact on the world price as well as national revenue, but the trend toward local and regional violence in both Delta and North, exacerbated by the proliferation of private or ethnic vigilantes, has set back any advances in human development and security, let alone human rights with the return to democratic civilian rule.

Following the assassination of Jonas Savimbi in northern Angola in February 2002, a ceasefire was negotiated internally in late

March and has largely held since, marking the end of a four-decade set of conflicts. However, the MPLA regime has become used to enjoying the fruits of corruption, so any improvement in popular human development and security is likely some way off still. A domestic peace dividend is still a distant dream for most Angolans, who still have to endure one of the most unequal and mined countries in the world.

The start of oil production and exportation from Southern Sudan in 1999 transformed and escalated the decades-old war in the south. There were IGAD peace talks in Kenya in the second half of 2002 and through 2003, partially in response to US diplomacy and opportunities but also to occasional battles; meanwhile, atrocities continue in the south, spilling over into child soldier raids and continued abductions in northern Uganda.

The embattled Canadian energy company Talisman used the pretext of peace talks to extricate itself from the quagmire of both Southern Sudan and vociferous NGO campaigns. In 2002 it sold its share of the oil field/pipeline to the Indian National Oil Corporation, which now joins fellow Chinese, Malaysian, and Sudanese state companies well away from NGO attentions. Corporations as well as communities are vulnerable to conflict in Africa as elsewhere.

Meanwhile, there has been a telling and inconclusive debate around oil flows and pipeline projects around Chad: can the World Bank in association with attentive NGOs and think-tanks ensure the honesty of the Chadian state as it faces massive new incomes? Likewise, with the Equatorial Guinean economy entering a boom period, can its new-found wealth be channeled toward popular human development and security rather than familiar corruption and embezzlement?

New Security: From HIV/AIDS to H_2O

In addition to contemporary conflicts over economic resources like oil and gas, Africa also faces a variety of more structural challenges, including the very immediate, such as HIV/AIDS, and the slightly more distant, such as ecological deterioration and scarce water resources. HIV/AIDS along with malaria and tuberculosis are the focus of a new global initiative with a concentration on Africa: the Global Fund to Fight AIDS, TB and Malaria.

Meanwhile, desertification and struggles over water in valleys like the Congo, Limpopo, Nile, and Zambezi have received insufficient attention but will lead to more overt conflict unless remedial steps are taken.

The indirect and direct effects of HIV/AIDS on old as well as new security are profound; they include high rates of infection in some armies, up to 75 percent in that of Zimbabwe. The fear of infection constitutes one largely unstated reason for peacekeepers from the North being reluctant to undertake missions on the continent; hence, as already mentioned, the evolving division of labor in which the North provides logistics and Africa the foot soldiers. HIV/AIDS also poses major implications for national and regional economies, along with companies, especially in mining, as revealed in the increasing corporate attention and finance for HIV/AIDS responses, especially from those companies dependent on a relatively skilled and stable labor force in sectors such as mining and oil and gas – hence the involvement of Anglo American, AngloGold, Anglovaal, Debswana and De Beers along with BP, ChevronTexaco, Eni, ExxonMobil, Statoil and TotalFinaElf, all of which are supportive of Botswanan, South African and Global Coalitions on HIV/AIDS.

Conclusions/Projections

This concluding section has two, interrelated parts. First, a brief reflection on implications of the African case for established disciplines. And second, a short prognostication about the near-term futures for the continent. First, then, as already noted earlier in the chapter, both terrorisms and the political economy of conflict pose profound challenges to the assumptions, explanations, and projections of established paradigms.[37] This is so for reasons of both analysis and policy, interstate and nonstate, local and global.

Likewise, they constitute fundamental dilemmas for disciplines and explanations, especially development and security studies, political science/international relations as well as international political economy (for example, IPE of conflict as well as of capitalism).[38] In the main this is because orthodox canons assume that states exist and are hegemonic; likewise, that the formal economy constitutes the whole economy and that regional cooperation and conflict are functions of states not nonstate actors and occur within neat, defined, recognizable, and stable boundaries. But the 9/11 nexus and related pre- and antiterrorist actions have complicated analysis as well as policy and practice even more than the end of the Cold War did. Internationalist scholars need to become more not less interdisciplinary and cosmopolitan in the new century and context.

Second, in terms of possible projections, high profile wars in the Middle East may yet work to Africa's advantage if it can contain any contagion from fundamentalist, terrorist networks. Certainly, current levels of violence on the continent, even in say "hotspots" like the Congo or Liberia, cannot match those in Afghanistan, Iraq, Israel, Kuwait, etc. Moreover, if the North can begin to learn that failed or failing states are not good for global security or stability, then it may once again begin to invest in "nation-building" and social capital rather than in simplistic market-driven policies. NEPAD might offer an agreed policy framework in which enhanced development aid and finance might flow to weak as well as stronger states; that is, not just to those who meet the good governance criteria of the review mechanism, but also to those regimes which are seeking to rebuild, such as Sierra Leone and Somaliland.

The corrosive effect of instability in one country on a whole region is apparent in the decline into chaos in Zimbabwe after the Mugabe regime lost the February 2000 referendum on the new constitution. The Southern African Development Community (SADC) had already lost its sheen or momentum because of its enlargement to include the "state" of Congo. But the controversial mix of corrupted and violent land "redistribution" and human rights abuse since the start of the new century in

Zimbabwe has complicated relations within as well as around the region, with regional regimes being uncritical while regional civil society and external associates have been critical, as revealed in the mix of Commonwealth, EU, UK and US "smart" sanctions. Meanwhile, the decline of human development/rights/security in Zimbabwe continues at an exponential rate.

But conversely, the "war on terrorism" may come to undermine globalizations as security preoccupations slow trade, especially from Africa, which can ill afford to meet all the proliferating "national security" requirements of the US. As already intimated, "Homeland Defense" may likewise erode globalizations as it raises the price and slows the passage of trade, including goods in air and ocean containers – preclearance is problematic coming out of Africa. Likewise, 9/11 poses profound dilemmas for assorted diasporas and civil societies, some of which may be quite fundamentalist themselves given romanticized memories of what they left behind. Conversely, if thereby globalization turns "regressive"[39] – only parochial, national interests and implications are to be recognized and considered – then other varieties are preferred such as those advocated by supporters or reformers, if not rejectionists.

Finally, it is important to note that assorted "globalizations" have had decidedly mixed effects in Africa: on the one hand, some new niches such as AGOA, fresh produce like flowers, fruit, and vegetables, and hard metals like platinum, but, on the other hand, a secular decline in the value of "colonial" commodities like cocoa, coffee, copper, tea, etc. Furthermore, the antiglobalization "movement" has developed less on the continent than elsewhere, in part because of the relatively underdeveloped character of civil society and the resistance of the state to the development and expression of nonstate sentiments.

Notes

This chapter is based on a presentation given at Goodenough College in November 2002 and has been substantially updated for this collection.

1 Bassam Tibi, "Fundamentalism," in Mary Hawkesworth (ed.), *Encyclopedia of Government and Politics* (London: Routledge, 2003), pp. 184–200.
2 "There is always something new out of Africa."
3 Graduate Institute of International Studies, *Small Arms Survey, 2001: Profiling the Problem* (Oxford: Oxford University Press, 2001); Graduate Institute of International Studies, *Small Arms Survey, 2002: Counting the Human Cost* (Oxford: Oxford University Press, 2002); Graduate Institute of International Studies, *Small Arms Survey, 2003: Development Denied* (Oxford: Oxford University Press, 2003).
4 Stefano Ponte and Peter Gibbon, *Africa, Value Chains and the Global Economy: Trading Down?* (London: Palgrave Macmillan, 2004).
5 Manuel Castells, *The Rise of the Network Society* (Oxford: Blackwell, 1996).
6 Timothy M. Shaw, "'New' Security Dilemmas and Debates in Africa beyond 9/11," in Albert Legault, Michel Fortmann and Gerard Hervouet (eds), *Les Conflits dans le monde/Conflicts around the World, 2001–2002* (Quebec: Laval for IQHEI, 2002), pp. 124–36.
7 International Institute for Strategic Studies, *Strategic Survey 2001/2002* (Oxford: Oxford University Press for IISS, 2002), p. 348.
8 Graduate Institute of International Studies, *Small Arms Survey, 2001; Small Arms Survey, 2002; Small Arms Survey, 2003.*
9 Rob McRae and Don Hubert (eds), *Human Security and the New Diplomacy: Protecting People, Promoting Peace* (Montreal: McGill-Queen's University Press, 2001).
10 Ken Booth and Tim Dunne (eds), "Worlds in Collision," in *Worlds in Collision: Terror and the Future of Global Order* (London: Palgrave Macmillan, 2002), p. 15.
11 Sandra MacLean, H. John Harker, and Timothy M. Shaw (eds), *Advancing Human Security and Development in Africa: Reflections on NEPAD* (Halifax: CFPS/Dalhousie University, 2002).
12 Marlies Glasius and Mary Kaldor, "The State of Global Civil Society: Before and After September 11," in Marlies Glasius, Mary Kaldor, and Helmut Anheier (eds), *Global Civil Society 2002* (Oxford: Oxford University Press, 2002), pp. 3–33.
13 Christien van den Anker (ed.), *The Political Economy of New Slavery* (London: Palgrave Macmillan, 2004).

14 Martin Shaw, "The Global Transformation of the Social Sciences," in Mary Kaldor, Helmut Anheier, and Marlies Glasius (eds), *Global Civil Society 2003* (Oxford: Oxford University Press, 2003), pp. 35–44.

15 Jorn Brommelhorster and Wolf-Christian Paes (eds), *The Military as an Economic Actor: Soldiers in Business* (London: Palgrave Macmillan for BICC, 2003).

16 Timothy Shaw, "Regional Dimensions of Conflict and Peace-Building in Contemporary Africa," *Journal of International Development*, 15.4 (May 2003): 487–98.

17 Tony Addison (ed.), *From Conflict to Recovery in Africa* (Oxford: Oxford University Press for UNU/WIDER, 2003).

18 Graduate Institute of International Studies, *Small Arms Survey, 2001.*

19 Graduate Institute of International Studies, *Small Arms Survey, 2002,* p. 142.

20 MacLean, Harker, and Shaw, *Advancing Human Security and Development in Africa.*

21 International Commission on Intervention and State Sovereignty, *The Responsibility to Protect*, Evans/Sahnoun Report (Ottawa: IDRC, 2001), at www.iciss.gc.ca, p. ix.

22 Sandra J. MacLean, "New Regionalism and Conflict in the DRC: Networks of Plunder and Networks for Peace," in J. Andrew Grant and Fredrik Soderbaum (eds), *The New Regionalism in Africa* (Aldershot: Ashgate, 2003), pp. 110–24.

23 Don Hubert, "The Landmine Ban: A Case Study in Humanitarian Advocacy," Watson Institute, Brown University Occasional Paper 42, Providence, RI, 2000; International Committee to Ban Landmines, *Landmine Monitor Report 2002* (New York: ICBL, 2002), at www.icbl.org.

24 Ian Smillie, "The Kimberley Process: The Case for Proper Monitoring," Partnership Africa Canada Occasional Paper 5, 2002.

25 Rob McRae and Don Hubert (eds), *Human Security and the New Diplomacy: Protecting People, Promoting Peace* (Montreal: McGill-Queen's University Press, 2001).

26 Andrew J. Grant et al., "Emerging Transnational Coalitions around Diamonds and Oil in Civil Conflicts in Africa," in Marjorie Griffin Cohen and Stephen McBride (eds), *Global Turbulence: Social Activists' and State Responses to Globalization* (Aldershot: Ashgate, 2003), pp. 124–39.

27   Tom Keating, *Canada and World Order: The Multilateralist Tradition in Canadian Foreign Policy* (Toronto: Oxford University Press, 2002).
28   Timothy Shaw, "Regional Dimensions of Conflict and Peace-Building in Contemporary Africa," *Journal of International Development*, 15.4 (2003): 487–98; Timothy Shaw, "The Commonwealth(s), Inter- and Non-state – at the Start of the Twenty-First Century: Contributions to Global Development/Governance," *Third World Quarterly*, 24.4 (2003): 723–42; Timothy Shaw, "Towards 'New Multilateralisms'? Globalisation, Anti-globalisation and the Commonwealth," *Commonwealth and Comparative Politics*, 41.3 (2003): 1–12.
29   Alexandra Magnolia Dias, "An African Interstate War in the Post-Cold War Era: Ethiopia and Eritrea (1998–2000)," Institute of Commonwealth Studies, London, 2003.
30   W. J. Breytenbach, "Rulers, Rebels and Mercantilists," *Africa Insight*, 32.2 (2002): 3–9.
31   Timothy M. Shaw and Jane L. Parpart, "African Studies/Scenarios at the Start of the New Century: Not Just Anarchy/Conflict," in MacLean, Harker, and Shaw (eds), *Advancing Human Security and Development in Africa*, pp. 233–54.
32   International Institute for Strategic Studies, *The Military Balance 2002–2003* (Oxford: Oxford University Press for IISS, 2002).
33   "Congo's Wars: Peace, They Say, But the Killing Goes On," *The Economist*, Mar. 29, 2003, pp. 59–60; MacLean, "New Regionalism and Conflict in the DRC"; Sagaren Naidoo (ed.), *The War Economy in the DRC* (Johannesburg: Institute for Global Dialogue, 2003).
34   Wolf-Christian Paes and Timothy M. Shaw, "Praetorians or Profiteers? The Role of Entrepreneurial Armed Forces in Congo-Kinshasa," in Brommelhorster and Paes, *The Military as an Economic Actor*, pp. 143–69.
35   Ian Smillie, Lansana Gberie, and Ralph Hazelton, "The Heart of the Matter: Sierra Leone, Diamonds and Human Security," Partnership Africa Canada, Ottawa, 2000.
36   Morten Boas, "The Task is Always to Revise," in James J. Hentz and Morten Boas (eds), *New and Critical Security and Regionalism: Beyond the Nation State* (Aldershot: Ashgate, 2003), pp. 203–12; Morten Boas, "Weak States, Strong Regimes: Towards a 'Real' Political Economy of African Regionalization," in Grant and Soderbaum, *The New Regionalism in Africa*, pp. 31–46.

37 Craig Calhoun, "Opening Remarks: Roundtable on Rethinking International Studies in a Changing Global Context," *SSRC Items and Issues*, 3.3–4 (2002): 1–4.
38 Shaw, "Regional Dimensions of Conflict and Peace-Building in Contemporary Africa."
39 Mary Kaldor, Helmut Anheier, and Marlies Glasius, "Global Civil Society in an Era of Repressive Globalization," in Kaldor, Anheier, and Glasius, *Global Civil Society 2003*, pp. 3–33.

9

Terrorism and International Law

Dinah PoKempner

Human bodies and steel girders alike are vulnerable to terror, and so too is the law. Terrorists have little use for law and are unlikely to be deterred by it – indeed, the project of spreading terror depends on violating basic norms and assumptions of our social existence, such as the norm against directing political violence against traffic police, bystanders, or children. The law is not designed by or for terrorists, but by and for the rest of us, who have some stake in things as they are. As an instrumentality for the suppression of terrorism, law is probably less effective than guns or even religious suasion. Indeed, law is often perceived as not merely ineffectual but as counterproductive in that it constrains official action to incarcerate or eliminate extremely dangerous people. For these reasons, it is to be expected that in times of national and international threat, there is often great dissatisfaction with law, leading to its suspension, derogation, revision, or reinterpretation.

That is not to say that law is irrelevant. If it is imperfect at deterring truly committed terrorists, it does articulate what counts in the sort of society in which the rest of us would wish to live: a society built not on terror and violence, but on humanistic values including rights, predictability, and tolerance. There is a value in criminalizing terrorist acts beyond deterrence, for to do so is to socially repudiate terrorism, as well as to provide socially acceptable means of incapacitating terrorists. Yet in a wider context, how law is revised to improve its utility in countering terrorism is important, for the law itself is a gauge of the degree to which our lives and liberties are constrained by terror. The law cannot describe a fantasy world, ignorant of real dangers – this is to make it a "suicide pact," as US Supreme Court Justices have warned.[1] But if we are not careful, in modifying law with the rationale of better intercepting terrorists, we will wind up creating a world more reflective of our fears than our aspirations.

Taking the view that law is a process of social construction, important not merely as an instrumentality to certain ends but as articulating norms that, in turn, shape social relations, this paper examines the impact of the so-called "war on terrorism" in three broad normative regions, each encompassing numerous principles. The laws of war, norms on detention, and privacy protections have all come under pressure, with shifts in state practice and some instances of statutory revision. And as years pass since September 11, 2001, there are also signs of counter-pressure from both courts and political movements. These sketches are not intended as an adequate description of the law's shift, but rather a way to provoke thinking about what that shift may entail, and why it should be the subject of further critical examination.

The Laws of (Real) War

The resort to actual armed conflict in the name of combating terrorism has been extremely controversial, first in Afghanistan, and even more so in Iraq, where the nexus between terrorist operations (or for that matter, weapons of mass destruction) and the state always appeared quite tenuous. There is no doubt that this aspect of the "war on terrorism" has raised important questions as to the status of *jus ad bellum* (justice of war) and whether the United Nations Charter has been violated, or manipulated, or reinterpreted to allow for inexplicit or post hoc authorization of military intervention. The issue of justified resort to force has always been contentious and highly politicized, so this chapter will focus on shifts in areas of the law that have been somewhat more stable and amenable to international consensus. Nevertheless, some of the themes that arise in the debate over the legality of these wars recur in other controversies.

One, a "new paradigm" argument, is that the new and extraordinarily destructive threat posed by private global terrorist networks is beyond what the law was designed to handle, and so the law must change or is changing. Some make the claim for large changes, others for tinkering, but the idea is that we must build a better mousetrap to catch the latest sort of mice. Of course, in the anxiety not to miss a single mouse, you may wind up with a very dangerous trap. Another strain is an argument for exceptionalism and against law, to the effect that certain actors must be liberated from certain legal constraints (the US from the authorization of the Security Council, the executive from judicial control) to handle the extraordinary threat. This follows the logic that if the bad guys are as bad as terrorists, unconstrained by law and morality, the good guys must be free of those bonds to cope with them. Yet another theme, often posed as a sort of zero-sum trade-off, is that we must be prepared to make sacrifices (of blood, of freedoms) to protect "our way of life" (our security). Unfortunately, the actual values of the trade-off (what freedoms? to get how much security?) are obscure. None of these ways of thinking about law adequately accounts for its function in constructing current realities and human expectations.

The law governing the conduct of hostilities is an important normative area under pressure. The Geneva Conventions and their protocols are among the most universally subscribed treaties, with many of their principles assuming the status of customary international law. The structure of *jus in bello* (justice in war) leans toward universal application, imposing obligations on each party to a conflict regardless of who is the aggressor, whether the enemy respects the law, or whether the war is formally declared or not.[2] In cases of internal armed conflict, the law is applicable also to the conduct of nonstate armed forces, without thereby conferring any political status upon them.[3] Reciprocity, the expectation that the enemy will treat your forces and civilians as you treat his, is an important motive for compliance with these norms.

The post-9/11 military interventions, however, have proceeded on different assumptions. The enemy was taken to be rogue, that is, without any incentive to follow civilized standards of conduct or the laws of war. Although the regimes of Afghanistan and Iraq were militarily weak, they were portrayed as capable of threatening immense devastation to the West, through sponsoring or equipping terrorists willing to make transnational attacks. The ambivalence towards the enemy – conceiving of him as easily crushed yet dangerous and utterly savage – found expression in the US invention of the "unlawful combatant," the combatant who forfeited even the right to determination of his Prisoner of War (POW) status by virtue of wearing no distinctive sign and fighting in forces known for their disregard of humanitarian law.

The United States (and in Iraq, its allies) considered rapid and decisive victories essential to maintain popular support for military intervention and to keep the enemy forces from adapting and learning to fight effectively as counterinsurgents. To that end, it counted on deploying overwhelming force, relying heavily on aerial firepower to obliterate infrastructure supporting the enemy forces, and an "effects-based" military strategy that emphasized not traditional battlefield objectives but end results, including political objectives such as "regime change."

This notion of a vicious and lawless enemy whose political base must be efficiently and speedily obliterated, of course, exists in tension with norms of limited war and the avoidance of direct attack on or disproportionate harm to civilians, foundational principles of international humanitarian law.[4] The tension between these two images of war was brought out vividly in Iraq, where the United States, although scrupulous in performing collateral damage analysis on preplanned targets, engaged in a series of "decapitation strikes" in urban areas that, due to reliance on inadequate intelligence, eliminated no political leaders at all, but did kill lots of civilians. The allies used cluster bombs with high dud rates in urban areas, reaping predictable waves of civilian casualties after the fighting was over. As in past wars, media outlets that appeared to be playing no military role were made targets of attack, on the flimsy justification that they could conceivably be put to such use.[5] These were tactics that had drawn criticism in the past, and did once again, as potential violations of the laws of war.

The traditional rule of proportionality, under which an attack is unlawful if the expected damage to civilian life and property would be excessive in relation to the direct and concrete military advantage to be gained, is also up for challenge in the new war paradigm. The US, and to some degree the UK, wish to equate the idea of an "attack" not with an attack on a specific target but with an entire campaign, an overall military objective, or even a political objective such as "regime change." This might appear more coherent in a context where the outcome of war is a foregone conclusion and the timeframe is measured in weeks or months rather than years. Most wars, however, don't follow this pattern. Moreover, such a shift in definition entails estimating the acceptable level of civilian death in relation to ultimate victory, which would swallow up the notion of proportionality entirely.

State practice informs the interpretation of international law, and in its most consistent patterns creates customary norms. Official statements are evidence of state practice as well,[6] and this is one reason it is troubling that the United States political leadership appeared to be in denial as to its role and duties as an "Occupying Power" under the Fourth Geneva Convention.[7] Those duties include protecting public order and respecting the fundamental human rights of the population,[8] duties we now know it has failed in significant ways.[9]

In Iraq, the coalition deployed far too few forces to ensure public safety even in urban areas. Those under the power of the coalition had the sense that they had been liberated only to fall prey to criminals, the dictates of religious fundamentalists, and the collapse of legal avenues of employment,[10] sensations familiar to Afghans now living under conditions of insecurity and revivified warlordism.[11] American soldiers, short of translators and not well trained to handle long-term deployment in an alien culture that supported persistent guerrilla resistance, fell prone to overreaction in using force against civilians and detainees.[12]

The language of "terrorism" permeated military descriptions of resistance attacks on coalition forces,[13] raising inappropriately the impression that these acts were somehow beyond the pale of war, deserving the most radical suppression. Americans began employing counterterrorism tactics whose dubious or marginal legality they had criticized when practiced by other states, among them detaining the relatives of fugitives,[14] destroying their homes,[15] and cordoning off whole communities.[16]

On the eve of the Iraq War, there was a moment of interest in revision of the Geneva Conventions to "fix" what were perceived discrepancies between the more conventional understanding of war and its law, on the one hand, and on the other, new circumstances of global terrorism and effects-based military doctrine. In January 2003, the Swiss government hosted at Harvard University an "informal high-level expert meeting" of state delegates and scholars (but not nongovernmental advocates) to examine some of these definitional controversies. Topics included how to assess proportionality between expected military advantage and civilian harm in an "attack"; what constitutes a military target and when does a civilian target change character; the definition of civilians and combatants; which combatants are entitled to the privileges of POW status; what law covers civilians who participate in hostilities; and what might signal the beginning and ending of the application of international humanitarian law in conflicts with transnational nonstate actors.[17] The most significant fact about this conference is that it galvanized European resistance to revision of existing international humanitarian law, and ultimately devolved into a lower profile research and conference enterprise.[18] This did not mean the controversies over definitional terms were over, but that they would be asserted more in the course of battlefield practice rather than diplomatic negotiation.

Constructive "War" and the Norms surrounding Detention

The only way to deal with terrorists, Rumsfeld said, is to hunt them down and capture or kill them before they kill more innocent Americans. . . . "The global war on terror is not something that is going to end precipitously," he said. "It is a war where we have no choice but to go after the terrorists where they are."[19]

The many strong norms that surround detention have also come under challenge through state response to terrorism, among them the ancient principle of habeas corpus, the norm against indefinite detention, the absolute prohibition of torture and cruel, inhuman or degrading treatment, and in the context of international armed conflict, the presumption that enemy combatants are entitled to POW status. The upshot is that it is becoming easier to detain individuals outside the constraints of judicial control, under conditions of secrecy and isolation that are amenable to severe and possibly torturous treatment, for an indefinite period.

At the heart of the controversies surrounding the detention of supposed terrorists lay the question of whether counterterrorism measures should fall under the paradigm of armed conflict or law enforcement. This distinction is crucial to regulating the use of force and the regime of detention. Under the laws of international armed conflict, one may shoot to kill an active enemy combatant, regardless of whether he is fighting or just eating lunch. But so long as the enemy is part of the regularly constituted armed forces, the opposing party may not prosecute him for mere belligerency, and must accord him the privileges of a POW until the war ends and he is repatriated. In a law enforcement scenario, the state may arrest and prosecute a rebel who takes up arms, but under international human rights standards, the authority to impose administrative detention in the interest of protecting national security is quite limited, and certainly cannot justify an indefinite detention. The international standards on the use of force for police or military personnel acting in a law enforcement constrain the use of lethal force to self-defense, to defend others against grave threats to life, or to arrest a perpetrator where less extreme measures will not suffice.[20]

Many of the 650 or so detainees who have spent time at Guantanamo's Camp X-Ray were apprehended in the course of a real war. The US government, to the dismay of many in its own military, decided to circumvent the requirements of the Geneva Conventions that these prisoners be presumed entitled to POW status until a competent tribunal established otherwise. Instead, it declared them, men and boys, taxi drivers and Taliban fighters, all *prima facie* ineligible for such status, and eventually constituted military tribunals that fall short of the guarantees of independence and fairness of US courts martial as well as international law. Their identities were withheld, and their persons confined in pens outside US territory to frustrate any effort to challenge their detention before regular US courts. Although the administration argued unsuccessfully before the Supreme Court that it was within the law in so acting, its attitude would more properly be described as exceptionalist, saying in effect that terrorism justifies detaining these individuals outside any regime of legal oversight whatsoever.

The United States is also detaining on its territory other "enemy combatants" it picked up far from a conventional battlefield. They are held without charge, without access to a lawyer, and without any end-point to their detention. So far, no clear rule has emerged from the litigation these cases are generating, with the government maneuvering to short-circuit the cases whenever a potentially adverse ruling may result.

Yaser Hamdi, a US citizen captured in Afghanistan, was transferred by the US to Guantanamo and then to military custody in Virginia and South Carolina and held without charge or the right to meet with an attorney. In June 2004, the US Supreme Court ruled that he could not be held indefinitely without the assistance of counsel and an opportunity to contest the allegations against him before a neutral arbiter.[21] Before litigation could proceed further on what procedures such review would entail, the government released Hamdi on October 11, 2004 and deported him to Saudi Arabia under an agreement whereby Hamdi renounced his US citizenship and accepted severe restrictions on his right to travel.[22]

The effort to avoid a definitive ruling was even more evident in the case of José Padilla, a US citizen arrested in 2002 as he arrived from Pakistan at Chicago's O'Hare Airport, according to the government's allegations with a purpose to hunt for targets al-Qaeda could hit with a radiological bomb. Classified as an "enemy combatant," Padilla was held in a military brig in South Carolina for three years without charge. The US Court of Appeals for the Fourth Circuit upheld the government's right to detain Padilla.[23] But two days before its response brief to Padilla's petition for certiorari to the Supreme Court was due, the government requested the Court of Appeals to grant permission to transfer Padilla to civilian custody on charges of conspiring to kidnap, murder and injure people abroad, in what appeared to be an attempt to short-circuit review of the Fourth Circuit decision in light of *Hamdi*. Judge Luttig, who had written the Fourth Circuit opinion on appeal, denied permission to transfer in a scathing opinion that pointed out the move called into question the government's rationale for holding him as an "enemy combatant." The Supreme Court approved the transfer, while leaving open the possibility for reconsidering the case should the government transfer Padilla back to military custody. Yet a third "enemy combatant" who is not a US national, the Quatari student Ali Saleh Kahlah al-Marri, is also being held in military detention in South Carolina as his lawyers send his case through the federal courts.[24]

If, indeed, the laws of war actually applied to persons apprehended far from any particular battlefront, like Padilla or al-Marri, it would have been in theory permissible to shoot them on sight at the airport or on the front lawn.[25] That we instinctively recoil from such a scenario suggests how attenuated the so-called global "war" on terrorists is from actual conditions of armed conflict. Indeed, in this constructive war, the government alone identifies the enemy, the battlefield, and when the war, if ever, is over.

Incommunicado detention outside of judicial control is the classic context of torture, and allegations of abusive treatment and harsh interrogation tactics emerged early regarding US holding centers at Bagram, Iraq, and Diego Garcia,[26] and subsequently as to Guantanamo. But there are more as yet unknown detention sites – and "disappeared" prisoners – than these.

The notorious photographs of abuse by US personnel of Iraqis at the Abu Ghraib prison were explained by US officials as portraying the misdeeds of a few "bad apples" on the night shift. Yet it soon became apparent that similar and worse abuses were rife in the context of the wars in Afghanistan and Iraq, not to mention the treatment of prisoners at Guantanamo.[27] This in turn has raised questions as to whether the abuse should be seen as merely random acts of soldiers under stress, or the calculated or entirely foreseeable result of coordinated government policies.[28] A particularly telling moment took place when the US government, in oral argument to the US Court of Appeals for the Ninth Circuit on the issue of Guantanamo, took the position that it was entitled to hold its captives on offshore territory without any form of federal court oversight – even if it were torturing or summarily executing them. The court wrote:

> To our knowledge, prior to the current detention of prisoners at Guantanamo, the US government has never before asserted such a grave and startling proposition. Accordingly, we view Guantanamo as unique not only because the United States' territorial relationship with the Base is without parallel today, but also because it is the first time that the government has announced such an extraordinary set of principles – a position so extreme that it raises the gravest concerns under both American and international law.[29]

Just as troubling is evidence that the US as well as European states have rendered terrorism suspects to countries known for rough interrogation and torture. This is perhaps a more surreptitious form of exceptionalism, where the legal norm against torture is not challenged directly, but evaded in practice.

These developments have not transpired without murmur. Two moments of governmental resistance deserve particular mention. Senator John McCain, a former POW who had experienced torture first-hand, sponsored legislation that prohibited cruel, inhuman and degrading treatment of detainees in the hands of the US government and required the Army Field Manual on Interrogation to guide the actions of all military interrogation. When the President in his signing statement to the legislation invoked a theory of presidential authority as Commander in

Chief and head of "the unitary executive branch," it threw into question whether the government would enforce the legislation in terrorism cases.[30]

In June 2006, Dick Marty, chairman of the Council of Europe's legal affairs and human rights committee, also issued a report implicating 14 European states in colluding with the US transfers of detainees to secret detention centers. Marty, who had no powers to compel governments to provide evidence, said: "Even if proof, in the classical meaning of the term, is not as yet available, a number of coherent and converging elements indicate that such secret detention centres did indeed exist in Europe."[31] The UN Special Rapporteur on Torture, the UN Independent Expert on the Protection of Human Rights and Fundamental Freedoms, and the Council of Europe Commissioner for Human Rights have all expressed concern about the practice of rendering terrorism suspects to countries with a record of torture.[32]

Privacy and Surveillance

Although Louis Brandeis is often credited with inventing the "right" to keep certain types of personal information out of the public eye in 1890,[33] the idea that a personal realm should be protected against the intrusions of the state is older and probably runs deeper. As an international norm, it is entrenched in international and regional human rights instruments as well as in many constitutions, although it is a relatively weak right that cedes to a host of other legitimate social interests.[34] The changeable content of the right in light of shifting social interests finds reflection in the language of US jurisprudence, which often frames the question in terms of whether people have a "legitimate expectation of privacy" in a given situation.[35] That formulation itself betrays the fact that actual expectations of privacy often exceed the legal protection of such expectations.

Granted that there has always been some disjunction between a litigant's expectations and a court's validation, there is little doubt that the realm of privacy has been diminishing apace. Long before 9/11, technology drove both the development of global communication and state interest in comprehensive surveillance. In debates over the control of strong encryption, for example, the threats of the global crime ring and the child pornographer were regularly debated as the rationale for giving governments keys to all such private padlocks. But the "war against terrorism" gave a compelling new vocabulary to governments seeking enhanced powers of surveillance.

The US Congress passed the voluminous USA/Patriot Act six weeks after 9/11 with virtually no debate or dissent, granting the executive extraordinary powers of surveillance that it had sought unsuccessfully in the past. Expiring provisions of the Act were reauthorized in 2006. Section 215 of the Act grants virtually unchecked authority to the FBI to obtain personal records from third parties – such as libraries, doctors, internet service providers – without the subject of surveillance being notified, and without any showing of need other than an assertion that the request relates to a terrorism or foreign intelligence investigation. This provision, as well as the provision allowing the FBI to demand personal records from internet providers without a court order on the basis of "National Security Letters," came under legal challenge. The executive gained new authority to conduct physical searches without advance notice, and to search and wiretap where gathering intelligence was only a secondary purpose to a domestic criminal investigation.[36] While the Department of Justice resisted giving open and meaningful answers to the House Judiciary Committee on just how these new powers were being implemented, it did prepare a draft of sequel legislation (the Domestic Security Enhancement Act) that would have further degraded the few remaining constraints on wiretaps and searches.[37]

These ominous legislative developments, however, were overshadowed by revelations in 2005 and 2006 of massive wiretapping and surveillance programs conducted by the US National Security Agency entirely outside the legal regime established by the Foreign Service Intelligence Act, on the executive's theory that Congressional authorization to go to war after 9/11 had placed the President at the "zenith" of his powers and permitted circumvention of other federal statutes.

These events also attracted lawsuits and, finally, Congressional protests.

The United States is hardly the only locale where privacy has been eroded in the name of preventing acts of terrorism. Broad new powers of surveillance, search and wiretapping were introduced in Europe, Australia, Canada, and India; the deployment of video cameras surveying public spaces reached new heights in the United Kingdom, Europe and Australia; collection and sharing of personal data of travelers between the European Union and the United States became institutionalized;[38] data retention in the course of terrorism inquiries increased in many countries, often with the data thereafter available for any other criminal inquiry; and Western governments renewed pressure on industry to build surveillance capability into communications infrastructure.[39] The European Parliament adopted in December 2005 a directive requiring communications providers to monitor and retain logs of all emails, calls and movements in cyberspace regardless of whether the subject of this surveillance was in any way under criminal investigation.[40] That, of course, is only half the picture: private collection of personal data also increased in response to the perception of insecurity and in the interest of showing compliance with the new laws on aiding terrorist activity.

One big question is whether all this additional surveillance is actually producing a serious increment in security in the form of deterrence or prevention of terrorist acts, for acquiring security is surely the justification for sacrificing privacy. So far, the evidence that we have a far improved mousetrap is scant. Deterrence is virtually impossible to gauge and there are not many claims that the new powers were necessary to actually interrupt crimes in progress. But even if one could point to cases where the proverbial ticking bomb had been stopped, one would have to ask whether the measures taken to discover it were disproportionate to the social harm inflicted in the effort. The comparison to the famous justification of torture is not accidental. One aspect of the social harm is that many innocent people's rights are inevitably abrogated in the search for the real terrorist. Another aspect is that the repeated derogation from the norm in the name of exigency – either the norm against torture or the norm against state intrusion into personal information – will ultimately erode its force in all contexts. This is particularly the case when, as in the case of the "war against terrorism," the propounded state of emergency appears to be without temporal or geographic boundary.

Transition from Justice?

This loose and incomplete sketch of terrorism's pressure upon numerous areas of international law and the domestic laws that inform international law is meant to suggest the broad scope of erosion in what have been thought to be fundamental norms. Developments in the United States merit particular attention, because by virtue of that nation's political dominance, they carry a unique global influence. The picture is not of a handful of egregious violations of the rights of disfavored minorities, although disfavored minorities are surely suffering such violation, but rather myriad holes suddenly appearing in the fabric of settled human rights and humanitarian law. The extent of the change makes one wonder whether this is not merely a swing of the pendulum, eventually to be reversed, but a more fundamental transition.

Theorists of transitional justice point to the inherent disjunctive quality that law bears at such times. It legitimizes political transition through rituals such as trial of the leadership, truth commission, lustration, reparation, and the like. While by their nature these events are a radical departure from what went before, they nevertheless reaffirm the rule of law and commitment to a liberal political order.[41] Yet if these terrorism-inspired legal developments point to any transition, it is one of a different order, one that is fundamentally illiberal.[42]

The world these new legal trends construct is one where rights are conditioned on personal status. Those who fall into the profile of a terrorist suspect – the alien, the immigrant, the Muslim, the irregular combatant, the activist – may find themselves excluded from the most basic individual freedoms. We may become comfortable with the notion of gunning down Mr Padilla at the airport. The moral repugnance of such a *nomos* can only be amplified by recognition that measures justified in terms of counter-terrorism can and are put to other uses, such as suppression of political dissent. Is this the world we want to defend from terrorists?

There are surely signs of resistance to such a transition. They include international reluctance to renegotiate the laws of war, international opprobrium over Guantanamo, judicial inquiry into the terms of detention, and populist resistance to the accelerating encroachments on privacy. Abuses that are acknowledged and remedied reaffirm the liberal norms. This is why we should welcome inquiries into and attempts to check indefinite detention, torture, disproportionate harm to civilians, and unjustifiable surveillance, and question why there have not been more.

Notes

This chapter was commissioned especially for this collection.

1 The observation that the US Constitution was not intended as a "suicide pact" was made by Justice Jackson, in the last line to his scathing dissent in *Termineello v. City of Chicago*, 337 US 1 (1949) objecting to free-speech protection of an incendiary speech of a Catholic priest that fomented a riot, as well as by Justice Goldberg, in his majority opinion in *Kennedy v. Mendoza-Martinez*, 372 US 144 (1963), striking down a law that permitted the government to denaturalize a draft evader without due process.

2 International Committee of the Red Cross, *Commentary on the Additional Protocols of 8 June 1977 to the Geneva Conventions of 12 August 1949* (Geneva: Martinus Nijhoff, 1987), Protocol I, Art. 1, paras 48, 51, 61, pp. 37, 40.

3 Ibid., Protocol II, part I(2), paras 4439, 4440.

4 See excerpt from Hans-Peter Gasser, "International Humanitarian Law: An Introduction," Henry Dunant Institute (Geneva: Paul Haupt, 1993), updated and posted at www.icrc.org/web/eng/siteeng0.nsf/iwpList104/B24E18B3F03914ABC1256B660059066B.

5   Human Rights Watch, *Off Target: The Conduct of the War and Civilian Casualties in Iraq* (New York: Human Rights Watch, 2003).

6   *Restatement of the Law, Third, The Foreign Relations Law of the United States* (St Paul: American Law Institute Publishers, 1987), sec. 102, note 2, pp. 31–2.

7   John J. Lumpkin and Dafna Linzer, "US Officials Were Reluctant to Call Troops Occupiers," Associated Press, Nov. 28, 2003 (citing internal review by 3rd Infantry Division (Mechanized) that blamed a refusal to acknowledge occupier status for the failure to order curfews, direct civilians back to work, and control local governments and populations); report also available at www.globalsecurity.org/military/library/report/2003/3id-aar-jul03.pdf.

8   Geneva Convention Relative to the Protection of Civilian Persons in Time of War, of Aug. 12, 1949, Art. 27.

9   See e.g. Joe Stork and Fred Abrahams, "Sidelined: Human Rights in Post-war Iraq," in *Human Rights Watch World Report 2004* (New York: Human Rights Watch, 2004), pp. 93–105, also at http://hrw.org/wr2k4/6.htm#_Toc58744955; Human Rights Watch, "Climate of Fear: Sexual Violence and Abduction of Women and Girls in Baghdad," July 2003; Human Rights Watch, "Northern Iraq: Civilian Deaths Higher since War Ended," Press Release, Apr. 27, 2003, at http://hrw.org/english/docs/2003/04/27/iraq5798.htm. Shortfalls in providing security were not attributable to the US alone, of course. See e.g. Human Rights Watch, "Basra: Crime and Insecurity under British Occupation," June 2003, at http://hrw.org/reports/2003/iraq0603/.

10 See, for example, Suzanne Goldberg, "A Land Ruled by Chaos," *Guardian*, Oct. 4, 2003.

11 Sam Zia-Zarifi, "Losing the Peace in Afghanistan," *in Human Rights Watch World Report 2004*, pp. 61–90.

12 See Michael Hirsh, "Blood and Honor," *Newsweek*, Feb. 2, 2004; Human Rights Watch, "Hearts and Minds: Post-war Civilian Deaths in Baghdad Caused by US Forces," Oct. 2003, at http://hrw.org/reports/2003/iraq1003/index.htm; "US Investigate Civilian Deaths in Iraq Military Operations," June 18, 2004, at http://hrw.org/english/docs/2004/06/18/iraq8872.htm; "Leadership Failure: Firsthand Accounts of Torture of Iraqi Detainees by the US Army's 82nd Airborne Division," Sept. 2005, at http://hrw.org/

reports/2005/us0905/; "By the Numbers: Findings of the Detainee
Abuse and Accountability Project," Apr. 2006, at http://hrw.
org/reports/2006/ct0406/.

13   See, for example, Gerry J. Gilmore, "Rumsfeld: Baghdad
     Terror Attacks Target Iraq Successes," American Forces Press
     Service, Oct. 28, 2003, at www.defenselink.mil/news/Oct2003/
     n10282003_200310286.html, and Jim Garamone, "Bremer Says
     Iraq Frontline of War on Terror," American Forces Press Service,
     Oct. 26, 2003 at www.defenselink.mil/news/Oct2003/n10262003_
     200310263.html. Although there is no one accepted international
     definition of terrorism, most uses of the term encompass attacks
     on civilians for the purpose of political influence. Attacks by a
     resistance or rebel force on the armed force of a state or Occupying
     Power describe conventional war.

14   See e.g. Rory McCarthy and Julian Borger, "Wife of Saddam's
     Henchman Held by US after Raid," Guardian, Nov. 27, 2003,
     p. 2.

15   John Daniszewski and Patrick McDonnell, "US Military Respond-
     ing More Fiercely to Iraqi Guerrilla Strikes," Los Angeles Times,
     Nov. 12, 2003.

16   Phil Reeves, "Americans Turn Tikrit into Iraq's Own West Bank,"
     Independent, Nov. 18, 2003.

17   List of topics can be found at www.hsph.harvard.edu/hpcr/ihl_
     research_meeting_topics.htm.

18   Dubbed "the Alabama Process" by the International Humanitarian
     Law Research Initiative, there have been three such conferences
     to date. See www.ihlresearch.org/ihl/portalhome.php.

19   Staff Sgt Michelle L. Thomas, USAF, "Rumsfeld, Myers Salute
     Success in Iraq, Warn Terror Threat Remains," American Forces
     Press Service, Dec. 23, 2003, at www.defenselink.mil/news/
     Dec2003/n12232003_200312238.html.

20   Basic Principles on the Use of Force and Firearms by Law Enforcement
     Officials, Eighth United Nations Congress on the Prevention of
     Crime and the Treatment of Offenders, Havana, 27 August to
     7 September1990, UN Doc. A/CONF.144/28/Rev.1 at 112
     (1990).

21   Hamdi v. Rumsfeld (03-6696) 542 U.S. 507 (2004), at www.
     law.cornell.edu/supct/html/03-6696.ZO.html.

22   A copy of the release agreement is available at www.humanrights-
     first.org/us_law/inthecourts/hamdi_briefs/Hamdi_Agreement.pdf.

23   Padilla v. Hanft, 423 F.3d 386 (4th Cir. 2005).

24 Ali Saleh Kahlah al-Marri, alleged to be an al-Qaeda accomplice-
    in-waiting, was arrested at his home in Peoria in 2001. Al-
    Marri was charged with a number of small crimes including
    possessing unauthorized access devices and making false state-
    ments. Sixteen months after these charges were filed, and while
    they were still pending, al-Marri was designated an enemy combat-
    ant and sent to a military brig in South Carolina. In July 2005,
    the US District Court for the District of South Carolina affirmed
    the government's authority to detain al-Marri in a military deten-
    tion facility, *Al-Marri v. Hanft*, 378 F. Supp.2d 673 (D.S.C.
    2005).
25 Kenneth Roth, "Drawing the Line: War Rules and Law Enforce-
    ment Rules in the Fight against Terrorism," *in Human Rights Watch
    World Report 2004*, pp. 177–93.
26 See Dana Priest and Barton Gellman, "US Decries Abuse but
    Defends Interrogations; 'Stress and Duress' Tactics Used on Ter-
    rorism Suspects Held in Secret Overseas Facilities," *Washington
    Post*, Dec. 26, 2002, and Mark Bowden, "The Dark Art of Inter-
    rogation," *Atlantic Monthly*, Oct. 2003.
27 See e.g. Human Rights Watch, "By the Numbers," detailing more
    than 300 cases of detainee torture, abuse or killing involving over
    600 US civilian and military personnel since late 2001, resulting
    in only a handful of prosecutions so far.
28 See Dinah PoKempner, "Command Responsibility for Torture," in
    Kenneth Roth and Minky Worden, *Torture: A Human Rights Per-
    spective* (New York and London: New Press and Human Rights
    Watch, 2005), pp. 158–72.
29 *Gherebi v. Bush*, US Ct. App. 9th Cir. No. 03-55785, Dec. 18,
    2003 at 18082, available at http://caselaw.lp.findlaw.com/data2/
    circs/9th/0355785p.pdf.
30 The struggle then shifted to whether the government would hold
    the CIA to such a standard, and whether the newly revised Army
    Field Manual would permit measures that would fall below
    Common Article Three to the Geneva Conventions of 1949 from
    whence the prohibition of "cruel, inhuman and degrading" treat-
    ment derives.
31 CNN, "Report: CIA Flights 'Spiders Web,'" June 7, 2006, at
    http://edition.cnn.com/2006/WORLD/europe/06/07/marty.
    rendition/.
32 See Human Rights Watch, "The Legal Prohibitions against Return
    to Torture or Ill-Treatment," in *Still at Risk: Diplomatic Assurances*

No Safeguard against Torture, Apr. 2003, at http://hrw.org/reports/2005/eca0405/3.htm#_Toc100558810.

33 This was the year of publication of his seminal article advocating the right, spurred by irritation with the intrusions of the society pages. Samuel D. Warren and Louis D. Brandeis, "The Right to Privacy," *Harvard Law Review*, 4 (1890): 193–220. The UK does not recognize a common law tort of invasion of privacy, but the tort of breach of confidence carries similar effect.

34 See International Covenant on Civil and Political Rights, Art. 17 (the right is protected against "unlawful" and "arbitrary" interference) and CCPR General Comment 16 (1988).

35 See e.g. *Minnesota v. Carter*, 525 US 83 (1998) (holding that visitors had no legitimate expectation of privacy in an apartment when police, looking through a partially drawn blind, saw them bagging cocaine). The term is a staple of both federal and state court decisions in the United States.

36 The law also created a sweeping new crime of "domestic terrorism" involving violence designed to "influence the policy of a government by intimidation or coercion" – a definition that could capture most direct action protestors – and allows prosecution or deportation of those who assist such "terrorists" by, for example, putting them up for the night or donating money to their cause.

37 American Civil Liberties Union, "Interested Persons Memo: Section-by-Section Analysis of Justice Department Draft 'Domestic Security Enhancement Act of 2003' also known as PATRIOT Act II," Feb. 14, 2003, at www.aclu.org/SafeandFree/SafeandFree.cfm?ID=11835andc=206. The draft was leaked to the public and generated intense criticism, after which it was withdrawn.

38 However, on May 30, 2006 the European Court of Justice voided the 2004 airline passenger data transfer agreement between the US and the EU on the grounds that it violated the EU 1995 directive on data protection. See http://curia.eu.int/jurisp/cgi-bin/gettext.pl?where=&lang=en&num=79939469C19040317&doc=T&ouvert=T&seance=ARRET.

39 For a comprehensive review of developments worldwide, see Cédric Laurent, *Privacy and Threats to Human Rights 2003: An International Survey of Privacy Law and Developments* (Washington: Electronic Privacy Information Center, 2003).

40 Privacy International, "European Parliament Approves Communications Data Retention," Dec. 15, 2005, at www.privacyinternational.org/article.shtml?cmd[347]=x-347-496240.

41 See Ruti G. Teitel, *Transitional Justice* (New York: Oxford University Press, 2000), pp. 219–28.
42 Ronald Dworkin has written eloquently of the immorality of the Bush administration's project of buying the majority's security by devaluing the lives and freedoms of the minority in his essay, "Terror and the Attack on Civil Liberties," *New York Review of Books*, 50.17, Nov. 6, 2003.

10

Global Terror and International Finance in the Immediate Aftermath of 9/11

Martin S. Navias

Introduction

In the war against international terrorism and al-Qaeda in particular, finance warfare emerged early on within the overall campaign as one of the core component strategies alongside the employment of military force, diplomacy, intelligence operations, and law enforcement. The rationale for this financial focus in its most basic and explicit form was articulated by then US Treasury General Counsel David Afhauser when he stated in Senate testimony: "You can stop the killing if you can stop the flow of money."[1]

Clearly terrorist groups need money. They need it for organizational reasons: to maintain and protect their structures as well as to grow them. And they also need it for operational purposes in terms of both planning and executing attacks. According to one study the costs of major al-Qaeda terrorist operations have ranged from $5,000–$10,000 for the USS *Cole* strike, to approximately $70,000 for the Bali bombing, to about $500,000 for the September 11 attacks.[2] These numbers are obviously small (given the impact of the operations), but estimates are that operations may account for only a small part of terrorist financial requirements (10 percent),[3] with the major amount being dedicated toward communications, networks, training facilities, and

protection. So, logically, by cutting off the flow of funds to terrorist organizations, it is to be expected that terrorist capabilities
will degrade both structurally and operationally.

Afhauser's argument is thus based upon a reasonable deduc-
tion and reflects the rationale of economic warfare – a strategically indirect approach that works by undermining one of the
core foundations of enemy fighting power and political resilience.
But terrorist organizations are not to be compared to states. They
do not have readily identifiable and large-scale economic resources
or means of production that are vulnerable to interdiction. There
are no production bottlenecks such as ball-bearing factories that
can be bombed or ports that can be blocked.

What international terrorist organizations such as al-Qaeda
developed in the 1990s, however, is a well-oiled and sophisticated machine for generating funds and also for exploiting loopholes in the increasingly interconnected international banking
system for purposes of moving these funds around the world in
support of cell sustenance and the propagation of terrorist activities. Counterterrorist finance warfare in the immediate aftermath
of the attacks of September 2001 therefore involved tightening
domestic legislation and enhancing international cooperation
with the aim of blocking terrorist fund generation capabilities and
preventing the movement across borders of these illicit monies.

In the immediate aftermath of 9/11 this proved to be a very
difficult task indeed. Closing down terrorist fundraising capabilities ran into a host of foreign policy problems. Tightening up the
banking system against money laundering by terrorists raised
civil liberties and practical business concerns. The results of
the finance war against international terrorism were decidedly
mixed.

The Immediate American Response

Finance warfare was one of the first elements of the counterterrorist war to be activated. Indeed, prior to the first ordnance
being dropped on Taliban and al-Qaeda positions in Afghanistan,
and well before any allied troops were deployed in theatre,

financial war was declared by the US and its allies on al-Qaeda. The US authorities had in fact been interested in identifying bin Laden assets since the East African bombings in 1998 but lack of political will and sense of urgency under the Clinton administration meant no significant steps had been taken to this end, though some al-Qaeda and Taliban funds had indeed been frozen.

Post-9/11 initial American practical action took the form primarily of freezing bank accounts believed to contain terrorist funds. Less than two weeks after the terrorist strikes, President Bush signed Executive Order 13224 which authorized the US government to block the assets of foreign individuals and entities that committed or posed a significant risk of committing acts of terrorism. In addition, authorization was given to block the assets of individuals and entities designated as providing support, financial or other services to (or otherwise associated with) designated terrorists and terrorist organizations. By January 8, 2002 the US had suceeded in freezing millions of dollars in assets belonging to more than 150 individuals and organizations suspected of being involved in terrorism. The Europeans followed this lead and also froze various accounts.

Freezing obviously amounted to superficial financial fire-fighting. Freezing was attractive because once the intelligence was available for identifying relevant accounts, freezing them could be easily and quickly effected. What was however needed was a proper means of locating accounts whose beneficial ownership was being masked, and even more importantly and ambitiously, identifying the means by which such monies were entering the American and European banking networks. As a result of this recognition the focus on account freezes was soon accompanied by an emphasis on the need to address deeper systemic vulnerabilities within the international banking system to terrorist financial penetration.

Following 9/11, the US Patriot Act became central to US efforts. This comprehensive piece of counterterrorist legislation provided both law enforcement and financial regulators with a new means to detect, investigate and prosecute money laundering, and broad legal authority to require the forfeiture of assets related to terrorism. It worked, inter alia, by requiring financial institutions to tighten their controls against money laundering, improve due diligence of their customer base, improve their record-keeping and upgrade their suspicious transaction reporting requirements. "Special measures" allowed the US Treasury to require any bank in the US, and indeed anywhere else, to divulge the most sensitive and private of their information records: accounts and transaction details of their clients. If a foreign bank did not comply it could be prevented from accessing the US banking system.

Also important were four counterterrorist lists that worked to help identify, and then to control, terrorist financial threats: (1) the Executive Order 13224, the freeze list referred to above; (2) the State Sponsors of Terrorism List of states which were in the US view guilty of abetting terrorist organizations; (3) the Foreign Terrorist Organization List of organizations the US government considered to be terrorist; and finally (4) the Terrorist Exclusion List, inclusion in which would lead to referred organizations being deported from the United States. This was complemented by the Rewards for Justice Program which in the financial context provided for $5 million in rewards for information leading to the disruption of terrorist financing operations.

In the UK objectives to combat money laundering were, in the aftermath of 9/11, achieved by way of the Proceeds of Crime Act 2002, complemented by various other pieces of legislation including, inter alia, the Anti-Terrorism Crime and Security Act 2001, the Financial Services Authority's money laundering rules, the Joint Money Laundering Steering Group's guidance notes, and various money laundering regulations.

Both countries also invested heavily in upgrading relevant bureaucracies, enhancing domestic cooperation between various agencies and stepping up coordination with international institutions committed to fighting terrorist financing. These institutions included the United Nations (most notably the special committee dedicated to dealing with international terrorism), the World Bank, the International Monetary Fund, the Financial Action Task Force ("FATF") of the OECD, and the Egmont Group (which shares financial intelligence between various national financial intelligence organizations).

The Money Laundering Threat

Efforts to deal both conceptually and instrumentally with these problems of illegal financing did not originate post-9/11. Indeed, the roots of the finance war against global terrorism are to be found not in specific antiterrorist financing measures but in initiatives against money laundering adopted during the 1970s to counter nonpolitical criminal rather than political terrorist money laundering – especially the massive amounts of drug monies that were being generated and needed to be both circulated internationally and legitimized.

According to one Home Office study, laundered money is equal to 2 percent of UK GDP (then approximately £18 billion).[4] Furthermore, according to the International Monetary Fund, sums being money laundered amount to between $600 billion and $1.5 trillion of funds annually (then equal to 2–5 percent of global GDP). One estimate is that the vast majority of this is derived from drug trafficking (60 percent); the next major category consists of funds derived from tax evasion (20 percent); and the rest is derived from all sorts of sources, including funds related to terrorism (which, as can be noted, make up a tiny percentage of the total). But in truth these are just estimates – no one can be really certain about the figures – and all the above may well be gross underestimates. Whatever the case, the ability of South American drug lords, East European mafiosi and others, including terrorist groups, to hide and transfer this really massive influx of cash was by the 1990s being radically enhanced due to the rapid integration of semiregulated and anarchic international banking and capital markets.

In order to appreciate the efficacy of steps dedicated to contain and root out terrorist financing that were taken in the immediate aftermath of 9/11 it is necessary to step back and investigate, albeit briefly, the concept of money laundering. Money laundering is the process by which the proceeds of crime are converted into assets that appear to have legitimate origins so that they can be retained permanently or recycled to fund further crimes. The money is, in the jargon, "cleansed," and so the ability to use the money trail to link a criminal to the crime is effectively broken.

The term, while gaining currency during the Watergate scandal in the 1970s, actually originated in Chicago in the 1930s when Al Capone, in order to hide ill-gotten gains raised in speakeasies, brothels and other illegal establishments, set up a chain of laundromats throughout the city. There was no means of gauging how many cycles each washing machine ran, so that one could not check the operating profit of each shop. Money that was actually being generated illegally appeared to have been earned entirely legitimately within the laundry shop. Meyer Lansky, the mob's accountant, took the money laundering technique somewhat further. He established companies in the United States to buy real estate. He then used a Swiss bank account into which he poured the illegal funds. The Swiss bank would then give loans to the American companies to buy the real estate. The origins of the funds were disguised behind protective Swiss banking laws while the money was transformed into legally owned and legitimate property.

Modern-day money laundering dedicated to hiding origins and transferring funds is somewhat more sophisticated, but tends to involve three distinct phases: placement, layering, and integration (see table 10.1). It is by way of a combination of

Table 10.1   Money laundering stages

Stage	Description	Activity
Placement	The disposal of cash proceeds derived from illegal activities	Such as small deposits into banks, bureaux de change; casinos
Layering	The financial structuring of complex layers of transactions to conceal the actual sources of funds	Such as shell companies, numerous transfers, lax offshore jurisdictions
Integration	The creation of apparent legitimacy by returning the proceeds into the economy as bona fide business funds	Puchase of high value items, legitimate investments

these processes that the monetary proceeds derived from illicit activities are transformed into funds with an apparent legal source. The key point here is that an element of criminality is central to this definition of money laundering. According to one US government analyst, writing in May 2001, money laundering is to be defined as "Legally . . . any attempt to engage in a monetary transaction that involves criminally derived property."

It is an unfortunate reality, however, that neither domestic nor international efforts – involving policies such as "knowing your customer" and the origin of his money, reporting suspicious transactions, and maintaining paper trails – have been particularly successful in targeting their original target, nonterrorist money laundering. According to some studies, outside the United States very little money laundered wealth has been interdicted and put beyond the reach of criminals. Furthermore, according to one British academic, in cases not involving drugs, the sums taken out of criminal circulation are less than 0.0001 percent of the amounts that are theoretically subject to the law.[5] The explanations for this are many: failure to properly implement existing legislation; the lacunae in existing legislation; limitations in strategic intelligence; the sophistication of the launderers and/or a dearth of sufficient international or domestic bureaucratic cooperation and coordination.

The dismal conclusion here is that efforts against money laundering have had no real impact on its level. On the underlying crimes, the view is that the efforts against money laundering focused on the war on drugs have had absolutely no impact upon the narcotics trade. The situation is not helped by international unevenness in anti–money laundering policy implementation. In a report in 2001 of the OECD's Financial Action Task Force (FATF) it was admitted that "money laundering is actively investigated in a limited number of countries . . . elsewhere the offence is not frequently prosecuted."[6]

This is not to say that efforts against money laundering have no, or will have no effect on terrorism. However, these efforts have proved to be relatively inefficient and, it will be argued, terrorist financing is in any case a very different beast from money laundering in relation to drug trafficking and will require its own specific instruments and focus.

To be fair, this latter necessity was recognized even before 9/11. FATF – an independent international organization set up in 1989 by the then G7 with its headquarters at the OECD – is the institutional centerpiece for global efforts against money laundering. In 1990 it published the so-called Forty Recommendations for all states and territories to adopt which are regarded as constituting the appropriate standard for anti–money laundering behavior. These recommendations included requirements for states to criminalize money laundering activities and to adopt customer identification and record-keeping practices. Countries and territories not maintaining adequate safeguards were to be sanctioned.[7] In 2001, prior to the September attacks, and for the first time, FATF began to focus specifically on terrorist financing.

One of the main objects of early FATF investigations into terrorist financing was to determine whether the reliance by terrorists on legal sources of funding impacted on countries' ability to employ existing anti–money laundering measures to target terrorist-related money laundering. Discussion unfortunately did not appear to have resulted in a consensus view. Some FATF experts argued that what terrorists were in fact doing did not actually constitute money laundering per se, as the source of funding was not criminal. Following from there it was reported that "There [was] no agreement on whether anti–money laundering laws could (or should) play a direct role in the fight against terrorism"[8] as "[s]ome countries, for example, are not able to use anti–money laundering legislation for tracking or restraining suspected terrorist money if the source of the funds was a voluntary contribution and not a criminal act."[9] In addition there was recognition by FATF of the political problem of definitions as to what constituted a terrorist, and that this would impact on a general financing consensus. On the eve of 9/11 many issues in relation to the specific category of terrorist financing and money laundering had been touched upon but as yet remained unresolved.

The Nature of Terrorist Financing

Terrorist financing, both in its fund generation and in its transfer contexts, differs in important respects from its nonpolitical criminal cousin. While the smuggling of illicit narcotics and the laundering of the extensive profits that result from that very lucrative trade are international crimes par excellence, they differ in their function from practices of global terrorism in that the genesis, motivations, and objectives of drug trading are at root neither political nor ideological in character, but rather mercantile. For terrorists, on the other hand, the pecuniary consequences of their actions are secondary to the achievement of their military and ultimate political goals.

It is important to recognize that the aim of the laundering process for criminals is to render dirty money clean, while for terrorists what is often originally clean money is dedicated to criminal ("dirty") ends. In some senses then the traditional process becomes inverted and terrorist financing becomes money laundering on its head. Not surprisingly, concepts and measures generated in response to nonpolitical criminal financing have proven not to be entirely sensitive to what is essentially a politically oriented and driven financing process.

Of course there is a nexus between the fund generation activities of terrorists and criminals. Terrorist organizations are known to tap into illegal sources of funding such as drug trafficking, extortion, kidnapping, robbery, fraud, gambling, and smuggling of contraband goods (see table 10.2). The Peruvian Shining Path has long funded its activities with sales of cocaine, as have the National Liberation Army of Colombia and the United Self-Defense Forces of Colombia. The IRA has a history of extortion and robbery; al-Qaeda, itself, relied upon the export of drugs from Taliban-controlled Afghanistan.

Despite these similarities, there are however three major sources of funds that appear unique to terrorist organizations and serve to severely complicate the picture from a control point of view, in that they do not in themselves constitute criminal activity in many a domestic context.

Table 10.2 Terrorist financing: examples of the criminal nexus

Criminal activity	Examples of terrorist groups
Drug trafficking	Shining Path, NLA (Colombia), USDF (Colombia), IRA, al-Qaeda, FARC (Colombia)
Extortion	Abu Sayaff Group, ETA, IRA Continuity IRA, Revolutionary People's Liberation Army (Turkey)
Kidnapping	Hezbollah, Harakat ul-Mujahidin (HUM) (Pak.), Lashkar-e-Jjhangvi, ELN (Col.), LRA (Ug.), Islamic Army of Aden, Loyalist Volunteer Force, HUJI (Pak.), Al Ittad al Islami (Som), ADF (Ug.), ALIR (Interahamwe)
Robbery	Abu Sayaff Group, ETA, 17 November (Gr.), IRA, Revolutionary People's Liberation Army (Turkey), GRAPE (Sp.)
Fraud	IRA
Smuggling	IRA, Shining Path, FARC, United Self-Defense Forces (Col.)

State support　The financial support of terrorist organizations by states for ideological, political or military reasons – both in terms of the provision of funds and of various financial services, including transmission and laundering of funds – is one of the key characteristics of the terrorist financing typology. By providing the full range of complex and integrated state-controlled financial services, large sums of money may readily be integrated on behalf of the terrorist organization into the international financial system – whether the origin of those funds be the state itself or some other legal or illegal source – and this makes the challenge of control much more difficult. Countries identified by the US State Department in the immediate aftermath of 9/11 as supporting international terrorist organizations were Iran, Syria, North Korea, Cuba, Sudan, Libya, and Iraq.

Legitimate business   Terrorists may also engage in legitimate business activities to both raise and distribute funds. While criminal organizations may seek to move from illegitimate activities into legitimate business activities for both financial and security reasons, among terrorists it may well be the case that the businesses are legitimate from the start and that only the purposes to which the money is put are illegal. This makes both identification and control extremely difficult. Legitimate businesses owned by terrorist groups have included construction companies, honey shops, tanneries, banks, agricultural commodities businesses, trade businesses, bakeries, restaurants, and bookstores.

Charities   Terrorist organizations often rely on donations from supporters as a means of funding activities. Because of their political and military objectives, terrorist groups are able to attract voluntary funds from supporters of those goals. (This is unlike nonpolitical criminal organizations, which when seeking funds do so by coercive techniques, such as protection rackets, which are themselves illegal.) Significantly such funds may be generated in the target itself. In the latter situation the terrorists disguise, from the authorities and sometimes even from contributors, the true objective of finance. This is in many instances achieved by differentiating between the political and military arms of the organization, the political wing often having a legal basis by creating charitable or educational foundations which appear as the object of the contribution. These institutions also serve a role of helping direct funding to the terrorists under the cloak of legitimacy. Hezbollah has certainly employed this strategy as a means of widening its political support within Lebanon by using such funds both to conduct operations and to abet wide-ranging social, economic, and medical programs.

Fund movement   There are clearly similarities between how terrorists and how criminals exploit the international banking system to move monies around the globe. Physical transportation, credit and debit cards, alternative remittance systems, and correspondent accounts all play a role.

International terrorist organizations have been especially active in the moving of funds through the vast network of alternative remittance systems. Alternative remittance systems (sometimes known as hawalas) refer to nonbank financial institutions that transfer funds through their own private networks. It is essentially a paperless system involving unregistered lenders in at least two countries, prepared to move money across borders. As there are no official bank records there is no proper trail to the source of funds. For example, it has been argued that the hawala network operating between London and Pakistan has served not only to channel finance in relation to drug trafficking but also so support Sikh and Kashmiri secessionists.

Correspondent banking systems in the formal sector are subject to significant regulations which require greater knowledge of whom a bank is doing business with at the other end and the retention by the bank of a paper trail dealing with the clients' transactions. In practice these careful procedures were not always followed. Banks have not always carried out proper due diligence procedures in respect of the correspondent bank with which they have had a relationship even if that correspondent bank was located in a jurisdiction with regulatory controls known to be lax. Thus by "nesting" in a bank with a correspondent banking relationship in a targeted country, terrorists can access the banking system of that country – a strategy that has been facilitated in the past not only by poor but in may cases effectively nonexistent investigatory procedures exercised by banks over their correspondent relationships. Terrorist organizations have shown a sophisticated understanding of how these systems work and their vulnerabilities.

In terms of fund movement one of the major differences between terrorists and drug cartels lies in the amounts of monies moved. Terrorists need much smaller amounts of funds, making those amounts more difficult to identify since they often do not reach reporting thresholds. Some of the financing amounts received by 9/11 hijackers were valued at less then $10,000. Transactions were thus neither quantitatively nor by category of the type which required, without other indicators, additional scrutiny by the financial institutions involved.

Certainly nowhere are the particularities of terrorist financing more evident than in the case of al-Qaeda.

Al-Qaeda Financing

The key point about al-Qaeda financing is its global nature and its sophistication. Al-Qaeda has cells in Africa, the Middle East, Asia, Europe, and North America. Since 1998 it has carried out operations in Africa, the Middle East, Asia, and North America and therefore, for structural and operational reasons, requires funds to be raised and delivered globally.

Such a wide range of international operations would not have been possible without bin Laden's knowledge of the functioning of contemporary international banking and financial practices. In an interview he gave to the Pakistani paper *Karachi Ummat* he stated that "he was aware of the cracks inside the western financial system as they were aware of the lines in their hands."[10] Certainly our understanding of bin Laden was firstly as a financial entrepreneur. A 1996 CIA profile of bin Laden was entitled: "Islamic Extremist Financier."[11] His family, originally from Yemen, had grown wealthy in the construction business in Saudi and it was in this context that he had gained financial experience, developed financial and political relationships with the Saudi government, and ultimately inherited a significant amount of money.

Bin Laden's jihad activities in Afghanistan in the late 1980s provided him with enormous experience in employing funds (amounts of them his own) in relation to the movement of both men and military material across borders. By 1986, bin Laden had channeled many millions of dollars from individuals, governments and charities to his Afghan Services Bureau, which provided logistical support to those fighting in Afghanistan against the Soviets. His acolytes traveled extensively, setting up support branches in many countries. This experience and framework was later reinforced by bin Laden's financial and logistic involvement in conflicts in East Africa and the Balkans, during which he honed his skills as the world's leading financial terrorist.

Following the end of the war in Afghanistan he returned to Saudi Arabia, where he busied himself with a mixture of illegal terrorist and legitimate business activities, including construction and import and export businesses. As a result of growing friction with the Saudi authorities over his terrorist activities, he was forced to move to Sudan in 1991, where in his relationship with the radical fundamentalist regime we can note the emergence of the phenomenon of terrorist sponsorship of a state, both in terms of direct sponsorship of the government by the terrorist organization and in terms of the intertwining of state and terrorist financial means and methods.

In Sudan, bin Laden's financial network reached new heights. Important to his operations was the al Shamal Islamic Bank in Khartoum. The bank was capitalized by bin Laden when he secured a major shareholding in the new institution. There are various views as to the origin of this funding. Some say it was bin Laden's own finances; others that it was a payoff by the Saudis to stay away from their country.[12] Foreign currency accounts were set up at al Shamal for a number of companies belonging to bin Laden, including the al Hijira Construction and Development Co. Ltd, which was involved in major construction work in the Sudan. The accounts were replenished from sources in the Gulf. Then by relying on al Shamal's correspondent relationships with a variety of reputable institutions, including, in the United States, Citibank, American Express and the then Arab American Bank, in Africa, Standard Bank of South Africa, in Europe, Kommerzbank in Germany and Crédit Lyonnais in Switzerland, in Asia, the ING Bank in Indonesia – all of which had their own various correspondent relationships – bin Laden was able to move cash around the globe.

To support his operations bin Laden also set up a group of more than a hundred wealthy individuals based in the Gulf and surrounding areas who were prepared to allow their legitimate companies to be used to move money internationally for al-Qaeda.[13]

In 1996 al-Qaeda was forced out of the Sudan and back into Afghanistan. Here again we see the phenomenon of terrorist sponsorship of a state rather than visa versa – this time in connection with the Taliban rulers in Kabul. Bin Laden's correspondent banking network remained in place, but we also see al-Qaeda using alternative remittance systems – indeed al-Qaeda developed its own alternative remittance system linked to its al Taqwa set of companies.

Despite the growing attention (including attention on al-Qaeda financial operations) following the 1998 terrorist bombings in both Kenya and Tanzania, al-Qaeda continued to generate and transmit funds in support of administrative and operational activities.

At this stage al-Qaeda fund generation came from three main sources: (1) legitimate and illegitimate businesses; (2) charities; and (3) state support. Firstly bin Laden continued to engage in legitimate business. For example, a company called Wadi al Aqiq served as a holding company for various legitimate businesses, including furniture, bakery and cattle breeding. Then there was an illegitimate element, especially sales of heroin emanating out of Afghanistan.

Secondly there were charitable donations. Charities here served fund generation and transmission purposes. These organizations were originally based upon the al-Qaeda foundation, a charity established by bin Laden in the 1980s whose purpose was both to raise funds from wealthy individuals in Saudi Arabia and the Gulf, and to steer them to Islamic fighters in Afghanistan and Pakistan. After the war against the Soviets in Afghanistan ended, these charities were not dissolved but appear to have been diversified and expanded both in their fundraising and disbursement capacities. The US authorities have identified related charitable organizations in Pakistan, Afghanistan, Kuwait, the United States, Europe, Asia, and of course, Saudi Arabia.

The Saudi charitable connection emerged as the most sensitive of all, both because of the magnitude of the support for al-Qaeda goals, and also because of the relationship of the Saudi charities to the Saudi government and what the Saudi government knew – or chose not to know – about the purposes of these charitable organizations in relation to al-Qaeda and other terror groups. Given the enormous potential economic and strategic ramifications of any US–Saudi confrontation on this issue, Washington chose to tread warily. Nevertheless, in Congressional hearings in 2003 a senior official in the Bush administration described Saudi Arabia as the "epicenter" of terrorist financing.[14] The US accused the Saudi government of turning a blind eye to a number of state-sponsored charities, including the World Association for Muslim Youth and the International Islamic Relief organization. Saudi sources were believed to be funneling millions of dollars a month to al-Qaeda, though following the May 2003 terrorist attacks in Riyadh, which killed 34 people, the authorities started to act upon these sources. Certain accounts were frozen and a joint US–Saudi financial task force has been set up to deal with the financing problem. The Saudis also promised to begin curbing the unregulated charity organizations in their country. They further promised to ban cash contributions in local mosques and to remove donation boxes for charities from shopping malls, important sources of al-Qaeda cash. Still, the Americans believed that nine out of all the top ten al-Qaeda financial supporters were at this time Saudi.[15]

The assault on al-Qaeda structures in Afghanistan which began soon after 9/11 resulted in the al-Qaeda cell structure loosening further. Local cells appeared to be heavily dependent upon their own sources of funding rather than any centrally sourced funds. Many of these local groups relied on petty crime, drug trafficking, and extortion. The amount of funds they began to raise was far more limited than the large sums bin Laden was able to generate in the Gulf during the 1990s, but as these groups appeared intent upon hitting softer targets the requirements for large sums of money were lessened.[16]

The Finance War: An Interim Balance Sheet (2001–2003)

The results of the financial war against terrorism in the immediate aftermath of 9/11 are difficult to determine but were probably not particularly good. Claims were made for various successes but such claims may simply have been measuring progress in their own terms and not against a proper grasp of the scale and scope of the problem.

Much attention was paid to the success of freezing terrorist bank accounts. By the end of 2002 the US had blocked approximately $36 million in assets of the Taliban, al-Qaeda and other terrorist entities and supporters. The rest of the international community in turn blocked more than $88 million of assets. Yet, while funds continued to be frozen, the momentum in relation to al-Qaeda slowed down as relevant intelligence dried up. Terrorists in any event began taking preemptive steps. (Lashkar-e-Taiba, for example, appears to have got wind of information that its funds were to be frozen and moved monies out of its accounts in Pakistan into, inter alia, real estate.) In any event, what all this meant was dubious: the claim that over $100 million had been frozen may have been effectively irrelevant if the actual pool of terrorist funds was far, far larger.

Whatever the case, the publicity attractions of freezing were clear and its popularity as a counterterrorist tool consequently increased. So for example in September 2003 even the Palestinian Authority, whose own funds were being frozen by the Israeli government, announced a freeze on Hamas accounts. Indeed, soon after 9/11 numerous members of the United Nations set blocking orders in force against suspected accounts and funds, and over 500 accounts were soon blocked.[17] But whether these were the right accounts, or whether there were other accounts in the same names as the beneficiaries, or other accounts in other persons' or organizations' names was most uncertain.

Moving beyond freezing tactics, what is evident is that unilateralism in this aspect of the antiterror campaign was meaningless given the global and interconnected nature of the international financial system. The United States by itself could not hope to constrain the generation and movement of terrorist funds without the help of allies in both the developed and developing world. Furthermore, it was not possible to sideline international financial and political institutions in the manner such bodies were marginalized in prosecuting other aspects of the antiterror campaign.

To be sure, the international community soon got behind the finance war in a way they had never done in the political and military spheres. The United Nations certainly did not shy away from taking relevant finance steps. United Nations Security Council Resolution 1373 passed on September 28, 2001 required all states to work to prevent and suppress terrorist activities. One month later, the OECD's Financial Action Task Force began to focus more fully and specifically on terrorist financing and in quick order adopted eight special recommendations (see box 10.1) for states to adopt in relation to such financing (complementing the existing 40 recommendations and indicating that terrorist financing required special and particular measures). While these reflected measures already in place in North America and Europe, they – as with the original 40 recommendations – helped set the international standard for antiterrorist financing measures.

Of course, it was one thing to agree on generalities such as those in box 10.1; it was quite another to agree on how to implement them and against whom they should be implemented. Political and economic pressures often intervened to undercut international consensus on broad generalities. Thus, for example,

---

Box 10.1   Financial Action Task Force special recommendations

1   Take immediate steps to ratify and implement the relevant United Nations instruments.
2   Criminalize the financing of terrorism, terrorist acts and terrorist organizations.
3   Freeze and confiscate terrorist assets.
4   Report suspicious transactions linked to terrorism.
5   Provide the widest possible range of assistance to other countries' law enforcement and regulatory authorities for terrorist financing investigations.
6   Impose anti–money laundering requirements on alternative remittance systems.
7   Strengthen customer identification measures in international and domestic wire transfers.
8   Ensure that entities, in particular nonprofit organizations, cannot be misused to finance terrorism.

United Nations member states were supposed to submit names of individuals and organizations associated with al-Qaeda and the Taliban to the UN's Counter Terrorism Committee, and these names were then to be placed on a special United Nations list and subjected, inter alia, to travel bans and financial freezes. In fact, by the end of 2002 it was reported that only 84 states (about half the membership) had submitted such reports. In addition, only 372 names had been put on the list although allegedly 4,000 individuals linked to al-Qaeda had been arrested by member states of the United Nations.

FATF recommendations were also implemented in a less than consistent fashion. It was central to FATF arrangements that those countries that did not implement its recommendations were placed on a blacklist, making them subject to sanctions and other penalties by the international financial community. Shortly after 9/11, Lebanon was however removed from the blacklist arguably before proper anti–money laundering measures were introduced in that country. Egypt remained blacklisted but no sanctions were applied by FATF against it. In the broader strategic scheme of things other political realities dominated. Nor were efforts always sensitive to the realities of international competition. An important issue here was whether governments in differing jurisdictions were enforcing the "know your customer" and "suspicious transaction report" requirements fairly. In the UK it was noted with some disquiet that both Russia and South Africa obtained approval for FATF membership, placing them on a level playing field in terms of anti–money laundering efforts and regulation with the City of London. The concern was that jurisdictions with laxer controls could benefit from an unfair commercial advantage.

It was however at the national level that the main difficulties were being encountered. Thus in the US the Patriot Act "special measures" were during the period rarely employed in an antiterrorist role, partly at least due to overriding political concerns not to overly antagonize allies or important states. It can be argued that during the period Riyadh never felt the brunt of Patriot Act sanctions – this despite the general consensus in Washington as to the role of Saudi charities in the support of al-Qaeda.

At one point, the US General Accounting Office strongly criticized US government agencies for still reportedly failing to come to terms with how terrorist funds were hidden and moved within the financial system. Furthermore, the report concluded that these agencies failed to properly gather and share information and were not, despite all their efforts, preventing terrorist financial transactions. In response to such criticisms, one Justice Department official was quoted as saying that tracking terrorist financing where operations could be conducted for as little as $50,000–$70,000 was a virtually impossible task.

Implementation of antiterrorist financing measures also ran into domestic opposition in the financial community, which baulked at the erosion of confidentiality practices regarded as critical to the proper functioning of the industry. There was also a suspicion among the finance community that some of these measures were adopted without a proper appreciation of the workings of the banking systems. Banks complained that they were being forced to bear too great a burden in this fight and the demands being placed upon them were often totally unrealistic.

It was also one thing to require suspicious transaction reports from banks and financial institutions, it was another thing to invest sufficient funds in resources to analyze those reports. Backlogs in review both in the US and the UK undermined both the efficacy of the antiterrorist financing system and the confidence of the finance community in that system. There were certainly not enough staff dedicated to suspicious transaction reports in the United Kingdom, let alone in other countries. For the banking and legal systems to function properly the parties needed speedy responses from the authorities to their reports, but this was not happening at the time because these authorities were being deluged by suspicious transaction reports. In the US, for example, banks filed 274,000 suspicious transaction reports in 2002 and 74,000 in the first quarter of 2003. In the United Kingdom it was reported that in May 2003 there were nearly 60,000 suspicious activity reports that had yet to be finally dealt with. In addition, it was estimated that a further 130,000 such reports were to be submitted to the authorities during 2004.

Significantly, in the United Kingdom responsibility was placed on the reporting financial institution or business for the decision as to whether to report a transaction. The institution was then caught on the horns of a dilemma. To report such a transaction would impact upon the critical issues of client confidentiality and the efficient progress of the underlying transaction. Not to report would lead to trouble with the authorities and open the firm up to various sanctions. Institutions found themselves being forced to report defensively – that is, to report where there was the slightest doubt as to whether a particular transaction was suspicious. Reports of questionable value to antiterrorist campaigns were regularly submitted.

Instituting proper anti–money laundering procedures, including staff training and the appointment of money laundering officers, also proved not only very time-consuming, but costly and difficult. New money laundering regulations in the UK extended suspicious transaction reporting requirements to lawyers, insolvency practitioners, auditors, tax advisors, company formation agents, estate agents, casinos, and in certain circumstances dealers in high value goods. This also led to an informational deluge, which did not necessarily ease the task of discerning the dangerous transactions.

It was therefore not surprising that one of the major criticisms made by the financial community of the antiterrorist financing focus was that it did not treat financial relationships in a realistic way. For example, it was pointed out to the author by one anti–money laundering professional that while, for example, correspondent banking networks had come in for severe criticism, one only had to view the then current backlash by consumers on the UK high street to see that financial institutions had to rely upon the efforts of other institutions to speed up transactions and to avoid alienating their own clientele. Antiterrorist financing requirements clearly had both efficiency and cost implications.

In any event, not all firms could afford the technological tools required to make the necessary checks. The biggest danger was for the middle-sized firms, which were too small to have the

technology but too large to actually know all their customers.
How these increasing demands by the antiterrorist financing legislation were to be translated into workable and usable intelligence remained to be seen.

Financial intelligence appeared very difficult to secure, or at
least to translate into employable legal material, and this sometimes led to embarrassment. For example, an Islamic charity
known as Interpal had its accounts frozen in the UK in August
2003 after the US government accused it of funding Hamas. In
September, however, these accounts were unfrozen by the
Charity Commission after Washington failed to provide evidence
substantiating the claim that the organization was involved in
political or militant activities.

There were two major reasons for these general difficulties:
Firstly, as noted, terrorist financiers only need to deliver small
amounts of funds to cell groups to carry out terrorist actions. This
makes detection more difficult than in the case of drug monies.
Secondly, because as noted this is money laundering on its head
– moving money from legitimate to illegitimate purposes rather
than vice versa – legally much depends upon proving intent. As
the sources are often legal, this becomes very difficult. FATF
Guidance in April 2002 admitted that "financial institutions will
probably be unable to detect terrorist financing as such."[18] FATF
elsewhere acknowledged that, given this legal source of funds, it
was possible that "there are few, if any, indicators that would
make an individual transaction or series of transaction stand out
as linked to terrorist activities."[19] Consequently, institutions were
often reduced to profiling transactions on the basis of geography
and ethnicity.[20]

Finally, what did all this mean for the actual finance war on al-
Qaeda in the 24–36 months after 9/11? Specifically in relation to
al-Qaeda, a US Council of Foreign Relations report concluded in
2002 that al-Qaeda remained financially robust and that blocked
al-Qaeda accounts represented only a small fraction of its funds.
In the same year a UN report on al-Qaeda's finances painted an
equally gloomy picture. "A large portfolio of ostensibly legitimate
businesses continue to be maintained and managed on behalf of
Osama bin Laden and al-Qaeda by a number of as yet unidentified

intermediaries and associates across North Africa, the Middle East, Europe and Asia."[21]

A UN study leaked to the *Financial Times*[22] at the end of 2003 stated that the finance war against al-Qaeda was being undermined by continuing inadequate cooperation, legislative loopholes, and lack of political determination. Al-Qaeda businesses and charities continued to operate (including Al Taqwa related companies). The report went on to state that "Al-Qaeda, the Taliban and those associated with the network are still able to obtain, solicit, collect and transfer and distribute considerable funds." Furthermore, there remained "continuing serious weaknesses regarding the control of business activities and assets other than bank accounts." Difficulties encountered in the finance war in the period immediately after 9/11 indicated that while, one day, the war on al-Qaeda could well be won, the financial front would probably not be the front where most progress was going to be made to that end.

Notes

This chapter was commissioned especially for this collection.

1   Quoted in Hudson Morgan, "Laundry Bag," *New Republic*, Apr. 14, 2003.
2   *Terrorism Financing*, Report Prepared for the President of the Security Council, United Nations, Dec. 19, 2002, New York, Jean-Charles Brisard, JCB Consulting.
3   Ibid.
4   Home Office, Money Laundering Bulletin, July–Aug. 2003, p. 5.
5   See comments by Professor B. Ryder in *Money Laundering Monitor*, no. 25 (Oct. 2001).
6   Anne Ashwara, "Money Laundering Fight Being Lost," Times Online.
7   As at October 6, 2003 the list of noncooperative countries and territories consisted of the Cook Islands, Egypt, Guatemala, Indonesia, Myanmar, Nauru, Nigeria, the Philippines and Ukraine.
8   *Financial Action Task Force on Money Laundering*, Annual Report 2000–1, June 22, 2001, p. 16.
9   Ibid.
10 Morgan, "Laundry Bag."

11 See Walter Laqueur, *No End to War* (New York: Continuum, 2003), p. 122.

12 Gerald Posner, *Why America Slept* (New York: Random House, 2003), p. 122.

13 Ibid.

14 Douglas Farah, "US–Saudi Anti-Terror Operation Planned," at Washington Post.com, Aug. 26, 2003.

15 Posner, *Why America Slept*, p. 124.

16 "Terrorism Inc.," *Washington Post*, Nov. 21, 2003.

17 US Dept of Treasury/US Dept of Justice, "National Money Laundering Strategy," 2002.

18 Cited in "Money Laundering," Oct. 2003, p. 4.

19 See ibid.

20 Ibid.

21 Quoted in Douglas Farah, "Al Qaeda gold Moved to Sudan," *Washington Post*, Sept. 3, 2002.

22 "UN Says Lack of Co-operation is Aiding Al Qaeda," *Financial Times*, Nov. 14, 2003.

11

Intelligence and International Security after 9/11

Christopher Mackmurdo

Introduction

The imperative to prevent terrorism-related threats to international peace and security has given rise to a new intelligence role in international security affairs. In a post-9/11 world, the emergence of a potentially catastrophic terrorism/WMD threat nexus has necessitated the development of preventive security strategies at state and UN levels. Intelligence has two basic functions in facilitating prevention. The first function is strategic: as James Sutterlin has pointed out, it is "patently impossible to prevent something from happening if there is no knowledge that it might happen."[1] Prevention requires "knowing the enemy" before the enemy has actually struck. The second function is societal: prevention needs to fit with the institutions of international society, including international law and war. Intelligence has the power to legitimize post-9/11 security strategies by demonstrating threats that may require prevention, and, if necessary, making the case for the anticipatory use of force. These two strategic and societal functions of intelligence similarly combine like a double-helix to represent a new dimension to the nature of intelligence after 9/11.

The purpose of this essay is to explore intelligence's new role in international security affairs, considering the threat posed by terrorism and the functions of intelligence in combating it. To do this, I will examine how the idea of the "war on terrorism" has impacted on the concept of intelligence as a type of knowledge, a type of activity, and a type of organization.

Intelligence: Knowledge, Activity and Organization

Intelligence is often described as being a type of knowledge, a type of activity, and a type of organization.[2] As a type of knowledge, intelligence is special.[3] The kind of information intelligence represents is secret, is usually of secret things and is useful insofar that it succeeds in supporting policy goals and informing policy-making processes. As a type of activity, intelligence is a multitude of individual but intimately entwined industries. The cultivation of sources and the utilization of various methods in the collection of information (the kind of tradecraft that is commonly associated with the popular idea of spying) are complemented by a number of other activities that make up the intelligence cycle. These activities include the exploitation, analysis, assessment and dissemination of information. As a type of organization, intelligence can be understood in terms of institutions that undertake intelligence activities and produce intelligence knowledge. These institutions generate what Michael Herman has coined "intelligence power": intelligence organizations possess the "capacity to produce effects that are more advantageous than would otherwise have been the case."[4]

It is interesting to ask, in view of recent events, what intelligence power means in the twenty-first century. What are the effects that intelligence organizations have the capacity to produce that provide advantage to states acting within the contemporary security environment? The surprise terrorist attacks against New York and Washington on September 11, 2001 marked the arrival of a new kind of threat, but also an intelligence failure. The failure to predict and prevent the 9/11 attacks has been compounded by intelligence failure in Iraq. The unsuccessful accumulation of evidence of Iraqi weapons of mass destruction programs, the existence of which was indicated in intelligence assessments worldwide and used by the United States and Britain to bolster support for military action against Iraq in March 2003, has increased public cynicism and distrust of intelligence in general, and its use by politicians in particular. The issue of intelligence abuse is continuing to steer political discourse and stir public debate on both sides of the Atlantic, and featured at the heart of both the Hutton and Butler inquiries in Britain and the investigation in the United States into Iraq-related intelligence on weapons of mass destruction commissioned by President Bush in 2004. In terms of the broader play of international relations, the intelligence-fueled war in Iraq split the transatlantic alliance and challenged the unique authority of the United Nations Security Council to determine and respond to threats to peace, thereby undermining existing international order. Coalition forces are continuing to suffer casualties in Iraq years after it was announced that the major fighting was over. Against this backdrop, one would be hard-pushed to describe the effects produced by the use of intelligence as being "advantageous" for any responsible state within the international system. One might be tempted to conclude that, all things considered, the use of intelligence to drive state practice has actually led to a breakup of international consensus and a worsening of the global security situation.

But to draw such a conclusion is to misunderstand the nature of the new role of intelligence in international security affairs. In the war on terrorism, the need for states to possess the ability to investigate and obtain knowledge of the existence of threats has never been greater. The capability of states to collect and exploit, analyze and assess and disseminate intelligence in support of policy goals and to inform policy-making has never been more urgent. And the organization of intelligence at the international level has never before been a strategic requirement for the legitimate management of threats to peace and security. The problem, however, is that intelligence-driven, preemptive responses to maintain international security fit with neither self-defense nor collective security institutions, as calibrated in the UN Charter. The *imperative* of prevention and, therefore, of *necessarily* intelligence-led action to maintain international security in the face of global terrorism (as well as of other serious challenges to stability such as the proliferation of weapons of mass destruction, ethnic conflict, and international crime) is recognized by the international community, but the *logic* of prevention continues to rub the wrong way against the conventions underpinning international society.[5] Political legitimacy is not automatically afforded to preventive measures that are undertaken in anticipation of, rather than in reaction to, breaches of the peace. The new intelligence role in meeting the challenge of prevention is crucial and it is an international one; but, unlike the terrorism threat, intelligence knowledge, activity, and organization have not been internationalized.

Terrorism and Intelligence Knowledge

Knowing terrorism

Terrorism is not a new threat to international peace and security. On January 31, 1992, the UN Security Council, sitting at the level of heads of state and government, identified terrorism as a challenge to the international community and urged collective action to deal with it effectively (UN S/23500). The UN Secretary-General Boutros Boutros-Ghali responded to the Security Council's edict by publishing, five months later, *An Agenda for Peace*, in which fact-finding missions, early-warning systems and preventive deployment of armed forces were proffered as essential components of the UN's strategy to maintain peace and security in a post–Cold War world. Twelve years on, the UN's High-Level Panel on Threats, Challenges and Change outlined a strategy for meeting the challenge of prevention in a post-9/11 world. In its report *A More Secure World: Our Shared Responsibility*, published in December 2004, the High-Level Panel found that "terrorism attacks the values that lie at the heart of the Charter of the United Nations: respect for human rights; the rule of law; rules of war that protect civilians; tolerance among peoples and nations; and the peaceful resolution of conflict,"[6] and called upon states to support stronger measures to increase international cooperation to prevent the root causes of terrorism and preempt terrorist threats if and when they are judged imminent. It was in this spirit that, on March 26, 2004, the Security Council had announced the revitalization of its Counter-Terrorism Committee in Resolution 1535 and reaffirmed that "terrorism in all its forms and manifestations constitutes one of the most serious threats to peace and security." A month later, on April 28, the Security Council passed Resolution 1540 which for the first time prohibited the acquisition of weapons of mass destruction by nonstate actors.

Outside of the UN system the severity of the threat posed by terrorism has received equal recognition. The Organization of African Unity has a Convention on the prevention and combating of terrorism, as does the Organization of American Sates. The Arab League signed the Accord to Fight Terrorism in 1998 and the European Union has declared terrorism to pose one of the most serious threats to European security.[7] In July 2002, the British government published *The Strategic Defence Review: A New Chapter*, which was devoted to the new international terrorism threat. On the other side of the pond, the United States government dedicated an entire section of its September 2002 National Security Strategy to the issue of terrorism, and complemented that in February 2003 with a separate document entitled *National Strategy for Combating Terrorism*. The terrorism and weapons of mass destruction nexus has given rise to the prospect of "ultimate terrorism," terrorism that utilizes WMD.[8] The spread of nuclear, chemical, or biological materials, money and expertise from states into the hands of terrorist groups threatens the soft underbelly of the sovereign state system, and its prevention demands an international response.

It is arguable that the threat posed by terrorism is internationally acknowledged. But what is it to say that a terrorism threat to international peace and security exists? It is certainly different from saying that interstate conflict exists. According to Article 51 of the UN Charter, a state has the right to use force in self-defense "if an armed attack occurs." Under that scenario, the Security Council has the responsibility to restore peace and security once an aggressor has been determined and a breach of the peace has occurred. In other words, interstate conflict constitutes a threat to international security when damage has already been done. It is the very act of perceiving the occurrence of damage that brings into existence a threat that can be reacted against, whether in self-defense or through collective security machinery. Terrorism, on the other hand, does not mean war between states. Terrorists are not territorially fixed political entities. Terrorists do not possess any military institutions, at least as conventionally understood in terms of armies, navies and air forces. Terrorists do not rule over populations within inviolable sovereign borders. Terrorists are not members of the United Nations and do not subscribe to international law. Rather, terrorism, as the Central Intelligence Agency understands it, means "premeditated, politically motivated violence perpetrated against noncombatant targets by subnational groups or clandestine agents, usually intended to influence an audience," as contained in Section 2656f(d) of Title 22 of the US Code. To put it another way, terrorists transcend state borders, operate in secret and aim to instill fear and inflict injury by damaging targets that are incapable of defending themselves. Moreover, weapons of mass destruction could act as a force multiplier for terrorist groups who seek to cause the utmost devastation.

Considering the nature of terrorism, the conventional understanding of what constitutes a threat to international peace and security needs revision. On an ontological level, terrorism constitutes a threat because it is perceivable, rather than perceived. This means that terrorism threats exist because they are capable of being perceived, not because, like threats posed by interstate conflict, they are perceived. As such, terrorism threats exist even when states do not perceive them. Even more significantly, terrorism threats exist *because* states do not perceive them. This might sound like a strange thing to say, but there are reasons why it is useful to think of terrorism threats in this way. Firstly, operatives like those who crashed into the Twin Towers on September 11, 2001 are successful when their activities are undetected until the actual point of impact and damage occurs. The efficacy of terrorism relies, in part, on secrecy. Secondly, the point of impact might be far removed from the place where the threat originated. For instance, on 9/11, damage occurred in New York and Washington but the planning of the attacks and the operatives involved originated in a number of places around the globe, including Afghanistan, Europe, North Africa, the Middle East and across the US.[9] Thirdly, it is the recognition of the reality of a clandestine and globalized threat that gives rise to the onus for states to investigate and verify the existence of danger in order to act effectively against it.

Describing risk

The function of intelligence knowledge in the war on terrorism can be explained by conceptualizing the terrorism threat in terms of risk. Ontologically speaking, terrorism is a potentiality, as well as an actuality. Terrorism is a phenomenon that exists independently of state perception, and terrorism threats do not cease to be real when states do not happen to observe them. As I have suggested, terrorist threats exist because they are perceivable, not because they are perceived. Terrorism means the risk of damage as well as the occurrence of damage.[10] Countering terrorism means, therefore, responding to the risk of damage as well as reacting to the occurrence of damage, and because the point of impact is not necessarily the same as the point of origin, the risk presented by terrorism can appear invisible to everyday perceptions.[11] Indeed, understanding terrorism in terms of risk does not weaken or obscure the ontological integrity of terrorism as a phenomenon: to describe terrorism using the language of risk is not to claim that terrorism isn't real. As the Director-General of the UK Security Service, Eliza Manningham-Buller, told the annual conference of the confederation of British Industry on November 8, 2004: "Be under no illusion. The threat is real and here and affects us all."[12] The value of intelligence knowledge in the war on terrorism can be measured in terms of its capacity to break illusions and enable states to describe threats in a meaningful way, and respond to them effectively.

Terrorism and Intelligence Activity

Collection and exploitation

Awareness of terrorist activity prior to the materialization of terrorist attacks is achieved through the collection of information. Since successful counterterrorism means preventing the occurrence of damage, the collection of information is crucial to dealing with terrorism effectively.

Collection is the bread and butter of intelligence work. There are three main kinds of intelligence collection, each with its own types of sources and methods that are used to obtain information. Firstly, there is human intelligence (HUMINT), which describes the methods and type of information associated with the cultivation and exploitation of human sources. These sources are, typically, either informers, who possess and pass on information, or agents, who are tasked to acquire information. This is what is popularly known as espionage. Secondly, there is signals intelligence (SIGINT), a term that covers the collection of information through the interception and monitoring of communications (COMINT) and electronic emissions (ELINT). The final major collection category is imagery intelligence (IMINT), which involves the gathering of information through satellites and other image-capturing devices. The exploitation of information, sometimes called processing,[13] refers to the transformation of raw information into intelligence that is capable of being analyzed, assessed and disseminated. In order to make sense of the vast amount of information that is collected, information needs to be sifted. This process separates what one might describe as the wheat from the chaff, and is essential to the flagging and following up of information. Indeed, it is arguable that ineffective exploitation of information prevented the US intelligence community from piecing together the 9/11 terrorism plot with segments of information that it had already collected.[14]

The role played by the collection and exploitation of information in the war on terrorism is a vital one. Hunting terrorists is, however, a difficult task.[15] Terrorists are not easy intelligence targets. Terrorists, unlike troop movements and missile silos, are not readily identifiable from space. Terrorists who are well versed in operational security procedures are not likely to discuss plans over the telephone. The penetration of terrorist groups is also tricky and highly dangerous to attempt. The "subnational groups and clandestine agents" that carry out terrorism operate in ways that make the job of approaching and cultivating insiders a challenge that is not easily met. However, the acknowledgement of the need to strengthen collection capabilities, especially human intelligence, in the face of terrorism has been made by the leading Western intelligence services, including the CIA. The so-called "Deutch rules," for instance, which were instituted in 1995 by the then Director of Central Intelligence, John Deutch, to prohibit the recruitment of any HUMINT asset who was associated with serious crime and other undesirable activities, were effectively scrapped in 2001. These rules have been highly criticized for limiting the ability of CIA operatives to penetrate terrorism groups, an intelligence role that is vital to the waging of a war on terror.[16]

Analysis and assessment

Intelligence analysis is the process of the intelligence cycle that turns information that has been collected and exploited into intelligence that is relevant to the requirements of policy. Intelligence assessment is understood here to mean the process by which judgments are made on the basis of intelligence analysis, and the product that is available to intelligence customers for the purposes of supporting policy goals and informing policy-making.

The judgments expressed in intelligence assessments constitute an important part of modern political decision-making processes.[17] These judgments have in the recent past led to the determination of threats that were deemed, at the political level, to necessitate military responses. Notwithstanding then US Secretary of State Colin Powell's presentation "Iraq: Failing to Disarm" before the UN Security Council on February 5, 2003, the most obvious example of such an assessment is the British document *Iraq's Weapons of Mass Destruction: The Assessment of the British Government*, published on September 24, 2002, which was used to assist in justifying the use of force by Britain against Iraq in March 2003. It is arguable that this assessment had little, if anything, to do with terrorism, but rather was an account of Saddam Hussein's noncompliance with UN Security Council resolutions regarding WMD proliferation. However, it is unquestionable that the events of 9/11 have shaped a global security landscape within which the proliferation of weapons of mass destruction constitutes an unacceptable risk to the international community, considering the existence of a type of determined and undeterrable actor intent on inflicting the gravest possible damage. Within this landscape, countering terrorism and nipping the prospect of "superterrorism" in the bud means preventing the spread of WMD. Many also argue that the British dossier was not an intelligence assessment at all but, rather, a public relations exercise.[18] This, in a way, is true: the information contained in the dossier was intended to be communicated to the public for the purposes of evidencing a particular line of argument and persuading an audience to view an issue in a certain way. Again, however, it is unquestionable, too, that the dossier drew on genuine and current intelligence analysis, that the Joint Intelligence Committee approved the contents of the document, and that the JIC chairman, John Scarlett, claimed to have "owned" the document throughout the time of its compilation, development and release.[19]

Whatever view one has of the British dossier, its existence and the part it played highlight the controversial relationship between intelligence and evidence. The current edition of the *Concise Oxford English Dictionary* defines "evidence" as "information indicating whether a belief or proposition is true or valid." Can this definition be used to successfully describe intelligence? The answer to this question is yes, and no. Intelligence can certainly be described in terms of information, as has been discussed above: intelligence knowledge is an essential part of intelligence power. Intelligence can also be understood as something that indicates whether a belief or proposition is true or valid: intelligence activity can be said to be about providing "truth to power," and supplying policy-makers with the facts they need to make rational decisions. However, the kinds of information and the kinds of propositions whose veracity intelligence seeks to indicate are special, insofar that they are secret, and usually relate to secret things. Unlike evidence information, intelligence information is not supposed to be "used to establish facts in a legal investigation or admissible as testimony in a law court." Intelligence knowledge and intelligence activity are devoted to serving purposes that are sometimes inconsistent with the procedures and purposes of courtrooms. Moreover, intelligence information is collected and processed in such a way that the indications it provides are very rarely clear-cut or of the quality required by the judicial system.

However, in the face of global terrorism, the burden has been imposed on intelligence of providing evidence of threats in order to satisfy public interest and the demands of due process.[20] In some cases, terrorist plots have been disrupted and terrorist suspects have been arrested, charged and brought before the courts.[21] In other cases, the requirement to prove the existence of a threat stretched intelligence to breaking point, and led to a situation in the run-up to the Iraq War where "more weight was placed on the intelligence than it could bear."[22] In January 2005, the UK Home Secretary Charles Clark refused to lift the ban on the use of information gleaned from intercepts because "it isn't always possible to bring charges given the need to protect highly sensitive sources and techniques."[23] The demand on intelligence to provide evidence information relates to the need of governments to be capable of being seen to resort to the preemptive use of force, if judged necessary, in a politically legitimate and law-abiding way. The emergence of terrorism and WMD proliferation as serious threats to international peace and security affects the way in which the rules governing the use of force in the international system are understood and applied in two key ways.[24] Firstly, states, under international law, have the peremptory right to defend themselves from harm. The problem, which has been mentioned above, is that the right to self-defense, as currently codified in Article 51 of the UN Charter, enables states to use force "if an armed attack occurs." This provision afforded by Article 51 is not in line with the determination of terrorism as a threat to international peace and security that requires a proactive and preventive response.[25] States' right to self-defense in the face of terrorism means, rather, the ability to use force, if deemed necessary, in response to threats prior to their materialization. The problem with this reconceptualization of the right to self-defense, however, relates to the condition of necessity. Ever since the *Caroline* case in 1837, when the British destroyed an American ship, the *Caroline*, to curtail raids into Canadian territory, there has had to exist "a necessity of self-defence, instant, overwhelming, leaving no choice of means, and no moment for deliberation."[26] In the war on terrorism, the fulfillment of these conditions is not met by the public manifestation of damage; it is met by assessing the necessity of military responses in the management of risk identified through the collection and analysis of information.

Secondly, the declaration by the UN Security Council of terrorism as a threat to international peace and security has not only affected the right to self-defense, it has also impaired the ability of the UN Security Council to carry out its responsibilities under international law. Collective security machinery is not calibrated to assess intelligence of clandestine activities; as such, the Security Council is incapable of determining and responding to clandestine activities, such as terrorism and WMD, that the Security Council itself has judged to constitute serious threats to peace. The resulting situation is that states have little choice but to bypass UN machinery and respond to current threats outside of the collective security framework. This has placed further pressure on intelligence analysis and assessment to support policy goals, inform policy-making, and evidence policy decisions in the public domain.

Dissemination and consumption

If the determination and evidencing of clandestine threats require the analysis and assessment of intelligence, who needs to know intelligence in order that these threats are responded against effectively and legitimately? Intelligence dissemination is the stage of the intelligence cycle that refers to the distribution of intelligence to customers and other producers. The consumption of intelligence is, generally and crudely speaking, the point at which intelligence assessments are received by policy-makers and incorporated, or otherwise (depending on the views of the policy-makers), into decision-making processes. In the face of clandestine and transnational threats, and considering the imperative of prevention, intelligence sharing between producers has increased and the dissemination of intelligence has been widened to include a greater variety of customers.

Cooperation in the field of intelligence analysis and assessment has led to greater information sharing between different intelligence producers.[27] This increased cooperation has been necessary in light of the nature of the threat posed by international terrorism. Firstly, terrorism represents a transnational problem. Understanding the terrorism phenomenon in terms of risk is useful in this regard: the point of impact is not necessarily the same as the point of origin. Therefore, in order for an individual state to make a meaningful assessment of its security situation it needs to process information pertaining to individuals and events existing in far-off places at any given time. No single state has the power to collect and exploit this type and volume of information; intelligence sharing between states has become essential even from the perspective of the most powerful intelligence producers, such as the US. In addition to intelligence sharing, collaboration between intelligence services is growing in the field of covert counterterrorist action to monitor, disrupt and foil terrorist plots, arrest terrorist suspects and degrade terrorists' capabilities.[28] The dissemination of intelligence information between intelligence producers is a crucial element of the war on international terrorism. Intelligence sharing encourages competitive analysis of global issues, seeks to ensure that judgments are based on the broadest possible range of available information, and makes it more likely that policy-makers receive accurate and reliable threat-assessments.[29] Intelligence is also required to track down and target terrorist networks that ignore national borders, span the globe and are intent on acquiring the capability to disrupt the international economic and political systems on which the market state depends.[30]

The issue of evidence raises other matters relating to intelligence dissemination and consumption. Perhaps the most controversial and problematic area of concern covers intelligence's role in public affairs. Is there a need for members of the public to be, in certain situations, intelligence customers? Should intelligence services involve themselves in public relations? Should concerns relating to public consumption ever figure in the assessment and dissemination processes of the intelligence cycle? These are questions that may sound odd considering the nature of the intelligence business, but they have occupied a central place in recent debates on the use of intelligence in democratic political systems, especially when intelligence is used as evidence to justify the declaration and waging of war.[31] The British dossier on Iraq's WMD opened a can of worms that British intelligence services are attempting to solder shut.[32] It is clear that the Joint Intelligence Committee and other constituent members of the British intelligence community grimace at the prospect of another Iraq dossier-type document being released in the future. However, considering the nature of the world, and pressing cases such as Iran and North Korea, intelligence will be used to justify the use of force some time in the future. It is important, therefore, that the public's right to engage in policy debates is protected, and this might mean the dissemination of intelligence assessments into the public domain. Working out how to strike the balance between the operational requirements of intelligence services and the rights of citizens in democracies to engage in intelligence-driven policy debates is a challenge that has yet to be met.

The war on terrorism has necessitated intelligence sharing between producers, but it has also necessitated the dissemination of intelligence to a wider range of decision-making bodies. In the field of international security, the decision-making body that requires intelligence (or, in intelligence parlance, has "a need to know") is the UN Security Council. The Security Council is the only political body under international law capable of authorizing the use of force in the international system. It is responsible for responding to threats to international peace and security; it is also responsible for determining them. It is simply the case that in order for the Security Council to function properly, its members must be able to make determinations based on information as well as on manifestations of damage. This is essential to meeting the requirements that the UN itself has laid down for the proactive management of new security challenges. Although the decision to invade Iraq was a political one,[33] the need to recognize and account for the role of intelligence in political decision-making processes at the international level is essential if the Security Council is to remain relevant and effective in the twenty-first century. Legitimizing intelligence-driven prevention means moving away from thinking about counterterrorism in terms of the right to self-defense, to thinking about prevention as a mechanism of collective security machinery.

In terms of intelligence dissemination and consumption, this might mean that the UN Secretary-General needs to be considered as an intelligence customer. However, at the present time, the reality is that intelligence is not shared with or within the UN even in exceptional circumstances. The most obvious case in point is the alleged withholding of information by the CIA during UN weapons inspections in Iraq in late 2002 and early 2003.[34] But the problem is wider than just an operational one; it is an organizational and cultural one. Despite its strategic intelligence requirement, the UN continues to have problems with intelligence because it equates intelligence with espionage instead of decision-making support. This understanding of intelligence is incompatible with the UN's role as a fair, independent and transparent broker. States have major problems sharing intelligence with the UN because the UN is not trusted as a place where secrets can be told, let alone kept; any information provider risks compromising assets, operations, sources and methods, as well as giving political and strategic leverage to competitors by sharing sensitive information. The allegation that British intelligence bugged UN Secretary-General Kofi Annan's office in the run-up to the Iraq invasion reinforces the impression that the UN remains an intelligence target rather than an intelligence customer or partner.[35]

Terrorism and Intelligence Organization

It is intelligence organizations that produce intelligence knowledge and undertake intelligence activities. In Britain, the three intelligence services are the Secret Intelligence Service (SIS or MI6), the Government Communications Headquarters (GCHQ), and the Security Service (MI5). Other members of the intelligence community include the Defense Intelligence Staff (DIS) and the Joint Intelligence Committee (JIC), with its supporting Assessments Staff located in the Cabinet Office. In the US, the intelligence community consists of the Central Intelligence Agency (CIA), the National Security Agency (NSA), the Defense Intelligence Agency (DIA), the National Geospatial-Intelligence Agency (NGA), the National Reconnaissance Office (NRO), the Federal Bureau of Investigation (FBI), and the Department of Homeland Security (DHS), with the State Department's Bureau of Intelligence and Research (INR) producing intelligence affecting US foreign policy, and the National Security Council (NSC) acting as the major intelligence/policy interface. The US military, coastguard, and departments of Energy and the Treasury each have intelligence components. Beyond Britain and the US, intelligence organizations constitute a fundamental and important part of governmental machinery in states around the world, with perhaps Israel, Germany, Canada, and Australia possessing the most developed intelligence apparatus outside of the remaining UN Security Council permanent members, China, Russia, and France.

The demands placed on intelligence knowledge and activities today are leading to significant organizational reform. The burden placed on intelligence organizations to produce knowledge of terrorist threats through the collection, exploitation, analysis, assessment and dissemination of information in support of policy goals, policy-making and policy evidencing is changing the way intelligence organizations are functioning. As mentioned above, intelligence cooperation is increasing. In Britain, the creation in June 2003 of the Joint Terrorism Analysis Centre (JTAC) has brought together 11 government departments and agencies to analyse, assess and disseminate terrorism-related intelligence. The Butler review of intelligence on weapons of mass destruction did not recommend any drastic changes to British intelligence machinery, but does emphasize the need to strengthen the analytical capabilities of the intelligence community.

In the US, however, significant intelligence reform is on the cards. The 9/11 Commission report has recommended an over-haul of the US intelligence community. Perhaps the most divisive issue at present is the prospect of a National Intelligence Director (NID) to oversee the entire US intelligence effort. Other innovations proposed by the 9/11 Commission include the establishment of National Intelligence Centres focusing on individual issues such as WMD proliferation, the Middle East, and international crime. On August 27 2004, US President George W. Bush passed Executive Order 13354 to establish a National Counterterrorism Center (NCTC) which brings together all terrorism-related intelligence analysis and builds upon the Terrorist Threat Integration Center (TTIC), which was created in 2003 to close the seam between the Department of Homeland Security, the Pentagon, the FBI's Counterterrorism Division, and the CIA's Counterterrorist Center. In both Britain and the US, the need for closer cooperation and an emphasis on analysis in the face of terrorism are forging new intelligence practices and institutions.

But it is not just at the national level that new intelligence practices are occurring. Bilateral and multilateral intelligence networks are emerging stronger, tighter and busier. The US–UK Joint Contact Group reinforces the already intimate Anglo-American intelligence relationship, facilitates a greater exchange of the information, and complements the national joint terrorism analysis centers that have formed in both countries. The Berne Club, which consists of 19 intelligence organizations drawn from

17 European states, has been revitalized after 9/11. In 2001, the Berne Club created a new organization called the Counterterrorist Group (CTG), which brings the United States, Norway, and Switzerland into the European security and intelligence fold, fostering a sense of community and developing trust, confidence and cooperative working relationships between intelligence organizations within the broader transatlantic alliance.[36]

At the overall international level, however, trust, confidence and cooperative working relationships are distinctly lacking. There is a complete absence of intelligence organization where, arguably, it matters most. Any amount of tinkering with national intelligence machineries will not resolve the problematic relationship between intelligence and *jus ad bellum*, or meet the demand to combat terrorism and related threats through collective security machinery.

The UN has never had an effective intelligence capability, despite some efforts to develop something like one. When in office as UN Secretary-General in the early 1990s, Javier Pérez de Cuéllar established the Office for Research and the Collection of Information (ORCI) to act in support of preventive diplomacy and to alert the Office of the Secretary-General about impending crises. When Boutros Boutros-Ghali entered office in 1992, he dissolved ORCI and handed over its functions to the Department for Political Affairs (DPA). In 1993 he created the UN Situation Center, which had its own information and research division staffed by seconded national intelligence officers. This division was shut down in the late 1990s when states stopped providing staff. Although the Situation Center still disseminates political, military, and humanitarian assessments to troop-contributing countries and others involved in peacekeeping, it has no strategic analysis function.[37] When Kofi Annan came to office, the idea of a UN Information and Strategic Analysis Secretariat (ISAS) was floated and seriously considered, but its establishment was thwarted by the Group of 77 (developing countries) in the General Assembly for fear that it would spy and intrude on their internal affairs. By 2004, the UN was no closer to achieving an intelligence assessment capability despite the growing need for the international community to work together to prevent crises from occurring. However, the UN High-Level Panel on Threats, Challenges and Change did call for "better information and analysis" of threats posed by interstate conflict and conflict within states, and argued:

> Prevention requires early warning and analysis that is based on objective and impartial research. Although the United Nations has some early-warning and analysis capacity scattered among different agencies and departments, the Secretary-General has not been able to establish any properly-resourced unit able to integrate inputs from these offices into early-warning reports and strategy options for purposes of decision-making. The best option for creating a coherent capacity for developing strategic options is to strengthen the Office of the Secretary-General through the creation of a Deputy Secretary-General for Peace and Security.[38]

The Deputy Secretary-General for Peace and Security would, the Panel goes on to say in its report, "integrate inputs from the various departments and agencies and prepare early-warning reports and strategy options for decision by the Secretary-General." Time will tell whether states will be prepared to invest in such an institutional capability at the UN level, or adhere to the normal practice of "intelligence-sharing, where possible."[39]

Conclusion

The imperative to prevent terrorism has given intelligence a new role in international security affairs. The capability of states to investigate and verify the existence of threats is vital to the prevention of terrorism attacks. Intelligence activities are crucial to disrupting terrorist plots, degrading terrorists' capabilities, arresting and charging terrorist suspects, supporting policy goals, and informing both policy-making and public debate. And the way intelligence is organized affects how intelligence activities are performed and intelligence knowledge acquired and applied. However, although terrorism has internationalized, intelligence power has not, and this has rendered the facilitation of preventive security strategies problematic.

Notes

This chapter was commissioned especially for this collection.

1   J. Sutterlin, *The United Nations and the Maintenance of International Peace and Security: A Challenge to be Met* (Westport: Greenwood Press, 1995).
2   S. Kent, *Strategic Intelligence for American World Policy* (Princeton: Princeton University Press, 1949).
3   M. Herman, *Intelligence Power in Peace and War* (Cambridge: Cambridge University Press, 1996).
4   Lawrence Freedman, cited in ibid., p. 2.
5   James Gow, "A Revolution in International Affairs," *Security Dialogue*, 31.3 (2000): 293–306.
6   UN High-Level Panel on Threats, Challenges and Change, *A More Secure World: Our Shared Responsibility*, 1 Dec. 2004, p. 48; text at www.un.org/secureworld/.
7   European Union Institute for Strategic Studies, *A Secure Europe in a Better World: European Security Strategy*, Dec. 2003; text at www.iss-eu.org/solana/solanae.pdf.
8   Jessica Stern, *The Ultimate Terrorists* (Cambridge: Harvard University Press, 1999).
9   National Commission on Terrorist Attacks upon the United States (also known as the 9-11 Commission), *The 9-11 Commission Report*, July 22, 2004; text at www.9-11commission.gov/.
10 Yee-Kuang Heng, "Unravelling the 'War' on Terrorism: A Risk-Management Exercise in War Clothing?" *Security Dialogue*, 33.2 (2002): 227–42.
11 B. Adam, Ulrich Beck, and J. van Loon, *The Risk Society and Beyond* (London: Sage, 2000).
12 Eliza Manningham-Buller, "Broadening the Business Security Agenda," speech at the CBI annual conference, Birmingham, Nov. 8, 2004; text at www.mi5.gov.uk/output/Page259.html.
13 M. M. Lowenthal, *Intelligence: From Secrets to Policy* (Washington DC: CQ Press, 2003).
14 National Commission on Terrorist Attacks upon the United States, *The 9-11 Commission Report*.

15 C. Cogan, "Hunters Not Gatherers: Intelligence in the Twenty-First Century," *Intelligence and National Security*, 19.2 (2004): 304–21.
16 Lowenthal, *Intelligence*.
17 W. G. Runciman, "What We Now Know," in Runciman (ed.), *Hutton and Butler: Lifting the Lid on the Workings of Power* (Oxford: Oxford University Press, 2004).
18 J. Morrison, interviewed on *The Today Programme*, BBC Radio 4, Oct. 28, 2004; see also M. Tempest, "Blair 'used intelligence as PR tool,'" *Guardian*, Oct. 28, 2004.
19 Lord Hutton, *Report of the Inquiry into the Circumstances Surrounding the Death of David Kelly C.M.G*, Jan. 28, 2004, text at www.the-hutton-inquiry.org.uk/content/report/index.htm; Lord Butler, *Review of Intelligence on Weapons of Mass Destruction: Report of a Committee of Privy Counsellors*, July 14, 2004, text at www.direct.gov.uk/assetRoot/04/01/46/86/04014686.pdf.
20 P. Hennessy, "The Lightning Flash on the Road to Baghdad: Issues of Evidence," in Runciman, *Hutton and Butler*.
21 Manningham-Buller, "Broadening the Business Security Agenda."
22 Lord Butler, *Review of Intelligence on Weapons of Mass Destruction*.
23 A. Travis and R. Norton-Taylor, "Ban Stays on Court Use of Phone Tapping," *Guardian*, Jan. 27, 2005.
24 Gow, "A Revolution in International Affairs."
25 Ibid.
26 M. N. Shaw, *International Law* (Cambridge: Cambridge University Press, 1997).
27 R. J. Aldrich, "Transatlantic Intelligence and Security Cooperation," *International Affairs*, 80.4 (2004): 731–53.
28 Manningham-Buller, "Broadening the Business Security Agenda;" Lord Butler, *Review of Intelligence on Weapons of Mass Destruction*.
29 Lowenthal, *Intelligence*.
30 G. F. Treverton, *Reshaping National Intelligence for an Age of Information* (Cambridge: Cambridge University Press, 2003).
31 R. Wilson, "Discussion," in Runciman, *Hutton and Butler*.
32 P. Wintour, "MI6 Anger over War Intelligence," *Guardian*, Apr. 7, 2004.
33 Lawrence Freedman, "War in Iraq: Selling the Threat," *Survival*, 46.2 (2004): 7–50.
34 Hans Blix, *Disarming Iraq* (London: Pantheon, 2004).

35 Christopher Mackmurdo, "Getting Facts," *The World Today*, 60.8–9 (2004): 22–5.
36 Aldrich, "Transatlantic Intelligence and Security Cooperation."
37 Mackmurdo, "Getting Facts."
38 UN High-Level Panel, *A More Secure World*, p. 37.
39 Ibid., pp. 114, 49.

12

Globalization and the War against Terrorism

Lawrence Freedman

"Globalization" was the buzz word of the 1990s; to be succeeded by "terrorism" in the 2000s. Both words suggest grand narratives of fundamental change at the macro level. There are a number of reasons to be nervous about this development. Terrorism, or antiterrorism, may come to define this era in the way that communism/anticommunism defined the Cold War period: meanwhile, talk about a "War on Terrorism" distracts attention from the political character of the situation we face. By the political character I do not simply mean the "causes," such as poverty or disaffection or the fear of modernization, that are used to explain why people adopt terrorist methods. The point is that it is not helpful to present the issue as a global struggle between those who want to engage in the mass murder of civilians and those who do not. Instead the struggle should be recognized as being with a particular political philosophy, which is inclined to violence against civilian targets as a tactic.

The impact of this ideological struggle is not that it comes as a surprise – the roots of Islamic militancy run deep – but that it seems so out of keeping with the expectations of a better world generated during the enthusiasm for globalization in the 1990s. After the end of the Cold War, discussions on the future of international politics verged on the euphoric. Instead of great power conflicts that had led to two world wars and the Cold War, we were moving to a much happier plane where great powers were friends with each other and worked together on peace and security. A new world order was in the making. The old disputes were being consigned to memory, liberal capitalism was triumphant, human rights were to the fore, the economy was booming, and extraordinary technological power was becoming available to everybody. Former trouble spots were coming to be known as emerging economies, and as they emerged their stock markets seemed to do very well. Indeed, everything seemed just fine and dandy.

Yet over this period a counternarrative developed which basically argued that while this may be all very well for the advanced industrial world, this "progress" was coming at the expense of the poor and exploited regions. The gap between rich and poor was widening and the environment was being ruined for future generations. Meanwhile vicious conflicts were taking place which were being ignored. Precisely because of the absence of great power confrontation and the consequent decline of the old strategic imperatives, there was no pressing reason to get involved in these conflicts.

This is not to say that states did not get involved, but if they did so it was a matter of choice and not necessity. The great challenges of the 1990s in terms of foreign policy seemed to be working out what ought to be done about the problems in the Balkans or in Africa. The constant issue was that of humanitarian intervention. It raised the question of the changing character of the state system. In a previous world dominated by a few great powers, sovereignty was the ultimate value and any suggestion of interference in the internal affairs of other states posed a challenge to that value. This value did not seem so precious in a world of numerous states, some 190, many of which were unable to fend for themselves however hard they tried. They suffered from social cleavages, economic failure, feeble political institutions, and so were at risk of being broken by internal conflict. The value of noninterference was regularly challenged, often in the name of human or minority rights.

This challenge began gingerly, first with the Kurds in Northern Iraq, followed by Croatia and then Bosnia. It was at first very tentative and uncertain, attempting to mask the intervention by casting it in the mold of traditional peacekeeping. But then Srebrenica underlined the dangers of caution. By the time that Kosovo was rocked by violence and refugee flows in 1998 there was a greater readiness to interfere in the internal affairs of other countries and use force, evident in NATO's air campaign the next year. A slightly different pattern was followed in Africa. There was a boldness with regard to Somalia, which seemed to go wrong, then followed by a lack of a response in Rwanda. Here it is estimated that 800,000 persons died (this is one where the margin of error seems to be in the hundreds of thousands of lives). Every time concern developed about a crisis in a Third World country a choice arose for Western countries about whether or not to get involved. Life could go on if they did not respond, but the neglect tweaked at the conscience if they did not. While in the Balkans it would be hard to say that vital interests were involved, here there were knock-on effects, in terms of population movements and some economic dislocation that added urgency to the discussion.

That debate went back and forth throughout the 1990s. I suspect that it is the constant debate of our time and will not go away. Today, it influences the approach to Afghanistan and Iraq, although the strategic stakes are higher in these two countries, and will lead us to worry about other countries in the future. Western involvement was by no means always welcomed or straightforward. It could smack of colonialism on the one hand, or moral indifference on the other. The large moral and strategic issues were handled on a case-by-case basis, as often as not, ineffectually. These interventions were often controversial. It is, however, worth noting that by and large they contradict the view, so central to al-Qaeda's propaganda, that these come down to the West versus the Muslim world. This just does not make sense. The West intervened in the Balkans on behalf of the Muslims, not the Serbs who were presented as the "bad guys." In the one case where intervention could be presented as anti-Muslim this was without it being realized. Indonesian oppression of East Timor was, quite understandably, the Great Left cause for many a year. Very few people thought of this in terms of a Muslim–

Catholic conflict but clearly, from certain perspectives, that is exactly how it did appear. Even in the Middle East, with the Arab–Israeli conflict, it is really only recently, with its aggravation after the failure of the 2000 Camp David Summit, that it has been seen as being central to international conflict. For much of the 1990s the Arab–Israeli problem was seen as difficult, but in the process of being sorted out. Nor was it an Islamic issue because the Palestinians, though largely a Muslim people, had a secular leadership.

The dominant critiques of Western policy during the 1990s were directed at globalization rather than intervention. The anti-globalization rhetoric was about the development of forms of economic power, and particularly the "giddy" sensation resulting from the unleashing of American capitalism, and capitalism worldwide, after some pretty tired times. With the burdens of the Cold War taken away, and information technology having an apparently transformational effect, impressive rates of economic growth were achieved and these were felt in a number of areas that had previously suffered under the stultifying effects of state socialism. A lot of the antiglobalization protest was muddled as it was inherently protectionist. By opposing free trade it was often opposing the best available means for addressing the problems of poorer nations. It remains the case that countries that have come out of poverty successfully (of which China is the most prominent example) have done so by taking full advantage of free trade and inward investment. Nonetheless, the need to pay attention to the adverse effects of trading with countries and peoples unable to stand up for their own interests against the power of multinationals, bound up with a keen sense of continuing levels of injustice and inequality, encouraged a sustained critique of Western policies from the left. Only the absence of such a critique would have been surprising. The problem was not what was found objectionable but the quality of the diagnosis and the consequent prognosis, which promised to make these problems worse rather than better. A serious problem with this critique is that it focused on the selfishness of Western countries and so did not draw attention to their own potential vulnerabilities in the developing international situation. In this sense there was a common thread tying both the impulse to humanitarian intervention and the critique of globalization together – an internationalist appeal to core values to alleviate wrongs being done to others. These were appeals to make a choice and to rise above narrow self-interest in external affairs. Their opponents argued that narrow self-interest was just fine. It was narrow self-interest that kept the wheels of the international economy turning and discouraged states from meddling in affairs that were none of their business and which they rarely understood.

The attacks of 9/11 challenged this debate because it removed the element of choice – at least for the United States. One of the problems is that Europeans still considered themselves operating in a realm of choice, while the Americans operated in a realm of necessity. Contemplation of 9/11 unavoidably reintroduced a strategic dimension back into the contemporary discourse on security. It suggested that the quality of intervention made a difference. Sins of omission or commission could come to haunt you. This was the line taken by the commentator Thomas Friedman (no relation) – you may ignore the Third World, but the Third World won't ignore you.

This shift can be demonstrated by considering the rather traditional conservative position with which the Bush administration came to power in 2001. Condoleezza Rice wrote a famous article in the January–February 2000 issue of the journal *Foreign Affairs*, describing the foreign policy philosophy of the Bush campaign. This was hardly an activist, interventionist, internationalist manifesto. The argument with regard to the "wars of choice" was that discretion should be exercised, by and large, to stay out. These conflicts were not judged to be as problematic as often presented and therefore did not require emergency interventions. Even Saddam Hussein, even Iraq, could be deterred. Armed forces have to be used carefully. If anything topped the agenda of the Bush administration, it was going to be China – in the very traditional concept of an ascending great power coming to challenge the primacy of the United States. The first major foreign policy squabble of the Bush administration was with China over a reconnaissance aircraft in April 2001. That all seems a long time ago. Tensions between the two have eased (although

Taiwan is not a settled issue) and relations are at least correct. The other big debate was over missile defense, over which there was an enormous fuss. With the death of the Anti-Ballistic Missile (ABM) Treaty would come massive instability. This issue evaporated very quickly when President Vladimir Putin said, quite sensibly, this program is a mistake but it does not really matter. As the main problem with missile defense (which is never going to be able to defend against much) was that it might upset Russia, Putin's decision not to be upset defused the controversy.

It could be argued that one of the achievements of the Bush administration, or at least of this period of international politics, is that great power conflict no longer figures as our dominant worry. The idea that we now have a generation that does not fear world war in the way that previous generations would have done is an enormous plus. As everyone goes about getting gloomy about the international scene, this is an extraordinarily positive element within the international situation. If there was a concern about the Bush administration when it came to power, it was largely its reluctance to recognize the end of great power conflict. Actually it has done the right things in that regard by reinforcing relations with Russia and with China. It is curious to recall that during the Cold War period talk of human rights in the East was often deemed to be extraordinarily dangerous and provocative. Reagan, the last American president to be barracked by the British left, was challenged because he was demanding change in the Soviet Union. Now the criticism is of hypocrisy, by cozying up to the Chinese and Russians, of ignoring human rights abuses in these countries. This is also an important debate. My point is only that it is quite interesting that those issues which dominated the lives of my parents and grandparents, in a way that was less personally challenging, are now strikingly absent, even as we have become inclined to think darkly about the future of the international system.

So the Bush administration came in with a very traditional foreign policy agenda, started to pursue it, but it did not get very far because 9/11 intervened. This was not an administration that would have expected to have troops in Afghanistan or even Iraq, and certainly not in the sundry other parts of the world where it now finds itself supporting a variety of regimes in the name of antiterrorism. This is not an administration that had any time for peacekeeping or nation-building, which was described as being for "sissies," the sort of thing that Europeans did but not the more manly Americans. That attitude can now be seen to be having its effect in terms of the poor preparation of the Americans for the role that they are now trying to play in Iraq. This sort of operation had not been addressed as a priority in Army doctrine and training.

All of this reflects the enormous difference 9/11 made to American thinking. It moved them into a readiness to engage in war as a matter of strategic necessity rather than moral choice. This matters because of American power. The Americans are the strongest power in the world. There is nothing much they can do about that: when they do not do anything or impede other people's actions, as with Rwanda, that's shameful; when they do things, that can also be shameful, as with Iraq. That is the problem of being a great power. You cannot expect to be loved. Nor were the British when they were a great power. In the days of empire, sins of omission and commission were also committed. The issue of American power therefore is always going to be with us. What made the difference with 9/11 was that the Americans felt that they were the victims of another entity's power. It was not that they declared a war on terrorism: terrorists had declared a war on the US.

How does globalization fit into this? Well, terrorism appeared as part of the underside of globalization. It was already becoming apparent that the consequence of the openness in the international system, economically as much as politically, was taking certain things out of state control. The result of globalization was the reduced power of states, the movement of capital and people around the world as governments opened up their borders. This created new opportunities for those who wished to inflict harm on the established order. It was evident with forms of trafficking, crime and drugs that there were advantages for well-organized groups whose main aim seemed to be to make a lot of money out of human misery.

The attacks indicated the possibilities, which had been there for some time, in terms of causing mass casualties. This was a twenty-first century event, but it was not the first attempt. The attempt had been made on the World Trade Center in 1993. All sorts of efforts were made during the 1990s to cause mass casualty terrorism, normally involving large buildings or airliners. The vulnerability of airliners goes back to the 1960s when the Palestinian Liberation Organization started to use them for terrorist purposes. By and large, until 9/11 the maximum levels of casualties caused were more or less equivalent to planeloads of people. As often as not, with hostage situations or attacks on buildings, mass casualties were not even the objective. The aim was to use threats to try to extract concessions from governments in pursuit of generally understood political objectives.

On September 11, 2001 our advanced technologies and our vulnerabilities were combined to create mass destruction using the oldest weapon of all – the knife. This made it fearful, as did the lack of clarity of purpose. What was this for? The attack was not actually claimed, although Osama bin Laden did not make a great effort to deny it. This lack of political demands directly connected with the attack encourages conspiracy theories about who was really behind it. By contrast, the linkage between political objectives and acts of terrorism was one of the features of the 1960s and 1970s. There is a nihilistic aspect to a preoccupation only with the levels of death and destruction that can be inflicted rather than the political objectives that might be promoted.

One consequence of 9/11, again challenging many of the ideas of how globalization had turned over the world to the capitalists, was the reaffirmation of the state. The state came back into fashion on the very day of 9/11 when the heroes were public service workers – the fireman, policemen and ambulance men. The basic welfare, emergency functions of the state became paramount. Also back to the fore was the question of the rights of citizens against the state. This became an issue in terms of civil liberties and the military role of the state, that is, its basic responsibility in terms of protecting its own citizens. In the name of "Homeland Security" controls came to be demanded on aspects of life people did not really expect to be controlled in quite that way. This is very apparent to anyone who tries to travel through airports and suddenly is seized by panic as holes in socks have to be revealed as shoes are removed in the name of security.

Mass casualty, nihilistic terrorism is extremely difficult to engage with politically. Terrorism is a tactic more than a strategy. It can also be argued that it is unacceptable as a tactic because of what it reveals in its adoption about the social theory and morality of the perpetrators. It defines them as reactionary against our concepts of progress and civilization. The disregard for innocent, civilian life is the other side of the coin to humanitarian intervention. The reasons for the discretionary interventions of the 1990s were to protect vulnerable, innocent civilians in the Balkans and Africa. The movement of war from combatant to noncombatant in the name of ethnic cleansing is an affront and should be resisted. At the same time, organizations like Hezbollah or Hamas taking potshots against Israeli soldiers, whether in southern Lebanon or the Occupied Territories, are generally considered to be less objectionable than somebody wrapping explosives around themselves and going into a discotheque or restaurant in Tel Aviv or Jerusalem.

The sort of tactics a movement is prepared to adopt therefore reveals much about its ethos and character. This is, however, implicit rather than explicit. One problem with addressing tactics first is that the question of political objectives only comes in behind. The policy problem then appears as thwarting the enemy tactics rather than the enemy politics. This may help explain the difficulties faced over the last couple of years in trying to be specific about what we need to do politically. Other than vague talk about "hearts and minds," no compelling narratives have emerged. Despite some attempts to make the new struggle fit, the popular pre-9/11 narratives do not work. This is clearly not part of the old globalization critique, except that this is a group of people who, for all their apparent antimodernism, know how to use modern communications, information technology and financial instruments to great effect. It is not about poverty. By and large terrorists have not defined themselves by this cause and, as often not, they do not come from poor countries or even poor families. Many truly poor countries do not have a terrorism problem: the everyday struggle for survival is just too demanding and political movements tend to be more populist and less dependent upon self-appointed vanguards. The regular claim that it is about the Palestinian issue picks up on a common rhetorical theme. There is scant evidence that al-Qaeda was ever that bothered about that issue – or more so than about the US garrison in Saudi Arabia, or about Kashmir, Chechnya, Kosovo or, now, Iraq.

The most dangerous assumption is that if only progress was made on the peace process the support for al-Qaeda would diminish. The peace process, by which most people mean a two-state solution, is exactly what the Islamists have been against because it would confirm the continuation of a Jewish state. For this reason the upsurges of terrorism in the Middle East, until recently, have been clearly correlated with progress on peace. Two-state solutions are opposed by extremists on both sides. This cause is not a recipe for order, although it is a recipe for justice and, over the long term, more political stability. I am opposed to the promotion of peace in the Middle East as a means of appeasing al-Qaeda and its ilk. It should be promoted because of the needs of those directly involved – the Israelis and the Palestinians.

The problem with addressing any of the complaints which are used to rationalize the activities of groups such as al-Qaeda is that there does not seem to be an obvious point of appeasement, of concession, of negotiation. It is not clear what a compromise with al-Qaeda and similar "jihadist" groups would look like. They are opposed to some regimes which are undoubtedly unpleasant and repressive, and others which are doing their best in testing circumstances. In all cases there can be no confidence that the jihadist alternatives would be anything other than deeply oppressive, misogynist, homophobic theocracies. In those places where strong theocratic, Islamic regimes have been put in place, by and large they seem to be rejected by their own people. In Iran, for example, the response to the Khomeini regime has hardly been one of growing approval and enjoyment of living under this particular type of regime. All the evidence is the opposite. We would probably say the same for Afghanistan under the

Taliban, leaving aside what one thinks of what is now replacing their rule.

What we are witnessing is not the "clash of civilizations" or the "West versus Islam" but an argument within Islam. A lot of the terrorism in recent years has been in Islamic countries. It is directed against the West on occasion, but not always, and often then as a means of undermining pro-Western regimes. The most poignant example of this is Saudi Arabia. For the Saudis promoted and exported an uncompromising version of Islam, in Wahabism, which they may now regret, as it is coming back and biting them. Western countries appear in this argument as the supporters of one particular faction. If this is the case then our options are even more limited because the battle is one that has to be led by "the other side" in this intra-Islamic struggle. This can raise some uncomfortable issues for the West. Here there are some similarities with the Cold War, at least once that confrontation moved into the Third World. Then all sorts of deeply unattractive regimes would appeal to the West on the grounds that if they were not helped the communists would overthrow them. Now it can be said that without help the terrorists will get us. This dilemma can be seen in some of the reporting back from countries in Central Asia, such as Uzbekistan, where the campaigns against local Islamist groups can become very vicious, accepting that these are groups that have a considerable potential for viciousness of their own.

Here then is the problem. By declaring a War on Terrorism we risk taking the politics out of the equation. As the potential victims of this terrorism we need to try to understand its political roots, but even when we do we must also recognize the limited quality of the political response available to us. There is an enemy – it is not a figment of a paranoid Western imagination and it is not one that should be underestimated, either in its political appeal or in its methodology. My argument is that it needs to be understood within its wider political context and addressed accordingly. Campaigns of terror are an effect, not a cause.

The last couple of years have been difficult and sobering, yet it is not all negative. It is good to be thinking more carefully about many states around the world that were all too easy to ignore before. It is easy to be rude about President Bush and his administration, but a learning process is underway. Iraq may be the most curious aspect of this, because having gone into a country believing that a call to democracy and opposition to terrorism and Saddam were enough, the United States has discovered just how complex politics can be and how sensitive you need to be to local political trends and factions. It may be that the earlier mismanagement of affairs in Iraq was too great to enable them to get out of Iraq in a way they would like, but at least there is a greater realism and less hubris in the American debate. The problem with Iraq was not the idea of regime change, but the confusion of this objective with the other claims made to justify the regime change, for example, on weapons of mass destruction, and the insensitivity to the society whose regime was to be changed. It demonstrates the danger of allowing the terrorism issue to be at the fore of every foreign policy issue addressed, because the policy was devised by working backward from such a dread scenario by which Iraq provided the worst weapons to al-Qaeda, instead of forward from the current state of Iraq and the best means of getting a stable transition to a post-Saddam regime. The Saddam question has been around for a long time. Every way of dealing with him had been tried, from appeasement during the 1980s to containment in the 1990s. At some point the Saddam issue would have arisen again and the issue of military intervention would have been raised. The roots of the problem, however, had little do to with any War on Terror.

Therefore, we need to liberate ourselves from the preoccupation with terrorism. It cannot be the filter through which we view the totality of our foreign policy. Whatever the anxieties and grievances we may feel in the aftermath of attacks, that will not in itself be an argument for supporting every initiative justified as our response in this War on Terror. This is not an argument for not taking the risks of terrorist outrages seriously, for ignoring security and how to protect the vulnerable. The openness of our societies does create vulnerabilities that were not there before. Intelligence communities need to work together and governments need to make the difficult judgments about how to combine a concern with our safety with support for our way of life and respect for our traditional liberties.

My conclusion is that neither the slogan of globalization nor that of terrorism is helpful on its own in thinking about the contemporary international system. The system has as its main characteristic the decline of great power confrontation, which is a great thing, and the independence of many states which were previously under imperialism, which is potentially also a great thing and in many cases already is. Unfortunately the failure of many of these states creates constant problems, first for their own peoples and then for the rest of the international community, which, at some point, finds itself trying to cope with the consequences. This was a key theme of the 1990s and I suspect will carry on being one for this century. Our record on this is not particularly wonderful, not because of bad motives, but because we have found it difficult to grasp the complexity of the political processes underway in critical parts of the world and to judge our interventions to make them effective and not counterproductive. For the moment the preoccupation with terrorism may be holding back this necessary adjustment. It gives far too much prominence and credibility to groups and individuals who would be disastrous in power and whose methods in the end will alienate them from likely supporters. Once we adopt the classic counterinsurgency approach, to find means of separating these militants from potential recruits and their natural constituency, then we will be drawn back into the underlying conflicts and problems that should be the real focus of our concerns. In this perhaps the best slogan comes from Mao Zedong: "Respect your enemy tactically but despise him strategically."

Note

This chapter is based on a presentation given at Goodenough College in November 2002 and has been substantially updated.

Index

Lightning Source UK Ltd.
Milton Keynes UK
UKOW030035150213

206303UK00006B/288/P